NATIONAL SOLUTIONS TO TRANS-BORDER PROBLEMS?

The International Political Economy of New Regionalisms Series

The International Political Economy of New Regionalisms series presents innovative analyses of a range of novel regional relations and institutions. Going beyond established, formal, interstate economic organizations, this essential series provides informed interdisciplinary and international research and debate about myriad heterogeneous intermediate level interactions.

Reflective of its cosmopolitan and creative orientation, this series is developed by an international editorial team of established and emerging scholars in both the South and North. It reinforces ongoing networks of analysts in both academia and think-tanks as well as international agencies concerned with micro-, meso- and macro-level regionalisms.

National Solutions to Trans-Border Problems?

The Governance of Security and Risk in a Post-NAFTA North America

ISIDRO MORALES

ITESM, Campus Santa Fe, Mexico

Routledge
Taylor & Francis Group

LONDON AND NEW YORK

First published 2011 by Ashgate Publishing

Published 2016 by Routledge
2 Park Square, Milton Park, Abingdon, Oxfordshire OX14 4RN
711 Third Avenue, New York, NY 10017, USA

First issued in paperback 2016

Routledge is an imprint of the Taylor & Francis Group, an informa business

British Library Cataloguing in Publication Data
National solutions to trans-border problems? : the governance of security and
risk in a post-NAFTA North
America. – (The international political economy of new regionalisms series)
  1. North America – Economic integration. 2. Border security – Mexican-American
  Border Region. 3. Border security – Northern boundary of the United States.
  4. Intergovernmental cooperation – North America. 5. United States – Foreign
  relations – Mexico. 6. Mexico – Foreign relations–United States. 7. Canada –
  Foreign relations – Mexico. 8. Mexico–Foreign relations – Canada.
  I. Series
  327.7–dc22

Library of Congress Cataloging-in-Publication Data
National solutions to trans-border problems? : the governance of security and risk in a
post-NAFTA North America / [edited] by Isidro Morales.
    p. cm. — (International political economy of new regionalisms series)
  Includes bibliographical references and index.
  ISBN 978-1-4094-0918-2 (hardback : alk. paper)
  1. Free trade—North America. 2. North America—Commerce.
  3. Border security—North America. 4. National security—North America.
  5. Risk management—North America. I. Morales, Isidro.
  HF1746.N38 2010
  355'.03307—dc22

                                                                2010035121

ISBN 13: 978-1-138-27872-1 (pbk)
ISBN 13: 978-1-4094-0918-2 (hbk)

Contents

PART 1 POST-NAFTA NORTH AMERICA. NATIONAL SOLUTIONS TO CROSS-BORDER PROBLEMS?

PART 2 THE GOVERNANCE OF CONTINENTAL SECURITY: IS IT POSSIBLE TO MOVE TO A COMMON APPROACH?

List of Tables

List of Figures

List of Contributors

Olga Abizaid is the Director of the Research Forum on North America at the Canadian Foundation for the Americas (FOCAL). Since 2004 she has undertaken extensive research on North American integration and has specialized in the Canada-Mexico relationship. She also has extensive experience working on different themes including Canadian foreign policy, the Mexican oil industry, and Mexican foreign and domestic politics. She holds a MA in International Affairs from the Norman Paterson School of International Affairs and a Licenciatura in International Relations from the Universidad Iberoamericana in Mexico City

John Bailey is Professor of Government and Foreign Service at Georgetown University, where he also directs the Mexico Project in the Center for Latin American Studies. His most recent publications include: "Corruption and Democratic Governability," in Stephen Morris and Charles Blake, eds., *Corruption and Democracy in Latin America* (University of Pittsburgh Press, 2009); "'Security Traps' and Democratic Governability in Latin America: Dynamics of Crime, Violence, Corruption, Regime, and State," in Marcelo Bergman and Laurence Whitehead, eds., *Criminality, Public Security, and the Challenge to Democracy in Latin America* (Notre Dame, IN: University of Notre Dame Press, 2009); and, "Evade, Corrupt, or Confront? Organized Crime and the State in Brazil and Mexico," *Journal of Politics in Latin America*, 2 (2009), 3-28.

Louis Bélanger is a Professor of Political Science at Université Laval, Quebec City. He is the author of numerous publications on Canadian foreign policy, regional economic integration, inter-American cooperation, and the politics of secession. He held visiting positions at Duke University, at SciencePo-Paris, at the Woodrow Wilson International Center for Scholars, and, as a Canada-US Fulbright Visiting Scholar, at the Paul H. Nitze School of Advanced International Studies. From 2000 to 2005, Professor Bélanger was the Director of Université Laval's Quebec Institute for Advanced International Studies (HEI). He is currently a member of the Advisory Council on National Security and the Military Police Complaints Commission of Canada.

Susana Chacón Domínguez is Professor at Tecnológico de Monterrey, Campus Santa Fe in Mexico City. Appointed as Secretary General to the Mexican Chapter of the Club of Rome since 2000, she has a BSc in International Affairs (Universidad Iberoamericana), along with specialties in international negotiation (Harvard University) and US-Mexico relationship (U.C.S.D.). Besides having graduate degrees on Economics and International Politics (CIDE, MSc), Public

Administration (Harvard Kennedy School of Government, MSc), History (Universidad Iberoamericana, PhD) and International Affairs (Georgetown University, post PhD), she has been Professor and Researcher in other institutions: (Tecnológico de Monterrey Campi Ciudad de México and Santa Fe and Universidad Iberoamericana) as well as guest researcher and visiting scholar to a number of higher education institutions (Colegio de México, Georgetown University, Harvard and CIDE). Professor Chacón has written extensively about the Formulation of Mexican Foreign Policy and US-Mexican relation in books such as *Between globalization and dependence: Mexican foreign policy 1994-2002; Energy, narcotics and finance: the hidden face of Mexican foreign policy, 2002; The conflict of cooperation: Mexico and the US 1940-1955: The cases of military, commerce and Bracero agreements, 2008; The Oil crisis in Mexico, 2008; México: One country, four scenarios, 2008.* Her more recent book is *Mexico and the Bicentenario: Ideas and Proposals, 2010.* She has also contributed to classic international affairs discussions in books such as *Diplomatic negotiation: Forgotten Art?, 2003* Her current research projects focus on oil, US-Mexican relation and Mexican foreign policy as well as conflict resolution and scenario analysis.

Stephen Clarkson is a professor of political economy at the University of Toronto whose work focuses on transborder governance and the economic relations between the three states of the North American continent. His recent books on these issues include *Uncle Sam and Us: Globalization, Neoconservatism and the Canadian State* (2002); *Does North America Exist? Governing the Continent after NAFTA and 9/11* (2008); and *A Perilous Imbalance: The Globalization of Canadian Law and Governance* (with Stepan Wood, 2010). His current research is assessing the extent to which Canada and Mexico construct and/or constrain US power. He is a fellow of the Royal Society of Canada and a senior fellow at the Centre for International Governance Innovation.

Elaine Correa is an Associate Professor in the School of Education at Medaille College, Buffalo, New York. She is also a Research Associate at the Centre for Research and Teaching on Women at McGill University, Montreal, Canada. Dr. Correa teaches in the fields of Canadian Studies, Women's Studies and Education in the US and Canada.

Imtiaz Hussain is Professor of International Relations in Mexico City's *Universidad Iberoamericana,* teaching mostly international relations, negotiations, and regional integration theories. He has published both books *Afghanistan-Iraq and Post-conflict Governance* (Brill 2010), *The Impact of NAFTA on North America* (Palgrave 2010), *North American Homeland Security: Back to Bilateralism?* (Praeger 2008); *Community, Diffusion, and North American Expansiveness* (Universidad Iberoamericana 2008), *Running on Empty Across Central America: Canadian, Mexican, and US Integrative Efforts* (University Press of America

2006), and *Globalization, Indigenous Groups, and Mexico's Plan Puebla Plan* (Edwin Mellen 2006); and articles in *Handbook of Global Security and Intelligence* (2008), *South Asian Survey* (2008), *Politics & Policy* (2008), *Journal of the Asiatic Society of Bangladesh* (2006), *Norteamérica* (2006); among others. A recipient of several fellowships (CONACYT, PIERAN, and Canadian conference grants twice each, North American Research Linkages) and teaching awards (University of Pennsylvania, and 6 from UDLA, Mexico), he received his Political Science PhD from the University of Pennsylvania (1989), and is from Bangladesh.

Alejandro Ibarra-Yunez holds the chaired professorship in Economics of Networks and Regulations, at EGADE Business School and the Department of Economics at Tecnológico de Monterrey, Monterrey, Mexico. His lines of research combine international economics and international economic policy, and industrial organization, network industries with market power and regulations. He has written ten books, and many articles in international academic journals. He has been advisor to sectoral and competition regulators, the government of Mexico and many firms in his country and elsewhere in the Americas.

Isidro Morales received his Ph.D. in France, from the Paris-based Institut d'Études Politiques. He worked as a researcher at El Colegio de México and other Mexican universities. He was a lecturer at the University of Copenhagen and guest researcher at the Danish Center for Development Research, the Watson Institute of the University of Brown and the John W. Kluge Center at the Library of Congress, in Washington D.C. From 2001 to 2005, he was Dean of the School of Social Sciences at the Universidad de las Américas-Puebla, in Mexico. During the academic year 2005-2006 he was a Fulbright Visiting Professor at American University, and a Senior Fellow of the Center for North American Studies, in Washington DC. Dr. Morales has published extensively on energy, integration and trade-related topics. His most recent book, *Post-NAFTA North America. Reshaping the Economic and Political Governance of a Changing Region*, was released by Palgrave/MacMillan in July 2008. Dr. Morales' main research areas are the following: the geopolitics and geo-economics of energy, trade and investment markets; the political economy of regional integration; Mexico-US trade relations; and US- Latin American relations. Dr. Morales is member of Mexico's National Research System, the Latin American Studies Association (LASA) and the Mexican Council for Foreign Affairs. He is currently Editor in Chief of Latin American Policy, a biannual journal distributed worldwide by Wiley-Blackwell, and professor at the Monterrey Institute of Technology (ITESM), Santa Fe Campus, in Mexico City.

José María Ramos. Director, Department of Public Administration Studies, El Colegio de la Frontera Norte, Tijuana, Mexico. Expertise on transborder management and public security in the Mexico-US in the US Mexico border.

José Luis Valdés-Ugalde. Former Director (for the period 2001-2009) and tenured lecturer-researcher of the Center for Research on North America (CISAN) at the National Autonomous University of Mexico (UNAM). Currently he is visiting scholar at the International Studies Division of CIDE (Centro de Investigación y Docencia Económicas). Political Scientist and internationalist. Dr. Valdés holds a MA in Political Sociology and a PhD in International Relations, both from the London School of Economics and Political Science (LSE). He is a regular member of the Mexican Academy of Sciences and Level 2 National Researcher of the National System of Researchers (SNI). His areas of expertise are theory of International relations, political theory, globalization, integration and security, history and foreign policy of the US, and North American studies. He has more than 60 publications as an author, joint author or editor. He is a member of the Latin American Studies Association (LASA), the International Studies Association (ISA), the Mexican Council on International Affairs (COMEXI) and Vice-president of the Mexican Association of International Studies (AMEI). He is founder of CISAN's Academic Journal Norteamérica and former Director of the magazine Voices of Mexico. In 2000-2001, he acted as Deputy National Security Advisor for Risk Analysis and Academic Liaison of the Presidential National Security Advisor's Office. He is a permanent analyst in the Radio Program Enfoque, in "CNN en español" and in the TV Channel 11, and a newspaper columnist in Excelsior.

D. Rick Van Schoik. Director, North American Center for Transborder Studies (NACTS), a consortium of seven Canadian, US, and Mexican universities headquartered at Arizona State University, the New American University P.O. Box 878105, Tempe, Arizona 85287-8105 (480) 965-1846, NACTS@ASU.edu, www.nacts.asu.edu. Mr. Van Schoik serves as the first Director of NACTS. His three decade-long experience in developing, funding, managing, and interpreting international programs enables NACTS to pursue complex, multidisciplinary, trinational research and policy work.

Bernadette G. Vega Sánchez has a BA on International Relations from Universidad de las Américas A.C. She is a regular member of the Mexican Council of Foreign Affairs and research assistant at the Centro de Investigaciones sobre América del Norte, UNAM, and the International Studies Center of the Centro de Investigación y Docencia Económicas (CIDE).

Carol Wise is an Associate Professor in the School of International Relations at the University of Southern California. She has written widely on issues pertaining to Latin American political economy, including four edited collections that analyze exchange rate regimes, trade integration, and political responses to market reform in the region. In 2003 she published *Reinventing the State: Economic Strategy and Institutional Change in Peru* (University of Michigan Press) and in 2007 she published *Requiem or Revival? The Promise of North American Integration* (with Isabel Studer, Brookings Institution Press). Prof. Wise is currently completing a book on China-Latin American political economic relations. In 2005 Prof. Wise was awarded two Fulbright Fellowships---the Carleton University Fulbright Chair in North American Studies and a Fulbright-Hays Senior Faculty Award at the Universidad de las Americas in Puebla, Mexico. She received her PhD in political science from Columbia University in 1991.

PART 1
Post-NAFTA North America.
National solutions to cross-border problems?

PART I

Introduction

Conventional wisdom says that regional integration, triggered by the North American Free Trade Agreement (NAFTA), prompted the governments of Canada, the United States and Mexico to redefine and adapt their public policies to the transnationalization and/or regionalization of all kinds of transactions. Now that North America has become a free trade area, after more than 17 years of progressively phasing out tariffs and other types of barriers, the governments and societies of the three countries have become more aware of the existence of shared sensitive issues, whose management and eventual solution can not be reached neither by current national-based governance institutions nor by NAFTA. Cross-border issues associated with commerce, such as migration, environment and security (among others), exceed the simple scope and capabilities of national policies and intergovernmental cooperation.

North American societies have realized that they constitute an economic, though differentiated space, without the policy or institutional mechanisms for dealing with the social, political, and cultural externalities provoked by the integrative trend. There seems to exist a sort of demand for deeper integration in some sensitive issues, such as migration, energy, and security- to name a few - with no equivalent supply of institutional and policy arrangements for accommodating those needs. The creation of a Security and Prosperity Partnership (SPP) in 2005, became the model of future cross-border cooperation for continental affairs, linking for the first time economic performance with security concerns. Under the SPP umbrella, trilateral working groups dealing with strategic areas for the three nations were created, including analyses on continental energy markets and the evolution of competitiveness of the North American economic space. Nonetheless, the profile and activities of the SPP remained heavily dependent on the political calendar and calculations of each North American government. It remained a top-down project in which the participation of non-government actors remained marginal. Furthermore, the upcoming of the economic crisis, first in the US and thereafter in the rest of North America and the world, and the departure of the Obama administration from previous Republican foreign policy commitments, vanished the continuity and possibility of a trilateral approach for the region and engulfed the future of cross border governance into the priorities of fragmented bilateral foreign policies.

The purpose of this book is to address these institutional gaps already existing within North-American affairs, focusing mainly on the governance and security aspects. It gathers the interdisciplinary work of various specialists working on continental issues within the three countries of North America. Their contributions highlight the transnational dimension of certain issues still managed under national-framed policies, and explore the possibilities and constraints for moving public policy into new cross-border governance strategies. Their research papers attempt to assess whether there is a real need to change the *status-quo* in an issue-area, mainly on security and natural resources management, into more innovative architectures of regional governance, thus exploring the risk and constraints for making such a change.

This proposal is originally the result of a workshop organized in Monterrey, Mexico, under the sponsorship of the Graduate School on Public Administration and Public Policy (EGAP) of Instituto Tecnológico y de Estudios Superiores de Monterrey (ITESM). I am grateful to EGAP's chair, Bernardo González-Aréchiga for all the support and enthusiasm he devoted when organizing the event. Thanks to the generous financial support of the Linkages Program of the Department of Foreign Affairs and International Trade (DFAIT) of the Government of Canada, and the Centre for International Governance and Innovation (CIGI), based in Waterloo, Ontario, Canada, most of the authors participating in this volume could gather in Monterrey in order to discuss the first version of their papers and establish a North American network of researchers, called the Tri-national Academic Group for the study of emerging governance institutions in North America (TAGGINA). I am especially grateful to Andrew Cooper and Daniel Schwanen, both from CIGI, for their kind support given to the original proposal and which made possible our successful encounter in Monterrey. From that time to the present the TAGGINA group has incorporated new participants and some of its members have gathered in different forums and conferences dealing with North American issues. This volume is the first collective product of the group and I hope many other joint publications and activities will come in the future.

This book is divided in three parts. The first one aims to assess what is at stake in cross-border governance issues in North America, and weather the integrative trend in the region will be maintained or stalled in the years to come. The second part explores the growing scope of security problems interconnected with borders, migration, terrorism and drug trafficking across the region. It highlights how Mexico and Canada are responding or adapting their policy choices to a continental security approach framed by the US after the terrorist attacks of September 11, and to the major concern of the Obama administration on organized crime activities and violence. Since we witness a return to bilateral relations for managing continental issues during the Obama administration, a third part of this volume focuses on the governance of territorial borders and bilateral affairs, i.e. Mexico-US and Canada-Mexico relations.

Four articles are included in the first part of this volume. Carol Wise's contribution makes a general assessment of NAFTA both as a benchmark and obsolescence. She highlights the impact of China to the overall trade exchanges for the region. Louis Bélanger's essay explores the possibilities for deepening economic integration in the region without having to build formal trilateral institutions. For so doing, states members should be able to build rule-making regional institutions with ample autonomy of the Executive branch from domestic politics. Isidro Morales' article explores the linkage between trade and security from the perspective of circulation regimes, in which strategies enhancing mobility trigger mechanisms of containment and deterrence and complement each other, as witnessed in North America by the establishment of the Security and Prosperity Partnership (SPP). Finally, this first section ends up with an analysis on the future of electricity markets in the region. Alejandro Ibarra highlights the need to supersede institutional restrictions in order to further continentalize an industry which is rapidly changing in the three countries.

The second part of this volume focuses on the possibilities and constraints of building common security architectures for the region, of which SPP has become a first generation model. Five contributions are included in this section starting with Stephen Clarkson's. He argues that security is not always a collective good, but sometimes a zero-sum commodity, as when the US drive for security begets the insecurity of others. He calls for a need to incorporate Canadian and Mexican interests in the development and execution of US security policies so that a continental agenda of shared sensitive issues can exceed the simple scope and capabilities of national policies. José María Ramos makes an assessment to what extent SPP has privileged security concerns over economic achievements. He argues that in spite of the lack of response from the Mexican side, several measures supported by the US government under the SPP framework have fostered investments and developed competition in Mexico. John Bailey makes a much needed comparative analysis of the similarities and differences between the Merida Initiative and Plan Colombia. Considered more as "half-brothers", Bailey raises the question whether the ad hoc responses may evolve into a more coherent regional or hemispheric security architecture. Rick Van Schoik analyzes the possibilities and constraints for building a continental defense, a zone of tranquility or confidence, a sort of an external perimeter which promotes what he calls a North American Continental Common Transborder Security. Finally, this section closes with a more general study on how September 11 produced a rigorous review of US security doctrine impacting not only North America but overall Latin America. Jose Luis Valdés and Bernadette Vega discuss how unilateralism dominated the security picture during Bush's years for the overall western hemisphere.

Elaine Correa opens the third part of this volume with a contribution suggesting that the management of borders between Canada and the US is framed under the paradigm of suspicion, through which identity, citizenship and risk is being intertwined for defining the mobility privileges of people. Imtiaz Hussain focuses his analysis on US migratory policies, both at the federal and state levels, impacting migrants coming from Mexico. Olga Abizaid's contribution explores the complexity of Canada-Mexico relations and explains the background of the recent imposition of visas for Mexican travelers, while Susana Chacón's article suggests the new fields in which future Mexico-Canada relations could evolve.

I am very grateful to all TAGGINA authors for their effort and patience in participating in this amazing volume. Their different perspectives and insights will make of this book and indispensable reference for the general reader and the professional researcher specialized in security issues, for understanding current North American affairs. Last but not least, I would like to acknowledge Melanie Slone's assistance for reviewing the language and editing of the thirteen chapters included in this volume, as well as for helping me to establish the general index.

Chapter 1
Sitting in Limbo: The North American Free Trade Agreement[1]

Carol Wise

Despite the emphasis that then-presidential candidate Barack Obama placed on the need to renegotiate the North American Free Trade Agreement (NAFTA) during the US Democratic Party primary debates in spring 2008, this promise has thus far come to naught. Once elected, and in line with longstanding protocol, President Obama's first foreign visit was to Mexico to confer with President Felipe Calderón. During this diplomatic foray Obama assured Calderón that the United States intended to upgrade those parts of NAFTA that were of most concern, particularly in the realm of labor standards and environmental protection. Yet, when the "Three Amigos" met in Mexico for their annual NAFTA summit, the agenda discussed by Obama, Calderón, and Canadian Prime Minister Stephen Harper was dominated by the problem of undocumented migration of Mexican workers into the United States and Canada and by the explosion of drug trafficking and cartel-related violence along the US-Mexico border (Lorber 2009).

As palpable as the domestic debate over the need for NAFTA reform may have seemed at the time of the 2008 US presidential election, the fact is that NAFTA is more or less beside the point at this political economic juncture. This is because 99 percent of all tariffs on those goods and services covered by NAFTA have basically been eliminated, and because politicians and policy makers in all three of the member countries (Canada, Mexico and the United States) have failed to institutionalize and update the agreement in ways that address problems that are to a large extent multiplier effects of NAFTA itself. These issues would include those same topics that invoked immediate tensions between participants at the 2009 NAFTA summit as well as the failure to promote economic competitiveness and to foster the development of NAFTA as a regional project proper. With NAFTA now fully implemented, the inability of political leaders in North America to renovate and expand on the accord has led it to be eclipsed by more recent and compelling global forces.

The most remarkable shift is the rapidity with which China has gained a foothold in sectors once considered "North American", such as electrical machinery,

1   An earlier version of this article was published by the author under the following title: 'The North American Free Trade Agreement', *New Political Economy*, 2009, 14:1,133–148

equipment and parts (Wise 2007: 38-39). Since China's 2001 entry into the World
Trade Organization (WTO) its exports have steadily surpassed those of Mexico
and Canada in any number of US market niches. Canada and Mexico remain the
most important trading partners of the United States overall, and together represent
the largest supply of US energy imports; however, when it comes to remedies for
today's economic pain, China, it seems, should be the main departure point for any
debate over the current sources of job dislocation and associated economic stress
in the United States and larger North American market.

Economic policy and public discourse across North America have yet to
register the full implications of China's rapid ascendance in regional markets.
Even though the prospect of the "China threat" has spawned a whole cottage industry of academic and popular books in the West,[2] apart from launching a series of
elite diplomatic dialogues and pressuring the Chinese to revalue their currency,[3]
Washington, Ottawa and Mexico City have been slow to react.

In sum, although competition from China may be the most obvious factor in
accounting for heightened job insecurity in both the United States and Mexico,
NAFTA still carries its weight in symbolic terms. Why else would political
candidates within the region continue to hammer away at it? Mexican presidential
contender Andrés Manuel López Obrador made the reversal of NAFTA a key part
of his failed campaign in 2006 and, tellingly, lost that race by less than one percent
of the vote. At the same time NAFTA conjures up some bitter disappointments
given the sizable gaps that have ensued in terms of expectations, implementation,
and outcome, while also representing some impressive benchmarks with regard to
trade liberalization and regional integration.

In this chapter I begin by analyzing NAFTA both as benchmark and
disappointment, a discussion that relies on substance as well as the numerous
symbols that have swirled around this single acronym over its 15-year lifespan.
From here follows an examination of the aggregate impact of NAFTA on the North
American region, including its variable effect on each of the three member countries.
I conclude with a section that looks at those regional and global trends that are
gradually contributing to NAFTA's obsolescence, notwithstanding its symbolic
staying power in public discourse and political debates across North America.

NAFTA: Substance and Symbol

Substance

The international context that framed the NAFTA negotiations from 1991 to 1993
was one of global recession and mutual frustration over the stalemate that had beset
the Uruguay Round of multilateral negotiations launched in 1986 at the General

---

2   Some examples of this genre are Gertz (2002), Menges (2005) and Lo (2006).
3   For more on this see Goldstein & Lardy (2008).

Agreement on Tariffs and Trade (GATT). Hindsight shows that the cleavages that divided trade negotiators back then are similar to those that have condemned the current Doha round, launched in 2001, to a hiatus that has now persisted for four years. With a growing number of developing countries adhering to the GATT, there was an ever-widening gulf between the newcomers' concern to achieve deeper concessions around "old" issues on the multilateral trade agenda (market access for agricultural and industrial goods) versus the push which emanated primarily from the Organization for Economic Cooperation and Development (OECD) countries to advance on the "new" issues (services, investment and intellectual property rights, or IPRs). Although the United States had always been a staunch proponent of the multilateral trade regime, its impatience with this standoff prompted it to pursue bilateral trade deals, first with Israel in 1985 and then with Canada in 1988. NAFTA, however, broke entirely new ground with the willingness of the United States to negotiate for the first time a bilateral free trade agreement (FTA) that included a developing country.

A second benchmark for NAFTA was Mexico's willingness to forgo any special or different treatment related to its developing country status at the NAFTA negotiating table (Cameron and Tomlin 2000: 61-63). It is difficult to exaggerate the extent to which this stance represented a complete U-turn in Mexico's approach to foreign economic policy. The decision reflected the advent of a new generation of more technocratic policy makers within the upper echelons of the state bureaucracy and the eagerness of this market-oriented cohort to lock in an entirely new set of policies based on liberalization, privatization, and deregulation (Pastor and Wise 1994). This paved the way for a final agreement that went well beyond what had been accomplished to date within the Uruguay Round. On this count, NAFTA's key innovations were the protection of IPRs, the liberalization of investment and trade in services, and the creation of mechanisms to resolve investment disputes based on binding international arbitration (Lawrence 1996).

When the Clinton administration was successful in getting the NAFTA bill approved by the US Congress in November 1993, US trade partners in Asia and Europe were reportedly caught off guard, as all outward signs had suggested that the NAFTA legislation would be killed in the highly polarized House of Representatives. However, with NAFTA now an approaching reality, East Asian trade partners faced the prospect of a US shift from a global trade liberalization strategy to one that favored regionalism; at the same time, the Europeans "feared the United States was turning away from its traditional Atlantic-first orientation" (Destler 2005: 208). Thus, it can be argued that NAFTA and its GATT-plus accomplishments were instrumental in the revival of the Uruguay round talks, the finalization of that agreement in 1994, and the creation of the WTO as a new institutional entity to better address those issues that now comprise the new trade agenda.

The third breakthrough was the negotiation and attachment of labor and environmental side accords to the NAFTA agreement, as the prospect of Mexico's entry into an FTA with the United States and Canada invoked valid worries about environmental dumping and the abuse of labor rights in these latter countries.

Historical in their own right, these labor and environmental agreements were offered up by the Clinton administration as side payments to garner congressional votes for NAFTA and to counter the political blowback on the domestic front that had arisen in regard to the steep asymmetries between Mexico and the United States. Although the incorporation of labor and environmental standards has now become commonplace in subsequent FTAs that the United States has negotiated with developing countries, the following section suggests that their effect in mitigating the electorate's fears around asymmetrical integration has been equivocal at best.

In sum, along with the side agreements on labor standards and environmental protection, the NAFTA accord promoted the free flow of goods, investment, and services within the North American bloc over a 15-year timeline that ended in 2009(Hufbauer and Schott 2005). In line with WTO rules, most barriers came down in the first 10 years of the agreement, by 2004. Tariffs and non-tariff barriers were eliminated on 65 percent of North American goods by the 5-year point; tariff reductions on automobiles occurred over a 10-year period, with the rules-of-origin stipulation that such vehicles must meet a 62.5 percent local-content requirement in order to qualify.[4] In the agricultural sector, sensitive products were allotted a 15-year liberalization schedule that ended in 2009. This included, for example, corn, dry beans and powdered milk on the Mexican side; sugar, peanuts and orange juice concentrate on the US side. In the end, negotiating tensions were such that sugar and dairy products were excluded altogether in trade between Canada and Mexico.

As for the liberalization of investment and trade in services, NAFTA adopted the principle of national treatment for member countries, removed performance requirements, protected intellectual property, and created dispute settlement mechanisms to arbitrate investment conflicts. The latter reflects the extent to which NAFTA was as much about the promotion of investment flows in North America as it was about spurring free trade. However, NAFTA still fell short of its mandate to liberalize substantially all trade between the three partners. First, administered protection persists in the setting of hefty percentages for local content under NAFTA's rules of origin in such sectors as autos, high-tech products and textiles and apparel. Second, as in the case of the 1988 Canada-US agreement that preceded NAFTA, little progress was made toward the elimination of antidumping policies and countervailing duties. Nevertheless, and despite the ability of special interests to secure these protectionist concessions, hindsight suggests that NAFTA has been a liberalizing force overall.

To frame NAFTA in the parlance of international relations theory, in the process of negotiating a revised set of rules to facilitate deeper trade and investment liberalization and the consolidation of a North American bloc proper, each partici-

---

4   In order to qualify for NAFTA's preferences, goods have to: (1) be produced entirely within the NAFTA bloc; (2) incorporate only those non-NAFTA materials that are sufficiently processed in North America to qualify for a tariff reclassification; and (3) satisfy a minimum-content rule.

pant was clearly looking to reduce transaction costs while simultaneously increasing the benefits of cooperation. Canada and Mexico saw an opportunity to secure access to the US market and establish clearly defined rules and procedures for resolving trade and investment disputes. The United States, while also concerned with promoting and rationalizing economic ties within the North American bloc, primarily sought to bolster the rules and norms that constituted the international trade regime codified within the GATT. Although pragmatic in the sense that all three parties sought to strengthen and institutionalize respective political-economic ties that had long been in place but had heretofore been managed in an ad hoc manner, the following section details the ways in which NAFTA also unexpectedly unleashed its own fair share of animal spirits in North America.

Symbol

From the launching of the negotiations in September 1991 to the ratification vote in the US House of Representatives in November 1993, the tone of the NAFTA debate was counter-intuitive. Economic integration theory suggests that both the United States and Canada, as larger, wealthier and more open Group of 8 (G8) economies, should anticipate marginal adjustments to occur. In turn, Mexico, as the smaller, poorer and more closed economy, should expect to undergo a more costly adjustment in the short term, but to realize considerable dynamic gains in the medium to long term (Bouzas and Ros 1994). From this theory it should follow that the debate over whether to pursue an FTA would be more heated in Mexico, the country that had the most at stake. Conversely, given that the United States and Canada had much less on the line, one would expect a fairly tame discussion about whether to negotiate an FTA that included Mexico. Paradoxically, the opposite scenario emerged.

In Mexico, the administration of Carlos Salinas (1988-94), which oversaw the period of NAFTA negotiations, was able to quell open debate over NAFTA by drawing on the authoritarian clout of its ruling Revolutionary Institutional Party (PRI) to reinforce informational asymmetries and marginalize dissenters. The PRI simultaneously sold NAFTA to the nation through the masterful manipulation of longstanding political symbols. By linking the core ideals of the Mexican Revolution–economic modernization, distributional equity, and social justice–with the neoliberal rhetoric embodied in NAFTA, Salinas and his team managed to convince the population at large that NAFTA was simply another phase in the realization of the country's long-term revolutionary goals (Wise 1998). This disingenuous exaggeration of the gains and low-balling of the losses from NAFTA would eventually lead to the unseating of the PRI in 2000 and the end of its seven-decade hold on the executive office (Cameron & Wise 2004). However, the point is that political symbols were a powerful catalyst, and perhaps even the "clincher," in enabling Mexico's transformative decision to enter into NAFTA.

In Canada and the United States, the NAFTA debate literally exploded. The Canadian government's announcement of its intentions to join the NAFTA negotiations reignited the same bitter exchanges over job impacts, economic liberalization, and the downside of US-Canadian relations that had surrounded the earlier negotiations for the Canada-US FTA. Similarly, in the US, a full-scale national debate ensued, one that approximated the heated controversy that surrounded the passage of the highly protectionist Smoot–Hawley Tariff in 1930 (Destler 2005: 11-12). As the debate on the US side bogged down in acrimony and data-slinging, a main upshot was the emergence of a blue-green coalition of grassroots labor and environmental activists that managed to insert non-trade issues onto the US trade policy-making agenda like never before.

This grassroots coalition gathered steam on two fronts. First was a realistic reaction to the miserable working conditions and badly polluted *maquila* factory sites that lined the US-Mexico border. If NAFTA signified the free flow of goods, services, and capital between all three countries, what was to stop the flow northward of environmental pollution and sub-standard working conditions? Why risk the lowering of labor and environmental standards that workers and consumers had fought to achieve since the 1930s? To the chagrin of free trade purists (Bhagwati 2008), it was this coalition that compelled the administration of George H. Bush to expend political capital on border cleanup and the enforcement of much higher environmental standards. With the election of President Bill Clinton in 1992, this ante was upped to include the formal negotiation of labor and environmental side agreements to accompany NAFTA as a *quid pro quo* for the blue-green endorsement of the 1993 NAFTA-implementing legislation.

The second front was largely symbolic, akin to that witnessed in Canada with regard to the Canada-US FTA, whereby NAFTA came to embody all that was cumulatively wrong with the US political economy at the outset of the 1990s. What had started out as an issue-oriented blue-green coalition in 1991 blossomed into a full-blown anti-NAFTA movement that included everyone from job-seeking college graduates to downsized business executives, laid-off factory workers, teachers' unions, pensioners and welfare mothers. Regardless of the actual effect that NAFTA would have on any of these constituents, they were united in the perception that they had somehow been excluded from the prosperity that surrounded them in the late twentieth century, and they were understandably angry about it.

NAFTA's self-appointed "losers" have thus kept the opposition to further trade liberalization alive, as witnessed in the pandering to these constituents by various candidates in the 2008 US presidential primary debates. But beyond this phenomenon of NAFTA coming to symbolize a general sense of downward mobility and free-floating economic anxiety in the United States, it is the tenacity of the blue-green coalition and its effect on congressional deliberations that perhaps best accounts for the testiness of US trade policy since the launching of NAFTA. Although this coalition won the battle in securing the attachment of labor and environmental side agreements to NAFTA, the lackluster enforcement of those agreements has further prolonged the trade policy war on the domestic side. Much of the fight has centered on correcting the institutional weaknesses in those earlier agreements, namely, the obligation of each country to enforce its own existing national laws but with little regard for strengthening and harmonizing North American labor and environmental standards overall (Hufbauer and Schott 2005).

First, the blue-green opposition has continued its fight for more binding commitments in enforcing labor and environmental standards, to the extent that this largely explains the decade-long refusal of the US Congress to grant the Clinton and subsequent Bush administration the Trade Promotion Authority (TPA) necessary to credibly negotiate further FTAs.[5] Second, the US insistence on incorporating labor and environmental stipulations into the pending Doha agreement, as well as the subsequent FTAs signed in the 2000s, can be attributed to this coalition. Finally, the irony is that the demands of the blue-green coalition have increasingly united congressional members of all political stripes against FTA expansion, either on the grounds that grassroots lobbying for the incorporation of non-trade issues has gone too far and should be resisted (business-backed Republicans) or in protest that these labor and environmental stipulations need to reach much further (Democrats beholden to labor and environment grassroots supporters). This messy merging of symbol and substance is one of NAFTA's key legacies, and it cast a disproportionate degree of difficulty over the Clinton administration's subsequent plans to negotiate a Free Trade Area of the Americas (FTAA) involving all 34 democratically elected countries in the region, which were finally shelved in 2005. Even seemingly easy US bilateral talks with countries that are otherwise ready and willing to constructively adhere to the full menu of blue-green demands (Panama, Peru, Colombia) have proved to be quite cumbersome.

NAFTA's Variable Impacts[6]

NAFTA's critics have arguably done a better job of advertising its failures than its proponents have done in touting the concrete material gains that have underpinned North American integration since the early 1990s. At least at the aggregate level, it would be difficult to paint NAFTA as anything but a success. This is especially so when NAFTA is judged according to its own goals, the creation of a free trade area in which all three partners have pursued an economic growth strategy via the liberalization of goods, capital, and services amongst themselves. Total NAFTA trade now accounts for some 30 percent of all US trade,[7] and the

---

5   Formerly known as the "fast-track" legislation, Trade Promotion Authority (or TPA) is granted to the executive by the congress. Once a trade agreement is negotiated with a foreign partner, the executive sends it to congress for an "up or down" vote, i.e. legislators are not given the opportunity to further amend or modify the bill.

6   Parts of this section borrow from Wise (2008) and Wise (2007).

7   TradeStats Express, International Trade Administration, Foreign Trade Division, US Centre Bureau, US Department of Commerce, Available at: http:tse.export.gov/ MapFrameset.aspx?MapPageNTDMap Display.aspx&UniqueURLpbstck551vkuf2mr2kz w0q55-2008-5-10-17-37-33 [accessed: 7 July 2008].

number of jobs gained in the US economy since NAFTA's implementation in 1994 towers over those jobs lost. "US trade in goods and services with Canada and Mexico tripled–from US$341 billion in 1993 to more than US$1 trillion in 2007–and inward foreign direct investment quintupled among the three countries and increased tenfold in Mexico between 1990 and 2005 (Pastor 2008: 85)." In terms of gross product, the NAFTA zone has surpassed the European Union (EU) to become the largest free trade area in the world. Within this zone, however, the impacts of regional integration have been quite uneven.

Again, when viewed from the dictates of economic integration theory (Bouzas and Ros 1994), it was expected that NAFTA would benefit all three countries, but especially Mexico, through the deepening of already strong ties in cross-border production and intra-industry trade. First, the elimination of barriers at the border would promote scale economies related to greater specialization, increased technological capabilities, and more rapid and efficient deployment of those factors for which Mexico has a comparative advantage (natural resources and comparatively cheap labor) (Chase 2003: 141). Second, it was argued that the blending of Mexico's abundant factors with the capital, technology, and know-how that Canada and the United States brought to the table would trigger a dynamic pattern of income convergence among the three members.[8] According to this largely neoclassical trade narrative, Mexico would readily advance up the industrial and technological learning curve, substantially increase its per capita income, and more authentically approximate the economic indicators of its fellow OECD members.

The data show that NAFTA has delivered rather erratically on these expectations. At the macroeconomic level, Canada and Mexico have clearly converged toward the more highly developed US standard in terms of aggregate growth, interest rates, exchange rate stability and the lowering of inflation to under five percent annually. For Mexico this is a considerable victory, given the explosion of consumer prices in the wake of the 1994 peso crisis. But the microeconomic data tell a different story, one that seems to vindicate those doubters of neoclassical theory (Mosley 2000, Wade 2004), while also highlighting the need for sound domestic policy reforms to complement and maximize on the opportunities intrinsic to a regional integration scheme.

As Table 1 shows, in all three countries per capita income has grown at a healthy clip since the 1990s. However, after rebounding from the disastrous 1994 peso crisis, the growth of per capita gross domestic product (GDP) in Mexico has hit a virtual standstill in the 2000s and is still 6.3 times lower than that of the United States.

---

8   See, for example, Sachs and Warner (1995).

Table 1.1   Competitive Inroads: United States, Canada, and Mexico, Various
              Years

		United States	Canada	Mexico
High-Tech Exports (% GDP)	1990	33.0%	13.0%	8.2%
	2000	33.0%	18.6%	22.4%
	2005*	34.0%	29.0%	19.6%
R&D % GDP*	1996	2.5%	1.7%	0.3%
	2001	2.8%	2.3%	0.3%
	2005	3.1%	2.0%	0.4%
Patents Granted	1999	153,487	13,778	3,899
	2001	166,038	12,019	5,479
	2005	143,806	13,060	8,098
Internet Users (per 1,000)	1994	49	25	0.4
	2001	551	512	36
	2005*	630	520	181
Productivity (output/hour) Index 1993 = 100	2000	145.8	125.8	145.9
	2001	149.9	121.9	144.8
	2002	161.3	124.8	154.0
	2003	171.6	126.2	159.2
	2004	177.0	132.8	168.2
	2005	185.9	137.6	170.7
	2006	192.5	138.3	176.1
Per Capita GDP Growth**	1980	21,000	16,539	3,282
	1990	26,141	19,229	3,187
	1995	27,404	20,117	2,637
	2000	34,445	23,537	5,799
	2001	35,163	23,048	6,326
	2002	36,033	23,535	5,956
	2003	37,423	27,403	5,878
	2004	39,722	31,030	6,478
	2005	41,917	34,028	6,771
	2006	43,883	35,568	6,937

Sources: World Trade Organization; International Labour Organization; INEGI Database, "Productividad de al mano de obra en diferentes paises," Available at: http://www.inegi.gob.mx/est/contenidos/espanol/rutinas/ept.asp?t=mano4&c=477

*OECD Statistics by Country and World Bank Country Profiles, Available at: http://devdata.worldbank.org/external/CPProfile.asp? Selected Country=Mex&CCODE=MEX&NAME=Mexico&PTYPE=CP

***Inter*national Financial Statistics (IFS), Washington, D.C., various years (all figures in US$).

Even Canada, despite its advantage as a G8 country, has lagged in this regard. Although Canadian income distribution is the most equitable in North America, Canada's per capita income remains about 20 percent lower than that of the United States and its productivity and investment ratios are similarly trailing.

While the roots of microeconomic under-performance appear to lie somewhere in the gulf between neoclassical trade theory–which assumes a state of perfect competition and constant returns to scale under NAFTA (Chase 2003)–and the concrete empirical obstacles that underpinned its launching back in the early 1990s, the persistent divergence between the United States and its NAFTA partners also can be chalked up to the nature of political institutions and policy making in these countries. The literature on regional integration argues that both Canada and Mexico, albeit in greatly varying degrees, are still in need of more proactive competition policies that spur rather than deter investments, increase ties between research and development (R&D), universities and private initiative, and promote the application of advanced technology to the extraction of natural resources and the production of goods.[9] Nonetheless, and in their own way, domestic politics in both cases has yet to fully embrace these prescriptions for promoting competitiveness.

In Mexico, the pending reform tasks inherited by the administration of Vicente Fox (2000-06) were waylaid by the unexpected difficulties that arose between the country's first democratically elected executive, a minority government, and the divided Congress which he was handed. This meant the delay of crucial competitiveness measures in the realm of energy sector modernization, fiscal restructuring, labor market mobility, and stronger technical support and credit access for those small and medium-sized firms that provide the bulk of Mexican employment. Although Fox's successor, Felipe Calderón (2006-12), has proven to be more politically adroit in navigating a divided Congress, the pace of micro-level reforms is still tediously slow and far too incremental.

Remarkably, the inability of all the relevant actors to overcome a longstanding collective action gridlock in reforming Mexico's energy sector has crippled the ability of this energy-rich nation to cash in fully on the latest oil price boom. Moreover, China, with its lower costs on utility inputs for industrial production, more favorable corporate tax rates, and blitzkrieg educational investment in the higher-skilled professions, is now burrowing through the more sophisticated sub-sectors of the US electronics market (computer peripherals, sound and television equipment, telecoms), which Mexico can no longer claim as its own (Martínez Cortes and Castillo 2004). As Table 1 shows, the penalties for reform delay have been steep, including a slowdown in productivity growth since 2004, a decline in high-tech exports as a percent of GDP, and the aforementioned plateau in the growth of per capita GDP.

---

9   On Mexico, see Lederman, Mahoney, Servén (2005), ch. 6; on Canada, see Roger Martin's January 2005 presentation at the World Economic Forum. Available at: http://www.competeprosper.ca/images/uploads/davos5.pdf [accessed 22 July 2007].

As for Canada, the most serious challenge that stands out in Table 1 is the mediocre productivity gains that the country has registered in the NAFTA era. Since 1997, and long before the current energy price boom, Canada has been the fastest growing G8 economy, registering a fiscal surplus for most of this time period. Thanks to a major fiscal overhaul and deep structural reforms implemented through the 1990s, public debt has been reduced by nearly 30 percent of GDP. In stark contrast to the US fiscal situation, Canada's public pension and healthcare systems are basically on sound footing. Despite registering a respectable increase in high-tech exports and holding the line on R&D spending as a percentage of GDP, the puzzle remains as to why these considerable feats have not spilled over into higher levels of per capita GDP, productivity and overall competitiveness.

In Canada's case, the bottleneck appears to lie in the breach between the candid and prescriptive insights offered up in the literature on Canadian economic policy and performance, and the constellation of political coalitions, special interests and regional factions that have succeeded over time–intentionally or not–in perpetuating Canada's low-productivity status quo. More specifically, the parameters of public policy debate in Canada still seem to juxtapose nationalist comforts and quality-of-life issues against the kinds of market-oriented economic measures that would reduce the numerous barriers to higher productivity and competitiveness (Wise 2008). These would include, for example, the reduction of inter-provincial trade barriers, the removal of restrictions on labor mobility, the loosening of controls on the production and distribution of public goods and services, and lower taxes on capital and income (Howitt 2007). Canadian politicians and policy makers have repeatedly postponed such measures, and in so doing have hampered opportunities for stronger growth of per capita GDP and upward mobility on the part of the average Canadian.

NAFTA's potential here is limited, as it seems safe to say that NAFTA has delivered its punch in terms of the role that enhanced levels of trade and investment can play in catalyzing further microeconomic change for both Canada and Mexico. Because of the minimalist institutional framework that all three members agreed to at the outset, NAFTA has basically been frozen in place and is sorely out of date when it comes to tackling today's structural challenges.

The bloom is already slightly off of Canada's aggregate growth rate, as the 2008-09 US financial implosion has placed downward pressure on Canada's real growth, although Canadian banks did succeed in fending off the worst of the financial contagion from the US turmoil and related global crisis. As for Mexico, still suffering from the effects of US contagion on both the financial and trade fronts, there are simply no grounds for the apparent complacency among political decision makers that NAFTA membership and Mexico's proximity to the US market will somehow guarantee that the integration gains made thus far are irreversible.

The Twilight of North American Integration

The importance of Canada and Mexico as US trade and investment partners is indisputable, and the impressive growth of North American gross product is testimony to the depth of these ties. At this point, however, NAFTA's operational tendencies are still more akin to two bilateral deals that have basically been cobbled together, meaning that the whole is no greater that the sum of its parts. Whereas the very creation of NAFTA is testimony to the possibilities of trilateral coordination based on the national interests of each trade partner (Studer 2007), all three countries adamantly resisted the option of strengthening this cooperation via the creation of European Union (EU)-style supranational institutions.

Canada and Mexico opposed the institutional formalization of NAFTA on the grounds that they would be pushed around and further disempowered by the United States if North America were to take the supranational institutional route. The United States reacted in its typical Anglo-Saxon fashion, pejoratively equating the creation of supranational institutions with the proliferation of the "Brussels bureaucracy" in North America. This insistence that NAFTA remain a free trade area in the absence of sound institutional moorings has thus stunted its evolution into a more compelling regional project and limited its success to the narrow parameters by which NAFTA was originally defined. Not surprisingly, the growth in NAFTA trade during the administration of George W. Bush (2001–09) was about 3 percent, versus the 9.8 percent growth rate registered in 1994–2000 (Pastor 2008: 87).

The difficulties of expanding or renovating NAFTA are such that a renewed tri-national effort to address today's difficult microeconomic realities was launched in March 2005 in the form of a parallel initiative–the Security and Prosperity Partnership of North America (SPP).[10] From there followed the creation of a North American Competitiveness Council (NAAC), which has focused on the need for a sweeping round of further deregulation. Unfortunately, these recent gestures mainly prescribe rather than mandate more coordinated policy approaches for enhancing productivity and competitiveness in North America, and each piles on new tasks with no concrete organizational mechanisms or significant financial allotments for implementing them. "If you measure progress by examining the growth in trade, the reduction in wait times at the borders, and the public's support for integration, all of these initiatives have failed miserably" (Pastor 2008: 87).

In light of this impasse, it seems safe to say that the authentic revival of NAFTA as a regional project would require that the United States, as the hegemonic member and industrial anchor, step forward with the necessary leadership and provision of public goods. Yet, the most visible US commitment in the Bush era was the construction of a double-layered wall and hundreds of miles of vehicle barriers along the 1,933-mile US-Mexico border meant to halt the northward flow of undocumented workers. Mandated by the Secure Fence Act of 2006 in the wake

---

10   See Clarkson (2008).

of failed efforts within the US Congress to reach bipartisan agreement over guest worker, amnesty clauses, and any number of other sticking points in the proposed immigration legislation, the US Department of Homeland Security expects to complete this project by 2011 at a cost of US$7.6 billion (Stables 2007). With long delays at the border post-9/11 and badly needed improvements in the highway infrastructure that links the three countries, this hefty US financial commitment to construct further border barriers has understandably enraged its NAFTA partners.

A final wedge is China, now a major trade and investment presence throughout the Western Hemisphere. Whereas China's trade relationship with South America is based on more traditional patterns of comparative advantage–China's export of lower-end industrial goods and its import of primary products from Argentina, Brazil and Chile, in particular–the China-NAFTA relationship is one of export similarity and fierce competition for manufacturing market share, especially with regard to Mexico and the United States.[11] For example, Mexico's export similarity index with China stood at 25.1 in 2004, versus 17.4 for Brazil or 7.0 for Argentina (Devlin 2008: 117-121).

With more than 80 percent of Mexico's exports destined for the US market this has become the locus of a fierce battle for market share, for Mexican and US producers alike. Between 2002-08, Mexico's share of the US import market slipped by 11 percent, from 11.6 to 10.3 percent, while China's share rose by 50 percent, from 10.8 percent to 16.2 percent (Watkins 2009: 4). As can be seen in Table 2, China is quickly encroaching on Mexico's US market share in computer hardware, telephone equipment, and apparel.

Given that nearly all of Mexico's manufactured exports to the United States are goods produced by companies that operate under the *Maquila* (two-thirds of manufactured exports) or Pitex (one-third of manufactured exports) programs, i.e. programs that were specifically designed to deepen US-Mexican integration in these sectors, it is incumbent upon both sides in this partnership to work jointly to combat these intense competitive challenges from China (Watkins 2009: 2).

An added pressure is the rapidity with which China is increasing the value-added content and technological sophistication of its manufactured exports. Along with China's outpacing of all other developing countries in its growth of manufactured exports from 2000-2006, it is now increasing its competitiveness in high technology exports at an even greater speed than in manufacturing as a whole (Gallagher, Moreno Brid and Porzecanski 2008). Although Mexico is the only Latin American country to rank amongst the top twenty developing countries in terms of the technological content of its manufactured exports, Kevin Gallagher and others report that as of 2006, 82 percent of Mexican exports in this category were under some degree of competitive threat from China (Gallagher, Moreno Brid and Porzecanski 2008). From 1985-2006, even the developed countries lost some 20 percent of their share of the high technology market to China, thus

---

11   See Phillips (2007), Santiso (2007), and Wise and Quiliconi (2007).

Table 1.2   Leading US Imports from Mexico and China in 2008

Mexico Category	Value Bill $	Share of total (per-cent) Percent	China Category	Value Bill $	Share of total (per-cent) Percent
Crude petroleum	37.6	17.4	Computers and parts	52.6	15.6
Motor vehicle parts	22.2	10.3	Textiles and apparel	36.4	10.8
Motor vehicles	22.2	10.3	Telephone equipment	24.0	7.1
Consumer electronics	19.7	9.1	Consumer electronics	22.2	6.6
Agricultural products	12.1	5.6	Toys and games	21.3	6.3
Telephone equipment	10.5	4.9	Chemicals and related products, including plastics	20.9	6.2
Chemicals and related products, including articles of plastics	6.8	3.1	Footwear	14.4	4.2
Computers and parts	6.6	3.1	Furniture	13.6	4.0
Textiles and apparel	6.0	2.8	Household appliances	7.4	2.2
Electrical circuit apparatus	4.8	2.2	Forest products	7.4	2.2
Medical goods	4.5	2.1	Steel mill products	6.0	1.8
Household appliances	4.4	2.0	Luggage and handbags	5.9	1.7
Steel mill products	3.3	1.5	Motor vehicle parts	5.8	1.7
Precious metal	2.8	1.3	Agricultural products	5.6	1.7
Measuring, testing, and controlling instruments	2.7	1.2	Sporting goods	4.1	1.2
Electrical motors	2.5	1.2	Lamps & lighting fittings	3.9	1.2
Air-conditioning equipment	2.4	1.1	Air-conditioning equipment	3.2	0.9
Non-automotive insulated wire	2.1	1.0	Electrical circuit apparatus	3.2	0.9
Electrical transformers	2.0	0.9	Electrical transformers	2.5	0.7
All other	41.1	19.0	All other	77.12	22.8
Total	216.3	100.0	Total	337.5	100.0

Source: Ralph Watkins, "The China Challenge to Manufacturing in Mexico," paper presented at "Global Perspectives Conference: Focus on China," Ellard School of Management, University of Arizona, April 3, 2009, based on data compiled by the US International Trade Commission from official statistics of the US Department of Commerce.

underlining the magnitude of the task that lies before Mexico and the developing countries overall.

The irony in Mexico's case is that the stated purpose of the country's 1994 entry into NAFTA was precisely to advance steadily up the industrial learning curve and to situate domestic producers more securely on the technological frontier. After all, a broad consensus has emerged within the literature concerning the importance of R&D, industrial learning, technological upgrading, and innovation for a given country's ability to trigger higher levels of sustainable growth (Rodrik 2007). What went wrong? A shorthand explanation seems to lie in Mexico's reliance on a market-driven, or "neoliberal" approach to technology acquisition and innovation (Wise 2007). Prior to entering NAFTA, trade and investment were liberalized, longstanding industrial policies were dismantled, and state firms were sold off. Under NAFTA, the innovation process, including technology transfer and R&D, was relegated to foreign direct investment (FDI) in Mexico's assembly plants, and it was envisioned that innovation would result from the dynamic spillovers and multiplier effects of heightened trade and investment flows (Gallagher, Moreno Brid and Porzecanski 2008).

However, sixteen years later, Alberto O. Hirschman's long-prescribed "forward" and "backward" linkages between foreign and domestic firms–a pre-condition for development-oriented capital accumulation and productive growth–have yet to be sufficiently forged (Franko 2007: 60). Expenditures on R&D have actually declined since 1994, and under the prevailing laissez-faire regime the country's Information Technology (IT) sector and firms have been decimated (Dussel Peters 2008). In light of its privileged access to the US market since 1994, Mexico's competitive capabilities may have advanced to the extent that it made it into the ranks of the top twenty developing countries in terms of technological inroads, but Table 1.2 suggests how quickly this is changing given the rise of China in both the US market and the global economy.

With US policy makers fixated on the completion of a highly symbolic wall along the Mexican border, and US public opinion closely holding on to its longstanding NAFTA grudge, Chinese investors are also quietly staking out their claims in the Mexican market. The overriding goal on both sides is to establish manufacturing operations in Mexico based on integrated global production chains, with an eye toward exporting to the US market.

For example, while still an incipient trend, the Chinese computer company Lenovo is establishing supply facilities in the northern Mexican state of Chihuahua, the Golden Dragon firm is constructing a plant to produce copper tubes in the state of Coahuila and, in the Mexican state of Hidalgo, China's Giant Engine Company has invested US$50 million to acquire an auto assembly plant (Ellis 2009). Through joint partnerships with companies such as Mexico's Grupo Elektra, a major distributor and financier of infrastructure, Chinese automakers like Zhongxing, the First Automobile Works, and others have set their sights on jointly producing some 1.6 million cars per year in Mexico by 2012.

Thus, by basically turning its back on Mexico the United States could soon be facing the worst-case scenario of all with regard to its mammoth commercial deficit: the displacement of US suppliers by Chinese firms in Mexico's *maquila* assembly plants–a trend that is now underway–and China's ability to offset Mexico's higher labor and production costs by meeting NAFTA's regional content requirements and thereby gaining duty-free access to the US market. Needless to say, this is a far cry from what NAFTA's architects originally had in mind.

Conclusions: The Legacy of NAFTA

As of 2009 NAFTA had met its prime objectives. Some 99 percent of goods and services in those sectors covered by NAFTA now flow duty-free between Canada, Mexico and the United States, and the explicit goals of increasing trade and foreign investment in North America have been met. Yet, for reasons that vary from the standpoint of each of the three members, NAFTA has fallen short of its original expectations. In the US case, the Clinton administration had announced its plans for NAFTA expansion in December 1994 with the hosting of the Miami Summit and proposal to negotiate an FTAA by 2005. Alas, domestic politics obstructed this plan and, despite the stipulation of Article 24 of the GATT that a preferential arrangement such as NAFTA should remain open to new members, there have been none.

Thus, the hopes of the United States to use NAFTA as a springboard for forging a hemispheric bloc and, in turn, the use of the latter to leverage important concessions around old and new trade issues at the Doha round, basically went up in smoke. The collapse of negotiations for both the FTAA and Doha round reflect in no small part the need to revamp the US trade policy apparatus in terms of organizational cohesiveness, leadership, and a more clearly defined set of US foreign economic policy objectives. In the bigger scheme of things and to the chagrin of Canada and Mexico, NAFTA has basically been a third-best option for the United States all along, one that counted for less than 1 percent of US GDP at the outset. This partially explains the pattern of benign neglect that has underpinned the US stance toward NAFTA. Moreover, despite paying lip service to the SPP and the need to forge ahead with new "NAFTA-plus" measures in the 2000s, the dominant US trade strategy since 2002 has been the negotiation of numerous bilateral deals in Asia, the Middle East, and Latin America.

For Canada and Mexico, the asymmetries involved have always meant that NAFTA is enormously more important for both. Hindsight shows that the decision of each to collude with the United States in opposing the creation of strong regional institutions stunted the possibilities for NAFTA's evolution into a more dynamic project.

Canada, in contrast to Mexico, did actively support the negotiation of an FTAA with hemispheric-level institutions to guide this process; however, Canada's impressive leadership efforts in the FTAA process and its hopes of counterbalancing

US dominance over NAFTA through the completion of a broader hemispheric accord were patently thwarted. Thus, on the regional integration front, and in light of heightened competition in the US market from China and a growing list of new US bilateral FTA partners, Canada still faces the prospect of remaining a mere spoke to the US trade and investment hub.

Since 2007 the Canadian government has responded by launching its own bilateral FTA strategy in Latin America and, given the continued anti-NAFTA sentiment reflected in US political discourse and public opinion polls, in late 2008 Canadian Prime Minister Stephen Harper signed an agreement to begin negotiating an FTA with the EU.[12] On the table are possibilities for the reciprocal opening up of air travel, government procurement and the two-way mobility of skilled workers across the Atlantic. While still incipient, a potential EU-Canada agreement may actually enhance Canada's quest to achieve NAFTA or WTO-plus measures that have stalled in North America.

Canada's progress in the NAFTA era has been such that it is gradually gaining the fame of a small, open economy that is very much on the move. Some of Canada's success since the mid-1990s had to do with NAFTA-induced restructuring and the country's having hit the commodity lottery in the 2000s, but the long-running boom is also a tribute to an earlier round of risk taking and tenacity on the part of the country's leaders. The micro-level indicators reviewed here confirm that it is now time to take this restructuring project to the next level. Canada's sophisticated economic institutions are an asset for undertaking another round of reforms to foster higher productivity and competitiveness. However, the domestic political incentives must somehow be realigned to support these micro-level reforms.

This analysis also emphasized the ways in which Canada has used its privileged access to the US market as an opportunity to restructure the economy despite the hefty political costs and to introduce sweeping changes to its historically mercantilist trade strategy. Mexico, in contrast, seized NAFTA membership as a way of locking in a new market-oriented reform model, one for which there has been insufficient preparation or follow-up. Sixteen years after the fact, numerous sectors of the Mexican economy (telecom, finance, petroleum, bread, tortillas) remain under monopolistic control. Mexican firms, moreover, trail their regional peers in the adoption of innovation and information technologies. To questionable avail, Mexico placed almost blind faith in neoclassical trade dictums and the power of geographical proximity to the US market to trigger higher growth and lift its population out of poverty.

According to the minimalist criteria of trade and investment expansion, Mexico used its NAFTA membership to effectively shift away from a heavy dependence on oil exports and toward a more diversified mix of higher value-added goods over the past two decades. As estimated in a 2005 report by Daniel Lederman and his colleagues at the World Bank's Latin America and Caribbean Division,

---

12   "Nafta-Plus." 2008. *The Wall Street Journal*, 20 October, A18.

Mexico's global exports would have been about 50 percent lower and foreign direct investment (FDI) would have been about 40 percent less without NAFTA. Also, the amount of time required for Mexican manufacturers to adopt US technological innovations was cut in half ... NAFTA made Mexico richer by about 4 per cent of its gross domestic product (GDP) per capita (Lederman et al. 2005).

However, although Mexico may arguably have been worse off had it not joined NAFTA, counterfactual analysis (that is, comparisons of Mexico with other Latin American emerging markets that did not join NAFTA) and the data in Table 1 confirm its pattern of under-performance.

NAFTA's critics have been quick to lay blame on the agreement itself, but Mexico's own reform record suggests that these shortcomings lie just as much in the frailties of domestic politics, institutions, and policy-making. In particular, trade policy makers were shortsighted in their adamant opposition to China's 2001 entry into the WTO and their aloof stance on the FTAA–thinking they could perhaps stall indefinitely the entry of other competitors into the US market. Instead, the United States actively sought bilateral FTAs around the world in the 2000s, thereby quickening the erosion of Mexico's preferential status, and China's rapid ascendance in the US market has further exacerbated these losses. In some fundamental ways, then, Mexico, rather than buckling down in executing a competition policy and other imperative reforms, squandered its preferential access to the US market.

Looking forward, a true revival of NAFTA would require that regional leaders agree on a continental strategy that taps labor markets across the three borders, tackles the huge asymmetries that continue to divide Mexico from its partners, and invests more vigorously in infrastructure and technology transfer. At this political economic juncture, such a strategy does not appear to be in the cards. Rather, it is the anti-NAFTA coalition in the US that has kept the continental debate alive. By skillfully conflating substance with symbol, anti-NAFTA public discourse in North America has steadily eaten away at this particular brand of regionalism. Unhappily, the daunting domestic and regional repercussions of the 2008-09 financial meltdown in the United States are sure to further stoke these flames. As Canada looks to the EU for answers and Mexico retreats into a survival-oriented mode, it seems safe to say that North America has officially entered the post-NAFTA era.

References

Bhagwati, J. 2008. *Termites in the Trading System: how Preferential Agreements Undermine Free Trade.* New York: Oxford University Press.

Bouzas, R. and Ros, J. 1994. The North–South Variety of Economic Integration: Issues and Prospects for Latin America, in *Economic Integration in the Western Hemisphere* edited by R. Bouzas & J. Ros. Notre Dame, Ind: University of Notre Dame Press, 1–45.

Cameron, M. and Wise, C. 2004. The Political Impact of NAFTA on Mexico: Reflections on the Political Economy of Democratization. *Canadian Journal of Political Science*, 37(2), 301-23.

Cameron, M.A and Tomlin, B.W. 2000. *The Making of NAFTA: How the Deal was Done.* Ithaca, NY: Cornell University Press.

Chase, K. 2003. Economic Interests and Regional Trading Arrangements: The Case of NAFTA. *International Organization*, 57(1), 137-174.

Clarkson, S. 2008. Maneuvering within the Continental Constitution: Autonomy and Capacity within the Security and Prosperity Partnership of North America, in *Canada among Nations 2007*, edited by J. Daudelin & D. Schwanen. Quebec: McGill-Queens University Press, 248-67.

Destler, I.M. 2005. *American Trade Politics* 4th Edition. Washington, DC: Institute for International Economics.

Devlin, R. 2008. China's Economic Rise, in *China's Expansion into the Western Hemisphere*, edited by R. Roett and G. Paz. Washington, DC: Brookings Institution, 111-147.

Dussel Peters, E. 2008. *Inversion extranjera directa en Mexico: desempeño y potencia.l* Mexico: Siglo XXI.

Ellis, R.E. 2009. *China in Latin America: the whats and wherefores.* Boulder, Colorado: Lynne Rienner.

Franko, P. 2007. *The Puzzle of Latin American Development.* Lanham, MD: Rowman and Littlefield, third edition.

Gallagher, K., Moreno Brid, J.C., and Porzecanski, R. 2008. The Dynamism of Mexican Exports: Lost in (Chinese) Translation? *World Development*, 36(8), 1365-1380.

Gertz, B. 2002. *The China Threat: How the People's Republic Targets America.* Washington, DC: Regnery Publishing.

Goldstein, M. and Lardy, N.R (eds). 2008. *Debating China's Exchange Rate Policy.* Washington, D.C: (Peterson Institute for International Economics.

Howitt, P. 2007. Innovation, Competition, and Growth: A Schumpeterian Perspective on Canada's Economy. *C.D. Howe Institute Commentary*, 246, 1-15.

Hufbauer, G.C and Schott, J.J. 2005. *NAFTA Revisited: Achievements and Challenges.* Washington, DC: Institute for International Economics.

Lawrence, R.Z. 1996. *Regionalism, Multilateralism, and Deeper Integration.* Washington, DC: Brookings.

Lederman, D., Mahoney, W.F and Servén, L. 2005. *Lessons from NAFTA for Latin America and the Caribbean*. Washington DC: World Bank.

Lo, C. 2006. *Phantom of the China Economic Threat*. New York: Palgrave Macmillan.

Lorber, J. 2009. Early Word: Three Amigos. The Caucus Blog-New York Time. com, August, 10. Available at: http://thecaucus.blogs.nytimes.com/2009/08/10/early-word-three-amigos/?scp=12&sq=NAFTA&st=cse [accessed April 24, 2010].

Martin, R. January 2005 presentation at the World Economic Forum. Available at: http: www.competeprosper.ca/images/uploads/davos5.pdf [accessed 22 July 2007].

Martínez Cortes, J.I and Neme Castillo, O. 2004. La ventaja comparativa de China y México en el mercado estadounidense. *Comercio Exterior*, 54(6), 516-28.

Menges, C. 2005. *China: The Gathering Threat*. Nashville: Nelson Current.

Mosley, P. Globalisation, 2000. Economic Policy and Convergence. *World Economy*, 23(5), 613-34.

Nafta-Plus. 2008. *The Wall Street Journal*, 20 October, A18.

Pastor, M. and Wise, C. 1994. The Origins and Sustainability of Mexico's Free Trade Policy. *International Organization*, 48(3), 459-89.

Pastor, R. 2008. The Future of North America. *Foreign Affairs*, 87(4), 84-98.

Phillips, N. 2007. Consequences of an Emerging China: Is Development Space Disappearing for Latin America and the Caribbean? *Centre for International Governance Innovation Working Papers*, 14.

Rodrik, D. 2007. *One Economics, Many Recipes: Globalization, Institutions, and Economic Growth*. Princeton: Princeton University Press.

Sachs, .J and Warner, A. 1995. Economic Convergence and Economic Policies, *National Bureau of Economic Research, Working Papers*, 5039.

Santiso, J. (ed.). 2007. *The Visible Hand of China in Latin America*. Paris: OECD Publishing.

Stables, E. 2007. Border Fence Construction Not Moving Fast Enough for Rep Hunter. *The New York Times*, 11 July.

Studer, I. 2007. Obstacles to Integration: NAFTA's Institutional Weakness, in *Requiem or Revival? The Promise of North American Integration*, edited by I. Studer and C. Wise. Washington, DC: Brookings, 53-75.

TradeStats Express, International Trade Administration, Foreign Trade Division, US Centre Bureau, US Department of Commerce. Available at: http:tse.export.gov/MapFrameset.aspx?MapPage NTDMap Display.aspx&UniqueURL pbst ck551vkuf2mr2kzw0q55-2008-5-40-17-37-33 [accessed: 7 July 2008]. ¼

Wade, R. 2004. Is Globalization Reducing Poverty and Inequality? *World Development*, 32(4), 567-89.

Watkins, R. 2009. The China Challenge to Manufacturing in Mexico, paper presented at "Global Perspectives Conference: Focus on China," Ellard School of Management, University of Arizona, April.

Wise, C. and Quiliconi, C. 2007. China's Surge in Latin American Markets: Policy Challenges and Responses. *Politics and Policy*, 35(3), 410-38.

Wise, C. 1998. Introduction: NAFTA, Mexico, and the Western Hemisphere, in *The Post-NAFTA Political Economy: Mexico and the Western Hemisphere*, edited by C. Wise. University Park, PA: Pennsylvania State University Press, 1-37.

Wise, C. 2008. The US Competitive Liberalization Strategy: Canada's Policy Options, in *Canada among Nations 2007: What Room for Maneuver?*, edited by J. Daudelin & D. Schwanen. Quebec: McGill-Queen's University Press, 225-47.

Wise, C. 2007. Unfulfilled Promise: Economic Convergence under NAFTA, in *Requiem or Revival? The Promise of North American Integration*, edited by I. Studer and C. Wise. Washington, DC: Brookings, 27-52.

Chapter 2
Governing the North American Free Trade Area: International Rulemaking and Delegation in NAFTA, the SPP, and Beyond[1]

Louis Bélanger[2]

Introduction

The North American free trade area appears to have reached an impasse. On the one hand, it is facing an institutional deficit that hinders its competitiveness. Deprived of adequate rule-making mechanisms, the three economic partners– Canada, Mexico, and the United States–cannot effectively adapt the regional trade and investment regime instituted by the now fifteen-year-old North American Free Trade Agreement (NAFTA). For the same reason, they have not yet been able to address pressing new problems adequately, the most important being the matter of regulatory coordination. Simply put, without serious institutional reform, the NAFTA compact is not sustainable (Bélanger 2007). On the other hand, because of the regional asymmetry of power, deeply ingrained attitudes toward sovereignty, and idiosyncratic treaty-making practices, any form of European-style supra-nationalism has unequivocally been ruled out as a conceivable way to administer the economic zone. The question is: Should North Americans abandon any prospect of deeper economic integration and expect an inevitable decline in free trade in the region?

1   This chapter was first published in *Latin American Policy. A Journal of Politics and Governance of a Changing Region.* Vol. 1, No. 1, May 2010.

2   I would like to thank Kim Fontaine-Skronski for her excellent research assistance on this project. This research was supported by grants from the Social Sciences and Humanities Research Council and the *Fonds québécois de recherche sur la société et la culture.* An earlier version of this text was presented in July 2009 at the 21st World Congress of the International Political Association in Santiago, Chile, and benefited from thoughtful comments and suggestions by panel participants and by Erick Duchesne, Richard Ouellet, and Jonathan Paquin. Finally, parts of this article draw on a study commissioned by the Canada-US Project at Carleton University (Canada-US Project 2009) and therefore benefited enormously from comments by the Carleton team, especially Fen Hampson, Michael Hart and Colin Robertson. I, of course, remain solely responsible for the content of this article and for any mistakes still present.

This chapter attempts to answer this question by first pointing out that supra-nationalism, or the international delegation of authority, is not in any way a necessary condition for effective international rulemaking. In fact, as will be seen, *ex post* or continuous rulemaking is almost never delegated in international cooperative agreements. The key ingredient for effective international rulemaking is not the external delegation of authority, but rather the level of domestic executive autonomy states are able to pool and coordinate through often sophisticated, but not necessarily legally binding, international institutions. As will be seen, this is the case even in the European Union, and because the United States can be considered our "hard case" here–theoretically and in the North American political context–I will discuss examples of international rule-making bodies to which the US is a party that are operating exclusively within the perimeters of the executive branch, even without the requirement of any form of legislative ratification.

Informed by this perspective on international rulemaking, this chapter offers an original assessment of NAFTA, and of the more recent Security and Prosperity Partnership of North America (SPP). In particular, it provides an in-depth comparative analysis of the level of executive discretion pooled in the SPP working groups and concludes that the SPP amalgamates enough executive autonomy to constitute a basis for the establishment of a non-treaty international rule-making body. It then suggests paths by which the three governments could upgrade the SPP design in such a way as to make it possible to break through the institutional "ceiling" (Moens and Cust 2008: 11) that has so far limited all attempts to deepen the process of North American integration, and provide the region with the rule-making capability it needs.

International Rulemaking and the Delegation Problem

Signing international treaties, or other binding instruments such as free trade agreements, is the conventional way for states to commit themselves to the rules by which they attempt to govern the global economy and other international issue areas. In the majority of cases, these international legal agreements are definitive; that is, they do not provide for any means of adding new rules or modifying existing rules apart from renegotiation, or its equivalent. However, renegotiation can be costly, and adaptation may be necessary in order to cope with a changing world. Therefore, although states value stable rules, they sometimes decide to opt for non-definitive, or flexible, international agreements that provide for *ex post* rule-making, or secondary ruling. They then create a decision-making body (a commission, council, general assembly, or conference of parties) and grant this entity the authority to decide on rules that were not initially stipulated in the original agreement.

When they do so, states in general jealously guard this *ex post* rule-making capability for themselves. The bodies to which the rule-making authority is granted are almost always collectives made up of all the members of the agreements themselves. Koremenos coined the expression "internal delegation" to describe this phenomenon and distinguish it from "external delegation," that is, delegation to a supranational third party (Koremenos 2008: 152). In a statistical survey recently conducted by this author on a sample of 97 international agreements, rule-making capability was found in the provisions of only ten. In all these cases, this capability was "internally delegated" rather than "externally delegated" (162). In another, more qualitative survey, Guzman and Landsidle, who dispute the very notion that "internal delegation" should be considered as delegation, reach a similar conclusion: "[T]o date states have delegated legislative or decision-making authority to supra-national entities in extraordinarily few instances. Moreover, in virtually every instance the delegation is narrowly cabined in terms of its scope, its importance, and its ability to actually influence state conduct" (Guzman and Landsidle 2008: 2).

Therefore, the process by which states organize *ex post* rule-making authority (the authority to add new rules) is radically different from the process by which they organize *ex post* adjudicative authority (the authority to interpret and enforce existing rules).[3] While states frequently and truly delegate adjudicative power to third parties (international tribunals or *ad hoc* panels), they maintain a firm grip on rulemaking by designing decision-making procedures in which they themselves remain the deciders. This means that, *stricto sensu*, there is generally no delegation involved in international rulemaking, if delegation is defined as it usually is in political science as "a conditional grant of authority from a *principal* to an *agent* that empowers the latter to act on behalf of the former" (Hawkins et al. 2006: 7; italics in original). There is usually no separate agent involved in "internal delegation". Therefore, this also means that states do not surrender significant degrees of autonomy or sovereignty when they engage in international rulemaking (see Guzman and Landsidle 2008).

If there is no real delegation and states retain to themselves the authority to modify or supplement existing agreements, what then makes these international rule-making mechanisms different from plain renegotiation? Basically, it is the fact that they provide for amending procedures that do not require full domestic ratification, often involving legislative action, on the part of the contracting parties. For example, many international agreements contain provisions for secondary ruling that explicitly isolate parts of the binding rules–more technical in nature and often set aside from the main body of the treaty in annexes or schedules–and allow for a more expedited and secure way to modify these rules than is normally required for more basic commitments. Sometimes the agreement itself provides for a simplified mode of domestic acquiescence for these types of secondary rules, but in other cases, new rules can become binding even without domestic action. A good example of the first case can be found in NAFTA itself. This otherwise inflexible agreement, which will be described below, permits some minor

---

3   On the distinction between the two kinds of "delegation," see Abbott and Snidal, 2003: 433.

modifications to the original classification of products for origin determination, or the schedule for tariff elimination, that do not require full ratification procedures. In the United States, this means that instead of going back to Congress for a vote, the adoption of the new rules simply requires a presidential proclamation preceded by consultations of the Committee on Ways and Means of the House of Representatives and the Senate Committee on Finance (House of Representatives 1993 sec. 103 and 202). An example of the second case can be found in international agreements containing "tacit amendment" procedures.[4] Tacit amendments become binding on a state if it acquiesces simply by failing to object after a given period of time, which means that there is no need for ratification. In a few other instances, such as in the case of the Montreal Protocol on Substances that Deplete the Ozone Layer, states cannot opt out of new rules even when the latter are adopted by a majority vote. However, as Guzman and Landsidle show, these provisions cover a limited number of highly technical and not very consequential rules (2008: 13-14). Lastly, there are many cases in which, the original arrangement having itself been concluded as an "executive" agreement without legislative approval, amending protocols can be swiftly negotiated.

Thus, states can and often do engage in international secondary ruling without delegating their decision-making authority and becoming entangled in supranational institutions. This is how and why the US, in spite of being so jealous of its sovereignty, does indeed engage, like other states, in "living" international arrangements. The main difficulty does not arise from the problem of *international delegation*, but from the problem of *domestic delegation*. In order to commit their respective states to new international rules, the executives participating in secondary ruling processes must themselves have the power to translate international commitments into enforceable domestic rules. In some instances, when the executive agencies already possess large amounts of authority, derived from constitutions or delegated by legislative bodies, the organization of international secondary ruling can be unproblematic. Nevertheless, when, on specific issues, agencies do not possess the constitutional or delegated authority to regulate domestically, international rulemaking is much more difficult. This is the case even in the European Union, despite the formidable development of European supranational institutions. A recent empirical analysis by Eberlein and Grande reports: "it is striking that the European agencies, insofar as they carry out regulatory tasks at all, are far from having the powers (rule-setting, implementation, dispute settlement) typical of classical independent regulatory agencies" (2005: 95). In the specific area of economic regulation, "[t]he bulk of regulatory activity here lies unambiguously at member-state level" (104). Therefore, European states achieve regulatory coordination more effectively through intergovernmental,

---

4   Some examples of these are the International Maritime Organization, the International Convention for the Regulation of Whaling, the Chemical Weapons Convention, and the Montreal Protocol on Substances that Deplete the Ozone Layer (see Bradley 2006).

rather than supranational, institutions. Thus, international delegation is not a prerequisite, whereas domestic delegation is critical:

> Externally, regulatory networks can perform their co-ordination function only on the precondition that participants be allowed a certain degree of independence and *de facto* room for manoeuvre in their decisions. A national regulatory authority that has no significant powers within its respective national regime, for instance, will find it hard to become effectively involved in transnational networks because it will lack the capacity for making credible commitments to partners. (103)

Because the US case will be central in the discussion below, it can be used as a useful example here. US constitutional practice gives the President, and therefore the executive branch, more autonomy to engage directly, and in a more flexible manner, in international rulemaking in the security area than in the trade area. National security clearly falls within the president's plenary powers as Commander-in-Chief, even though Congress retains the power of military appropriations (see Yoo 2005 chap. 8). The president's direct authority in this realm, as well as the cumulative effect of his power to make international agreements "as authorized by treaty", have contributed to the development of more flexible international commitments. For example, post-world-war treaties signed with allies have subsequently given legal legitimacy to several significant agreements negotiated as sole executive agreements (Yoo 2005: 285). One of these, the North American Aerospace Command agreement (NORAD), has gone as far as establishing a joint Canada–US military command for the defense of North American airspace and has regularly been amended without the need for legislative action (see Jockel 2007). The contrast with the situation pertaining to trade-related matters is striking. Congress has always exercised firm and direct control over tax and other revenue raising policies, and the House Committee on Ways and Means has closely guarded its rule-making authority in these areas. Therefore, traditional trade policy, comprising tariff measures, is a policy area in which the executive branch must content itself with particularly low levels of delegated authority. US legislators periodically delegate impressive levels of authority to the president for the negotiation of trade agreements, but once these deals are sealed, Congress keeps a firm grip on all matters related to customs and tariff regulations. Accordingly, traditional trade agreements negotiated by the US have been carefully crafted as definitive agreements, and Congress takes extra precaution, when passing the implementing legislations, to ensure that no *ex post* decisions coming out of the few bodies created by these agreements could be interpreted as self-executing.[5]

A different situation occurs in areas in which the legislative branch, while exercising its constitutional authority, is more willing to delegate regulatory

---

5   On self-execution and the recent treaty-making practice in the US, see the contrasting opinions of Bradley 2003, and Cinotti 2003.

matters to the executive branch. In such instances, it is easier for the executive branch to unilaterally commit itself internationally. In the US, this can be achieved by tacit amendment or, if needed, by "sole executive agreements" as well as "agreements made by virtue of an existing treaty", which are concluded solely by the president without legislative approval. For example, the successive Softwood Lumber Agreements negotiated with Canada have been ratified as sole executive agreements (Softwood Lumber Agreement 2006). Although they are trade related, these agreements essentially deal with anti-dumping (AD) and countervailing duty (CVD) determinations, an authority delegated by Congress to the Department of Commerce and the International Trade Commission. Although precise data on sole executive agreements are difficult to obtain, experts agree that the relative number of international agreements concluded by the president without congressional ratification has been significant and is on the rise.[6] Congress can, by law, also direct administrative agencies to implement international rules and standards, and assimilate these as domestic regulations. One authoritative jurist estimates that "[t]he US Code is replete with [such] international assimilations" (Swaine 2004: 1519).[7] It is important to note that international assimilation, as will be seen below, does not require the existence of an international, legally binding agreement.

To sum up this section, international rulemaking is complex, but, contrary to common wisdom, international delegation and the related issue of sovereignty costs are not the main factors underlying the difficulties. Domestic delegation–that is, the amount of authority delegated to the executive branch of the cooperating states and how this delegation is framed–plays a much more significant role.

Trade Liberalization with and without Rule-Making Capability

Currently, as will be seen in greater detail in the next section of this article, NAFTA and the SPP have almost no rule-making capability. Although one positive and reassuring aspect of this fixity is that it provides predictability and protects the NAFTA deal from opportunistic political maneuvers, such fixity also seriously limits the depth and benefits of this trade agreement. Thus, although the 1994 agreement is certainly exemplary of what can be achieved in the absence of continuous rule-making authority, there are levels and areas of trade liberalization that simply cannot be reached by relying exclusively on pre-established rules.

A first, patent, example of the suboptimal situations engendered by discarding secondary ruling capability can be found in NAFTA's rules of origin regimen. The most efficient way to create a free trade area is to establish a common external

---

6   For example, Van Alstine estimates that 15,000 sole executive agreements have been concluded "in the past 50 years", which means an average of 300 agreements per year (2006: 319), while according to Hathaway, only 5.5 percent of all executive agreements are of the "sole" type, which would mean an average of eight per year (2008:1287 note 130).

7   For examples, see US Congress 2004.

tariff for all member countries. In the case of NAFTA, there would be an immense advantage in administering the rules and tariffs applicable to non-regional products solely at their point of entry into North America and leaving the Canada-US and the Mexico-US borders free from tariff controls. However, a common external tariff requires continuous coordination in order to adjust it to evolving trade relations with third countries, which means ongoing rulemaking, or secondary ruling. To avoid this, NAFTA relies on the alternative rules-of-origin solution, which calls for discriminating at each intra-regional border between products that truly originate from the trade-zone member-countries (or that have been sufficiently transformed within their borders), and products that are simply imported from a third country. This is a second-best mechanism that is costly for governments to administer and for businesses to comply with. The overall cost of having NAFTA operate under a rules-of-origin system, in comparison with a common external tariff system, has been estimated, for Canada and Mexico respectively, at more than 1 and 5 percent of their GDPs (Ghosh and Rao 2004: 34). Moreover, it opens the door to protectionist manipulations of levels of "regional content" and therefore risks undoing precisely what the Free Trade Agreement is supposed to achieve.

Another clear example of the costs of avoiding rule-making capability can be found in NAFTA's approach to coordinating trade remedies. Ideally, countries in a free trade pact would exempt each other from the application of their respective AD and CVD laws and adopt a common system of rules and policies related to competition. Again, such a system would not only necessitate enforcement through a regional dispute settlement authority, but would also require the ongoing adjustment of regional rules on dumping and on other distorting practices such as subsidies. Delays have plagued the alternative, the dispute settlement mechanism established by NAFTA's Chapter 19, which provides for the review of the AD/CVD determinations of each country's national agencies. It has also been ineffective in bringing about the settlement of prolonged conflicts, such as the Canada-US softwood lumber or the Mexico-US high-fructose corn syrup disputes, which have hurt the economy and eroded political support for the agreement.

Rules-of-origin and protection against abusive trade remedies are important aspects of any conventional free trade agreement. However, the kinds of trade restrictions and distortions they are aimed at eliminating or reducing, mainly tariffs and subsidies, are now pretty much under control. They are, to paraphrase Pascal Lamy, "20th century issues" (Chen, et al. 2004: 2). The new 21st century frontier of trade liberalization is clearly the reduction of regulatory obstacles to trans-border trade. While over the last quarter century, privatization and market liberalization have led to a retreat of the state as a direct provider of certain public goods, the latter has reinvented itself as the "regulatory state" (see Eberlein and Grande 2005). "Protective regulations" (the regulatory activity aimed at protecting consumers, the environment, labor rights, public health and safety) (Vogel 1995) and "economic regulations" (the regulation of infrastructural and utility sectors such as communications, railways, energy, and water distribution) (Eberlein and Grande 2005: 95-96) have steadily increased, with a significant impact on trade. In some cases, being specifically designed to impose higher costs on some importers, regulations have been used as protectionist non-tariff barriers. More generally, though, regulations affect trade because differences in domestic regulations impose significant compliance costs on producers operating in different jurisdictions; in other words, there can be no true global, or regional, market without concordant rules. Hart has analyzed the costs of regulatory discordance for exporters and reports Organization for Economic Cooperation and Development (OCDE) data that estimate them at between 2 and 10 percent of overall production costs (Hart 2006: 9). In a recent communication to the World Trade Organization (WTO), the three North American governments estimated the amount of their reciprocal trade affected by regulatory non-tariff barriers to be $715 billion (WTO 2009: 2). Regulations also affect trade because they have become a central issue in trade policies. Indeed, trade policymakers must increasingly take into account the preoccupations of constituencies who fear that free trade will make it easier for economic agents to simply escape the reach of regulations by moving their activities to more accommodating jurisdictions. For all these reasons, regulatory coordination has become a central issue of trade liberalization.

The problem is that the coordination or harmonization of regulations–from those affecting food safety to those relating to professional accreditation aimed at guaranteeing the free flow of goods and services–cannot be carried out successfully without "dynamic rulemaking" (WTO 2009: 21). This is necessary for the simple reason that governments are permanently making new rules and unmaking others, and regulatory activity is a central and sensitive function of the modern state that cannot be preordained. In the United States alone, and only at the federal level, more than 50 agencies, employing nearly 250,000 people, produce 4,000 new rules every single year (US House Committee 2008: 106, See also Annex 2). National governments are acutely aware of the way regulations affect the competitive position of firms not only within a country, but also between or among different countries (Vogel 1995: 13). Thus, as has been recognized in several studies, effective regulatory coordination requires flexible, not definitive, international agreements.[8] Because it lacks secondary ruling capability, the concordance of regulations is an area that has largely been left out of NAFTA. Chapter 7B (Sanitary and Phytosanitary Measures) and Chapter 9 (Standards-Related Measures) do encourage parties to make their regulations compatible "to the greatest extent practicable," but fail to establish a mandatory process of harmonization. Instead, they provide for a fastidious process in which it is up to the exporting party to bear the burden of demonstrating that its own regulation should be recognized as equivalent to that of the importing party (Irish 2009: 338-342). As will be seen below, regulatory cooperation has been a central horizontal component of the SPP agenda, but seeking convergence simply through sharing information and raising awareness among regulators has obvious limits.

---

8   See the many studies conducted in the framework of the "Canada-US Regulatory Co-operation" project (Canada 2004).

Current Lack of Rule-Making Capability in NAFTA and the SPP

The institutional model under which NAFTA operates combines highly detailed pre-established rules and a quasi-absence of rule-making capability. The degree to which NAFTA was written down and has operated as a definitive agreement, rather than a flexible one, has already been described with great minutiae (see Abbott 2000, Bélanger 2007, Bélanger and Ouellet forthcoming). Basically, NAFTA is equipped with several technical working groups and a minister-level Free Trade Commission (FTC), which have almost no authority to create new rules or modify existing ones. The FTC has the mandate to monitor the implementation of the agreement and can settle interpretive disputes with the help of a panel system when required. Thus, NAFTA gives the Commission limited political interpretive authority. The FTC has no real mandate to modify the agreement in the future; the clause on modifications in the last chapter of the agreement makes no mention of this possibility (NAFTA 1993 art. 2202). This basically means that NAFTA does not provide for endogenous modifications: Additions or amendments to the agreement must be processed from outside the agreement's framework, through the same diplomatic channels and domestic ratification procedures required for brand new agreements. It is thus not surprising that no such modifications have ever been made. Although the FTC, in general, was not granted the power to amend the agreement, there are two specific instances in which alterations to the agreement require actions on the part of this Commission: It has a role to play in negotiating the eventual accession of other states (art. 2204) and, as mentioned above, in authorizing technical and limited tacit amendments, as in the case of modifications to rules-of-origin or customs regulations (art. 414 and 512). Apart from purely procedural rule making, the latter instance is the only real rule-making authority the FTC has.

The FTC used its interpretive authority in 2001 when it attempted to clarify some provisions pertaining to the operation of Chapter 11's arbitration tribunals (Canada 2001). The tribunals have since operated in accordance with the FTC's interpretive note, but this move has not gone unchallenged.[9] As for the FTC's authority to modify technical provisions such as the classification of products for origin determination or the schedule for tariff elimination, such modifications remain subject to the implementation procedures that apply in each state (House of Representatives 1993 sec. 103 and 202). The FTC does not directly enact these modifications. NAFTA has thus been carefully crafted to ensure that, even with regard to its most technical and trivial aspects, absolutely no measures or rulings deriving from the work of its institutions could be conceived as self-executing.

---

9 One panel's ruling clearly indicated that such clarifications could not, under any circumstances, be interpreted as modifications of the original text of the Agreement, thus setting clear limits on the use of interpretations to indirectly amend the Agreement (Pope & Talbot 2002: 23).

The North American leaders did not at first consider the necessity of supplementing the restrained coordination institutions of NAFTA. In 2000, soon after being elected President of Mexico, Vicente Fox tried to engage his US and Canadian counterparts in his "Vision 20/20" agenda, which proposed improved policy coordination and, among other things, the creation of a customs union (Wilson-Forsberg 2001), but the initiative was coldly received. A first post-NAFTA trilateral meeting took place in 2001, during the Third Summit of the Americas in Quebec City, but no immediate sequel followed. It took four additional years and the events of September 11, with their tightening effects on the US border, to bring the three heads of state and government together again. They gathered in Waco, Texas, in 2005, to launch the Security and Prosperity Partnership (SPP) with the objective of keeping North American borders closed to security threats but open to the movement of legitimate people and goods.

From its inception, the SPP was foreseen as essentially an agenda-led intergovernmental process. The Waco Summit established twenty trilateral working groups at the bureaucratic level, reporting to ministers on a semi-annual basis, and foresaw an "ongoing process of cooperation" that could be expanded "by mutual agreement as circumstances warrant", but no formal agreement was signed and no future or regular summits were planned (White House 2005). Decisions were subsequently made to convene in Cancun (2006), Montebello (2007), New Orleans (2008), and Guadalajara (2009). The Guadalajara Summit, however, the first to take place under an Obama administration, was conducted without activating the SPP apparatus of ministerial meetings and action plans, raising the question of whether the SPP process will be dismantled, redesigned, or rebranded. A loose structure of cabinet-level coordination has supported these agenda-setting summits at the presidential and prime-ministerial level, with one minister in each country responsible for each of the two pillars, security and prosperity, and one minister responsible for overall coordination. In the US (Figure 2.1), the Secretary for Homeland Security is responsible for the security pillar, the Secretary for Commerce is responsible for the prosperity pillar, the Secretary of State has overall coordination responsibility, and the Director for Western Hemispheric Affairs in the National Security Council has assumed bureaucratic coordination authority.

On conventional trade issues, the SPP agenda has not been ambitious enough to bring liberalization much farther than the limits established by NAFTA, but it has nevertheless attempted to reanimate some technical discussions and provide the kind of cooperation at the operative level that NAFTA's working groups have failed to sustain. The content of the economic pillar of the SPP, as set out, was "reflective of the fact that the soft political mandate for such negotiations [...] contained in NAFTA (the built-in agenda) had been insufficient" (Anderson and Sands 2007: 14), and it did not take long before there began to be pressure to move the new mechanism toward completing NAFTA. At first, this pressure took the form of a willingness to better activate NAFTA's own limited capacity to decide on secondary rulings. In their first *Report to Leaders* in June 2005, the US, Canadian and Mexican ministers announced that "[t]he three countries ha[d]

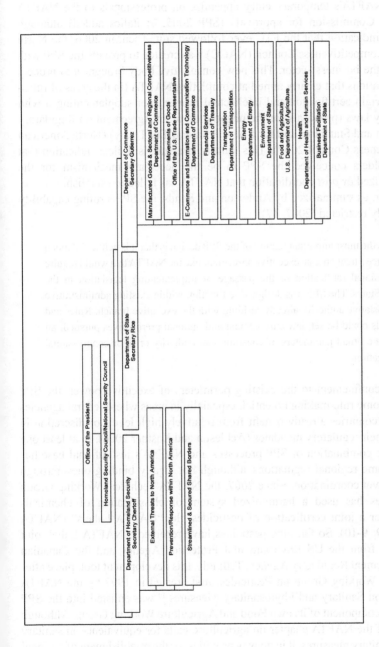

Figure 2.1   Security and Prosperity Partnership of North America US government Organization Chart

Source: US Department of Commerce, International Trade Administration, Freedom of Information Act Request for Record Production by Judicial Watch, September 25, 2006.

forwarded a trilateral document setting out each country's domestic procedures to *modify* NAFTA's temporary entry appendix on professionals to the NAFTA Free Trade Commission for approval" (SPP 2005: 7; italics added) although there is no indication that the FTC ever followed suit. Then, in 2006, the North American Competitiveness Council (NACC) was created to provide the SPP with input from the business sector. This new consultative body brought into process recommendations that clearly aimed at completing NAFTA (in the areas of rules-of-origin, origin certification and intellectual property) or supplementing it with new primary laws (proposals for the negotiation of an Agreement on Regulatory Cooperation and Standards and for a new Trilateral Tax Treaty) (North American Competitiveness Council 2007). This kind of pressure is a clear indication that the stakeholders conceived the SPP to be the necessary mechanism for the institutionalized *ex post* coordination that NAFTA has failed to establish.

However, as summarized by Anderson and Sands, the SPP's ruling capability was narrowly restricted (2007: 17):

> Perhaps the most important feature of the SPP design is that it is neither intended to produce a treaty nor an executive agreement like the NAFTA that would require congressional ratification or the passage of implementing legislation in the United States. The SPP was designed to function within existing administrative and legislative authority already residing with the executive branch. Rules and standards could be set, law enforcement and national prerogatives pursued, all within the broad parameters of constitutional authority or prior congressional authorization.

Despite its confinement to the existing perimeters of executive power, the SPP has shown some rule-making potential, especially in areas where federal agencies in the three countries already benefit from relatively high levels of discretion in exercising their regulatory mandates (Ackleson and Kastner 2006). In at least one instance, the combination of SPP processes and NAFTA's institutional base has produced some regional regulations—although not legally binding ones—through executive-level coordination. Since 2007, the NAFTA Technical Working Group on Pesticides has used a harmonized system of classification of chemicals as a basis for a joint certification of pesticides, the "NAFTA Labels" (NAFTA TWGP 2009: 9-10). So far, nine pesticides have received a NAFTA Label joint certification from the US Environmental Protection Agency and the Canadian Pest Management Regulatory Agency. Tellingly, this development took place after the NAFTA Working Group on Pesticides, first created in 1997 by the NAFTA Committee on Sanitary and Phytosanitary Measures,[10] was enlisted into the SPP process as a component of its own Food and Agriculture Working Group. Although Section B of the NAFTA chapter on agriculture calls for equivalence in sanitary and phytosanitary measures, it in no way provides for the establishment of regional

---

10   Pursuant to Article 722(3)(e) of NAFTA. See NAFTA TWGP 1997.

labels for pesticides. Therefore, the legal ground for the labels is found neither in NAFTA nor in the SPP but rather in the simultaneous registration of products by domestic agencies. This is exactly the kind of executive-level rulemaking that this article proposes should be enhanced and institutionalized on a larger scale.

Domestic Delegation and the SPP Linkages

Could NAFTA be reformed and the SPP re-launched in order to provide the North American free trade area with the necessary secondary ruling capacity it needs? As for NAFTA, as long as it is considered in US treaty-making practice as a traditional trade agreement, in spite of its scope, Congress will probably never accept loosening its grip and delegating significant levels of rule-making authority. That said, an upgrading of NAFTA–whether in its current or other form–to "treaty status" (see Schwanen 2004), which would give the US executive branch more discretion for its implementation, should not be totally excluded.[11] After all, the decision as to the appropriate ratification route for an agreement, either as an *Article II treaty* (requiring a supermajority vote in the Senate) or as a *congressional-executive agreement* (requiring a majority vote in both houses of Congress), remains a political, non-justiciable issue, and there is growing support in the US legal community for the principle of "interchangeability" between treaties and executive agreements. Moreover, although standard trade agreements such as NAFTA are always treated as congressional-executive agreements in the United States, this is not necessarily the case for all commerce-related arrangements. Over the past two decades, the United States has indeed ratified a significant number of agreements dealing with trade and investment issues as Article II treaties. A recent survey of the 1980-2000 period found 27 US treaties dealing with commercial issues and 43 dealing with investments. These two categories combined represent 18 percent of the Senate's treaty ratification activity.[12] However, although the convertibility of NAFTA is theoretically feasible, politically it remains a long shot.

As has been seen, contrary to NAFTA, the SPP has no legally binding foundations. However, rather than focusing on international delegation, any thoughtful evaluation of the SPP as an eventual regional rule-making body should take into consideration its potential in terms of domestic delegation. After all, as the European model suggests, regional economic rule-making capability more often resides with intergovernmental networks benefiting from strong domestic executive authorities than with supranational institutions. As regards domestic delegation, the most striking difference between NAFTA and the SPP is that the

---

11   The argument proposing that NAFTA, because of its scope, should have been ratified as an Article II treaty and should therefore be considered unconstitutional has been defended by prominent law scholars and been brought, without success, before the courts (see Stribe 1995, Ackerman and Golove 1995).

12   For a complete list, see Hathaway 2008: 1266.

latter significantly enlarges the scope of economic cooperation beyond traditional trade issues and, at the same time, mixes this enlarged economic agenda with security issues. The question is: What do these linkages bring to the table in terms of executive authority? This section offers an answer to this question by analyzing the first years of US participation in the SPP process. A complete analysis, also including the Canadian and Mexican cases, would have been more desirable, but an exclusive focus on the United States can be defended on two grounds. First, as will be seen below, precise information on each government's participation in the SPP working groups has been extremely difficult to gather. In these circumstances, the time and cost of including the three cases in the analysis would have been prohibitive, at least for a first-cut evaluation. Second, because of its relative power and the peculiarities of its political system of checks and balances, which imposes a high level of constraint on the executive branch, the United States is most certainly the hard case here: It is the level of executive autonomy in the United States itself that is likely to define the potential for secondary ruling capability in any tripartite cooperation scheme.

In order to assess the capability of the executive branch to engage in the kinds of rule-making collaboration that interests us here, we first need to identify the individual US agencies that have been involved in the SPP process. Over the SPP's first two years of existence, ten different agencies from the executive branch and four independent agencies were active, at different hierarchical levels, in one or more of the twenty SPP working groups. Tables 2.1 and 2.2 list the main participating agencies and Annex 1 provides a detailed listing of all the bureaus, offices and divisions involved. The US government has not made public any official list of agencies or contact persons. Thus, this compilation is based on information found in internal documents, disclosed following several Freedom of Information Act requests to the US federal government by Judicial Watch, and crosschecked against agency Web sites, organizational charts, and directories.[13]

---

13   This was a time-consuming and painstaking operation, in part due to the fact that the disclosed documents had often been subject to heavy editing. Therefore, a certain margin of error must be allowed for here, and these tables should not be considered as definitive, although the level of accuracy certainly suits the purposes of this chapter.

Table 2.1   Main US agencies participating in the prosperity pillar of the SPP
(overall responsibility: Department of Commerce)

SPP Working groups	Members 2005-2006 (US departments and agencies)
E-Commerce	Department of Commerce International Trade Administration Department of State United States Trade Representative Federal Trade Commission Federal Communications Commission
Energy	Department of Energy
Environment	Department of State Environmental Protection Agency
Financial Services	Department of Treasury
Food and Agriculture	Department of Agriculture Foreign Agricultural Service Department of Health and Human Services Food and Drug Administration
Health	Department of Health and Human Services
Manufactured Goods and Sectoral/Regional Competitiveness	Department of Commerce International Trade Administration
Movement of Goods	United States Trade Representative
Transportation	Department of Transportation
Business Facilitation	Department of State

Source: Author's compilation of data from: US Department of Commerce and Department of Homeland Security, Freedom of Information Act Request for Record Production by Judicial Watch, September 2006 and March 2007. Available at http://www.judicialwatch. org/SPP. See Annex 1b for detailed list of bureaus and offices.

Table 2.2   Main US agencies participating in the security pillar of the SPP (overall responsibility: Department of Homeland Security)

SPP Working groups	Members 2005-2006 (US departments and agencies)
Aviation Security	Department of Homeland Security Transportation Security Admin. Customs and Border Protection
Bio-protection	Department of Homeland Security Department of Health and Human Services Department of Agriculture
Border Facilitation	Department of Homeland Security Customs and Border Protection Department of Transportation
Cargo Security	Department of Homeland Security Customs and Border Protection Department of Commerce Nuclear Regulatory Commission Department of State Department of Energy
Intelligence Cooperation	Department of Justice Federal Bureau of Investigation
Law Enforcement Cooperation	Department of Homeland Security Customs and Border Protection Department of Justice
Maritime Security and Transport	Department of Homeland Security US Coast Guard
Critical Infrastructure	Department of Homeland Security Department of Energy Transportation Security Administration Department of Transportation International Boundary and Water Commission Department of Health and Human Services Food and Drug Administration Department of Agriculture Animal and Plant Health Inspection Service Food Safety and Inspection Service
Science and Technology Cooperation	Department of Homeland Security Customs and Border Protection
Traveler Security	Department of Homeland Security Customs and Border Protection
Transportation Security Admin.	Department of State

Source: Author's compilation of data from: US Department of Commerce and Department of Homeland Security, Freedom of Information Act Request for Record Production by Judicial Watch, September 2006 and March 2007. Available at http://www.judicialwatch.org/SPP. See Annex 1b for detailed list of bureaus and offices.

Unfortunately, there is no systematic and direct measure of the level of delegated authority entrusted in each of these agencies. However, an indirect measure can be created using Epstein and O'Halloran's index of "executive discretion" (1999: chap. 5 and 8). This index was computed for each congressional committee based on the average percentage of provisions appearing in bills passed in which authority was delegated to the executive branch.[14] In order to attribute a specific index to each agency, for the purposes of our analysis, agencies were linked to committees on the basis of the committees' legislative jurisdictions listed under House Rule X and on the basis of frequency of appearances of witnesses from each agency before committees from 1998 to 2005.[15] When more than one agency was involved in a single working group, the index was averaged. The result is graphically presented in Figure 2.2.

The data suggest that the agencies participating in the prosperity pillar of the SPP enjoy significantly greater executive discretion (24.3% on average) than those involved in the security pillar (17.6% on average). Historically, Congress has indeed maintained a relatively high level of control over domestic security and law enforcement policies and regulations.[16] The 9/11 attacks and the subsequent creation, in 2002, of the Department of Homeland Security (DHS) certainly boosted executive autonomy in the new "homeland" security area (CSIS-BENS 2004), even though Congress has since begun to reorganize and reassert its oversight over the Department's activities.[17] However, the redefinition of the security agenda in the context of North American cooperation has gone beyond even the newly conceived administrative limits of homeland security.

The DHS leads all of the working groups constituting the security pillar of the SPP and therefore dominates the process in a way that has no parallel in the

---

14   Epstein and O'Halloran 1999 used data from the 1947-90 period, and thus did not include an index for the more recent Committee on Homeland Security. Therefore, this committee was attributed the average index of the four main committees that transferred jurisdictions to the new Committee on Homeland Security when it was created in January 2005. They are, to use the old terminology applied by Epstein and O'Halloran: Internal Security, Judiciary, Public Work and Transportation, and Ways and Means. On transfers of jurisdiction to the benefit of Homeland Security, see Congressional Research Service 2005.

15   This was carried out using the GPO Access search engine, available at http://www.gpoaccess.gov/chearings/search.html.

16   The House Judiciary Committee and the defunct Internal Security Committee rank at the low end of Epstein and O'Halloran's classification of committees' lawmaking activity according to the levels of discretion granted to the executive branch. Yet they do not reach the bottom-rank positions occupied by committees such as the Ways and Means or Budget Committees (1999: 205).

17   Mainly through the creation of the Senate Committee on Homeland Security and Governmental Affairs in 2004 and the House Committee on Homeland Security in 2005. Notably, other committees, such as the House Ways and Means Committee and the Judiciary Committee, have retained important jurisdictions over key functions of the DHS (see Congressional Research Service 2005; Congressional Research Service 2004).

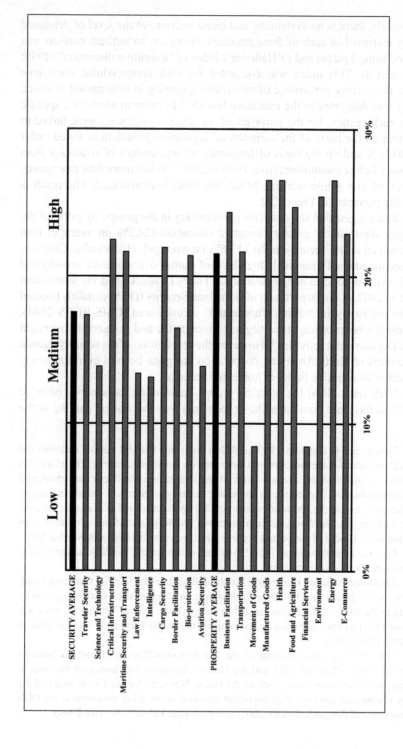

Figure 2.2   SPP Working Groups and Historic Executive Discretion in the US

prosperity pillar. However, despite the ubiquitous nature of its mandate, it has had to involve numerous other agencies in the process (see Table 2.2 and Annex 1b). For example, in the United States, representatives of the Department of Energy, the Department of Transportation, the Department of Health and Human Services, the Food and Drug Administration, the Animal and Plant Health Inspection Service, and the Food Safety and Inspection Service of the Department of Agriculture have been participants in the single working group on critical infrastructures.[18] These agencies bring significant levels of executive discretion with them to the table.

A close look at the prosperity pillar shows an important and fascinating discrepancy between "old" and "new" trade-related policy issues. Historically, as mentioned above, Congress has exercised firm control over traditional trade policy issues. By contrast, in complex and information-intense policy areas targeted by non-tariff barrier measures and economic regulatory cooperation, such as energy, consumer protection, transportation, or telecommunications, rulemaking is much more widely delegated. This is also the case, to an even greater extent, in more social regulatory areas such as public health, public safety, and environmental protection, where the incentives for members of Congress to delegate are high, perhaps because constituency-based political benefits are difficult to identify. Compare, for example, the 3,406 regulations promulgated by the Department of Transportation between 2005 and 2008 with the 673 promulgated by the Department of Treasury (Annex 2). Thus, an examination of the working groups constituting the prosperity pillar of the SPP reveals the involvement of agencies that are bringing to the table different levels of executive discretion. For example, the working groups on the environment, energy, e-commerce, manufactured goods competitiveness, and transportation bring to the table agents of the executive branch benefiting from relatively high levels of discretion. On the other hand, in the United States, the Department of Treasury, an agency operating under tight control by Congress, leads the working group on financial services. On the whole, however, it is evident that by departing from traditional trade issues and enlarging the scope of economic cooperation, especially toward regulatory convergence issues, the prosperity pillar of the SPP covers policy areas over which the executive branch of the US government has a considerable amount of delegated authority at its disposal.

The working groups with a higher index of executive discretion are also those that seem to have been the most effective. It is not possible here to carry out a rigorous assessment of each of the working groups' accomplishments. However, in August 2006, the ministers responsible for the SPP published their second Report to Leaders, to which was annexed a complete list of each of the working groups' initial objectives, with a mention of their level of achievement (SPP 2006). On this basis, it is possible to calculate the percentage of accomplished objectives for each group and to use the result as a convenient, although approximate, measure of

---

18   This working group was renamed "Protection, Prevention and Response Working Group" in 2006.

efficiency. Figure 2.3 compares each group's accomplishment score with its level of executive discretion.

On average, the working groups in the prosperity pillar, which also benefit from higher levels of delegated authority, show significantly higher levels of accomplishment (41% for prosperity vs. 14% for security). More importantly, almost all of the working groups at the top of the list in terms of objective accomplishment (*Environment*: 56%; *Energy*: 48%; *E-Commerce*: 45%; *Transportation*: 39%) have "high" scores on our executive discretion index. The only exception is the *Movement of Goods* working group, which combined an impressive 50 percent level of accomplishment with a "low" level of executive discretion, but is led in the United States by the Office of the United States Trade Representative, whose level of delegated authority is difficult to assess because of its status as part of the Executive Office of the President. The worst results are all for the working groups in the security pillar (*Aviation Security*: 0%; *Science and Technology Cooperation*: 0%; *Border Facilitation*: 6%; *Law Enforcement Cooperation*: 7%; *Traveler Security*: 7%), which scored "medium" levels of executive discretion.

To sum up, in contrast with international security, traditional internal security is a policy area over which, historically, the US executive branch has not secured the amount of discretionary authority on which innovative forms of international commitments can easily be built. As the SPP experience has shown, however, North American trilateral cooperation is evolving towards enlarged conceptions of homeland and regional security, and in the process, more autonomous sectors of the governments, at least in the United States, are being brought in. This is the case, for example, in the areas of transport security and critical infrastructures. Concurrently, in the prosperity pillar of the SPP, there has been a similar and even more pronounced evolution toward the amalgamation of new policy issues, for which the executive branch has inherited high levels of delegated authority, with more conventional trade issues, for which the legislative branch has always exerted tighter control. Insofar as they make it possible to build a base of delegated authority that could facilitate the transition toward the kind of institutions the region needs–institutions vested with the permanent rule-making capability required to sustain and reinvigorate the North American free trade area–these linkages are promising.

Non-Treaty International Rulemaking

As seen above, in spite of its potential in terms of domestic delegation, the SPP itself has not evolved to become a rule-making institution. It has essentially sought coordination simply through sharing information and raising awareness among agencies. When, at the 2007 Montebello Summit, the three North American leaders unveiled a new *SPP Regulatory Cooperation Framework*, it was made clear that this framework was "voluntary" and that its goal would be to encourage compatibility of national regulations rather than to produce truly regional ones (SPP 2007). The fact

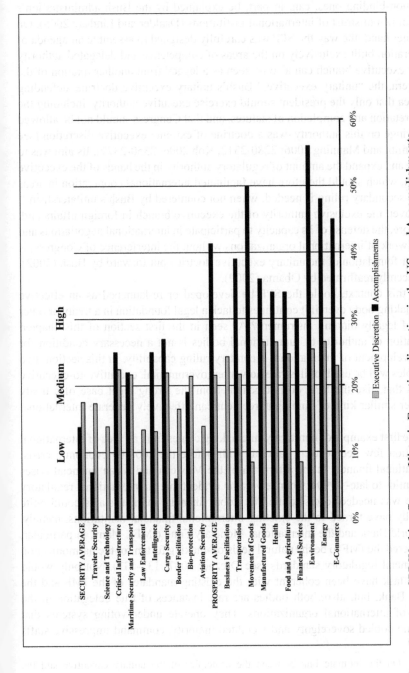

Figure 2.3   SPP Working Groups, Historic Executive discretion in the US, and Accomplishments

Note: The Business Facilitation Working Group did not report its accomplishments

that the SPP was prevented from clearly promulgating regional rules and standards, even non-binding ones, can, in part, be explained by the Bush administration's well-known mistrust of international institutions (Daalder and Lindsay 2005). On the other hand, the way the SPP was carefully designed to assemble an agenda of cooperation built exclusively on the areas of competence and delegated authority of the executive branch can also be seen as a legacy from another fixation of the Bush era, the "unitary executive." Bush's unitary executive doctrine–defending the idea that only the president should exercise executive authority, including the interpretation and completion of statutes, and that Congress should not be allowed to infringe on this authority–was a doctrine of extreme executive discretion (see Goldsmith and Manning 2006: 2280-2312, Koh 2006: 2350-2379). Its aim was to secure and expand the amount of regulatory authority in the hands of the executive branch, which should therefore have facilitated international cooperation in areas where secondary ruling is needed, when not countered by Bush's unilateralism.[19] Moreover, the exclusive authority of the executive branch in foreign affairs and, therefore, the defense of its capacity to participate in international negotiations and in the work of international organizations without the interference of Congress, is another foundation of the unitary executive doctrine put forward by Bush (2002), and recently reaffirmed by Obama (2009).

In this context, could the SPP be developed or re-launched as an effective rule-making body even if it continues to lack a legal foundation in a treaty or other kind of legally binding instrument? As seen in the first section of this chapter, delegation of authority to supranational bodies is not a necessary condition for the development of international secondary ruling capability. In this section, two examples will be used to illustrate how intergovernmental, executive-to-executive bodies that, like the SPP, do not benefit from the strong legal base of a treaty or other similar kind of binding agreement can effectively generate international rules.

The first example of non-treaty rulemaking comes from an area of international regulation few people were familiar with before the 2008-09 economic crisis: international finance. In the aftermath of the Mexican and Asian financial crises in the mid- to late- 1990s, when it became evident that an international regulatory regime was needed to discipline the global financial market, states could quite naturally have turned to the existing international financial institutions, namely, the World Bank and the International Monetary Fund (IMF). Many, in particular, considered the IMF to be the natural decision-making forum for the harmonization of financial regulatory standards (see Drezner 2007: 132-133). Not only would such a task have been coherent with the existing mandates of the IMF and the World Bank, but, also, both bodies are rare instances of true delegation in the world of international organizations. They operate under voting systems that combine pooled sovereignty and weighted majority, command impressive staffs

---

19   On the intimate link between the principles of the unitary executive and the regulatory activity of the state, see Gattuso 2008.

of highly qualified professionals, and are mandated, by treaty, to make legally binding decisions. In spite of this, in 1998, the major economic powers decided instead to create a new, stand-alone entity, the Financial Stability Forum (FSF). The FSF's regulatory activity had no international legal foundation. It was, in the language of Drezner, a "club-based organization" (2007: 75-78, 136). It was established by a non-legally binding decision of the G-7, itself an *ad hoc* political organization with no legally-binding foundations, not formally different from the North American Leaders' Summit that oversees the SPP process.[20] In 2000, the FSF promulgated a "compendium of standards" covering twelve areas of financial regulation, from insurance and banking supervision to money laundering. Some of the standards have remained untouched since their promulgation, but others have been continuously revised.[21] Recently, facing another major global financial crisis, the new G-20 again opted in favor of an enlarged FSF[22] –renamed the Financial Stability Board (FSB)– in order to broaden the scope of and tighten international financial regulations. The G-20 members declared that, compared to the old FSF, the new FSB would benefit from "a stronger institutional basis and enhanced capacity" (G-20 2009). It now has a permanent decision-making organ, the Plenary, with biannual meetings, a full-time Secretary General, and an enlarged secretariat (Financial Stability Forum 2009). It remains a non-treaty organization, however, and its decisions are politically, rather than legally, binding. Nevertheless, compliance with FSF regulations has been remarkable (Drezner 2007).

The second example of what can be achieved by cooperating through non-legal means is the Organization for Security and Co-operation in Europe (OSCE). The OSCE is an international forum for collective security vested with the mandate of fostering, among its member states, the observation of common standards in three areas (or "baskets"): human rights, politico-military affairs, and environmental and economic cooperation, including regulatory and border-crossing facilitation issues. The OSCE features almost all the characteristics of a full-fledged international organization. It has a Charter, an annual Council of Ministers and a Permanent Council made up of ambassador-level representatives, a rotating Chairman-in-Office, a Secretary General, a well-staffed secretariat located in Vienna, a respectable budget, and even its own international "Court of Conciliation and Arbitration." However, throughout the different institutional metamorphoses that

---

20   "At its inception, each G-7 member was assigned three members–one slot for a finance ministry official, one slot for a central bank official, one slot for a financial regulatory authority. Three other countries–Hong Kong, Australia, and the Netherlands– had a total of five members. The remaining sixteen members consisted of representatives from [international financial institutions], the [Bank of International Settlements] and its emanations, and pre-existing regulatory bodies" (Drezner 2007: 136).

21   A list of the different codes and standards is available at: http://www. financialstabilityboard.org/cos/key_standards.htm.

22   This was in order to make additional room for all G-20 members, as well as Spain and the European Commission.

the OSCE has undergone since its creation, it has retained its status as a political organization and is not based on any international legal commitments. The written agreements on which the organization was built, beginning with the 1975 Helsinki Final Act, were in fact all carefully crafted as politically-binding documents, rather than legally-binding treaties.[23] As the OSCE developed, especially following the new mandate and capacity it received to face the security challenges of a post-Cold War Europe, the issue of its legal status was often raised, but the essentially political nature of the institution has been preserved (Shapiro 1995: 631-637). This means that member governments, including the successive US administrations, have never had to seek formal legislative approval for their commitments to the OSCE process and that the international cooperation that takes place inside the OSCE framework falls exclusively within the realm of the executive branch of each state.[24]

One obvious effect of the legal nature of the OSCE is that, like the FSF/FSB, its decision-making bodies do not directly create legal "obligations," but rather lead to politically binding "commitments" to internalize the standards that have been collectively adopted. Consequently, enforcement cannot be ensured through judicial recourse; rather it is obtained through a system of continuous monitoring that involves transparency measures, appointed "rapporteurs," fact-finding missions, and a multi-stage problem resolution mechanism (Buergenthal, 1991). As seen above, member states can always translate their commitments into legal obligations by signing separate, formally distinct instruments, which may or may not require domestic legislative action, as took place, for example, in the case of the Open Skies Treaty. In fact, this nearly happened with the SPP; talks in the Border Facilitation working group led to the opening of formal negotiations on a land preclearance agreement between Canada and the United States, which never succeeded (SPP 2006: 74, GAO 2008). It should be said that, although non-legally binding rules cannot be enforced by means of judicial remedies, this does not mean that such rules are entirely without legal consequences. For example, they can be relevant in interpreting the disputed provisions of previous international agreements that are legally binding (Buergenthal,1991: 379). In the North

23   The 1975 Helsinki Final Act, as well as the 1990 Charter of Paris, contain the same provision, which calls for the transmission of the agreements to the Secretary General of the UN, but specify that they are not eligible for registration under Article 102 of the Charter of the United Nations.

24   In the US, ignoring objections raised by the executive branch, Congress created an independent Commission on Security and Cooperation in Europe with the mandate of monitoring the Helsinki process. This commission plays an active advisory role and exercises some level of oversight, but is not a standing committee of the House or the Senate –even if it looks like one– and, therefore, remains deprived of any legislative jurisdiction (see Paquin Granier 1980: 540). This hybrid commission consists of nine senators, nine House members, and one representative from each of the departments of State, Defense and Commerce (see Galey 1985).

American context, NAFTA's ad hoc tribunals could, for example, use rulings from an upgraded version of the SPP.

The SPP, with its annual leaders' summit, its mechanism of ministerial coordination and its working groups, possesses the embryonic structure of an international organization similar, in institutional and legal terms, to the FSF/FSB and the OSCE. In a sense, re-launching the SPP at a level of institutionalization similar to that of the OSCE would resemble the process by which the initial "Conference on Security and Co-operation" (1973-75), with its three main committees and eleven subcommittees, evolved to become the international institution of today. In order to achieve this goal, the three governments would have to negotiate and sign a political declaration that would have many of the classic characteristics of a treaty but would not contain the usual final clauses on ratification and entry into force. To make things even clearer and to reassure potentially worried domestic audiences, a provision could be added stating that the declaration does not affect the international rights and obligations of the three states and that, because it is not a treaty or an international agreement, it is not eligible for registration under Article 102 of the United Nations Charter. The most important provisions of the new declaration would transform the old informal SPP ministerial meetings into a formal "Council" or "Plenary", with rotating chairmanship, create a permanent "Board" or "Steering Committee" that would become the converging point for the deliberations of the working groups, and have the mandate to decide on politically-binding regional rules and establish a monitoring mechanism. Many other provisions could be added. For example, since there are already some levels of duplication between the SPP and the NAFTA working groups, the declaration could seek to establish clear institutional links between NAFTA and the newly created bodies.

Conclusion

NAFTA has led to the limited level of trade liberalization that is possible when parties to a free trade agreement stop short of providing for permanent rule-making capability in their cooperation scheme. The SPP has failed to make up for this institutional deficit, which ultimately hinders the free trade area's competitiveness in the world economy. Yet, the SPP amalgamates enough executive autonomy to constitute a serious basis for the establishment of a non-treaty international rule-making body.

From the perspective adopted here, the advantages of upgrading the SPP along the lines of the FSF/FSB or OSCE models would be significant. The new institutional forum would have the authority to promulgate regional standards that the three governments would then be politically committed to internalize. This commitment would be made at the highest political level rather than at the current bureaucratic level, and the decision-making process, at least its formal part, would be open and public. Decisions would not be legally binding, but a centralized mechanism of surveillance and monitoring, which does not currently exist in the SPP, would maintain a political pressure reinforced by the momentum of annual summits. In areas where the new organization acquired sufficient levels of technical credibility and efficiency, there could well be the development of a system of harmonization through assimilation, whereby domestic statutes would require federal agencies to consider regional standards when issuing their own standards, even if this practice were not formally inscribed in international legal obligations. Finally, such an institution would be a natural incubator for additional legally binding agreements. For example, when required, and depending on the level of discretion at the disposal of the executives in a particular policy area, the three governments would be well positioned to translate the politically binding decisions negotiated in the framework of the new organization into a legally binding executive agreement or even, if the circumstances were favorable, into a treaty.

The key feature of the new regional body would be that its authority to decide on new rules would not be "supranational". First, there would be no external delegation involved but only, to come back to Koremenos' oxymoronic terminology, "internal delegation". Second, because the pool of rule-making authority involved would be contained within the perimeters of the executive branch's authority, no legally binding ratification would be required. Such an institution would provide the North American free trade area with the flexible rule-making capability it so desperately needs.

Annex 1a Detailed list of US departments, agencies and offices that were members of the SPP working groups in 2005-06 – Prosperity pillar

SPP Working groups	Members (Department or agency affiliation)
E-Commerce	Deputy Under Secretary for International Trade (International Trade Administration, DOCª)
	Office of NAFTA and Inter-American Affairs (An office of Market Access and Compliance of the International Trade Administration, DOCª)
	International Spectrum Plans and Policy Division (An office of Spectrum Management of the National Telecommunications and Information Administration, DOC)
	International Communications and Information Policy Division (Under Secretary for Economic, Business and Agricultural Affairs, DOS)

	US Embassy in Ottawa (DOS)
	Telecommunications Policy (Assistant US Trade Representative for Industry and Telecommunications, USTR)
	Bureau of Consumer Protection (Federal Trade Commission)
	Regional and Industry Analysis Branch (Federal Communications Commission)
Energy*	Office of Policy and International Affairs (DOE)
	Office of American Affairs (A division of the Office of Policy and International Affairs, DOE)
	Office of Climate Change Policy & Technology (A division of the Office of Policy and International Affairs, DOE)
Environment	Under Secretary of State for Democracy & Global Affairs (DOS)
	Environmental Protection Agency (Independent agency)
Financial Services	Under Secretary for International Affairs (Department of the Treasury)
Food and Agriculture	Under Secretary for Farm & Foreign Agricultural Service (USDA)
	Regional & Bilateral Negotiations & Agreements Division (An office of the Foreign Agricultural Service, USDA)
	Policy Coordination & Planning Staff

(An office of Capacity Building and Development of the Foreign Agricultural Service, USDA)

Agricultural Marketing Service
(Under Secretary for Marketing and Regulatory Programs, USDA)

Office of International Programs
(An office of International and Special Programs of the Food and Drug Administration, DHHS)

Health   Office of Global Health Affairs
                           (DHHS)

Manufactured Goods   Market Access & Compliance
and Sectoral/Regional   (A division of the International Trade Administration,
Competitiveness   DOC)

                           Office of NAFTA and Inter-American Affairs
                           (An office of Market Access and Compliance of the International Trade Administration, DOC)

Movement of Goods   Assistant US Trade Representative for the Americas
(USTR)

Transportation   Office of International Transportation and Trade
                           (Assistant Secretary for Aviation and International Affairs, a division of the Under Secretary for Policy, DOT)

                           Maritime, Surface and Facilitation Division
                           (Office of International Transportation and Trade, Under Secretary for Policy, DOT)

Business Facilitation   Bureau of Economic, Energy & Business Affairs
                           (Under Secretary for Economic, Business and Agricultural Affairs, DOS)

                           Office of Andean Affairs
                           (Bureau of Western Hemisphere Affairs, Under Secretary for Political Affairs, DOS)

Source: Author's compilation of data from: US Department of Commerce and Department of Homeland Security, Freedom of Information Act Request for Record Production by Judicial Watch, September 2006 and March 2007. Available at http://www.judicialwatch.org/SPP.

[a] Please refer to the list of acronyms at the end of Annex 1b.

* The North American Energy Working Group was created in 2001 but incorporated into the SPP structure in 2005.

Annex 1b Detailed list of US departments, agencies and offices that were members of the SPP working groups in 2005-2006 – Security pillar

SPP Working groups	Members (main department or agency)
Aviation Security	Transportation Security Administration (DHS[a])
	Customs and Border Protection (DHS)
Bio-protection	Under Secretary Information Analysis and Infrastructure Protection (DHS)
	USDA (responsible office unspecified)
	DHHS (responsible office unspecified)
Border Facilitation Lead:	Customs and Border Protection (DHS)
	Private Sector Office (A division of the Assistant Secretary Office of Policy, DHS)
	US VISIT – US Visitor and Immigrant Status Indicator Technology (Under Secretary National Protection & Programs Directorate, DHS)
Subgroups: Pilots	Assistant Secretary Office of Policy (DHS)
Transportation Infrastructure	Customs and Border Protection (DHS)
	Transportation Security Administration (DHS)
	Private Sector Office (Assistant Secretary Office of Policy, DHS)
	DOT (responsible office unspecified)
Cargo Security Lead:	Customs and Border Protection (DHS)

Sub-groups:

Export Control	Customs and Border Protection (DHS)
	Assistant Secretary Immigration and Customs Enforcement (DHS)
	DOC (responsible office unspecified)
Nuclear & radiological	Domestic Nuclear Detection Office (DHS)
	Nuclear Regulatory Commission (Independent agency)
	DOS (responsible office unspecified)
	DOE (responsible office unspecified)

Intelligence Cooperation	Under Secretary for Intelligence & Analysis (DHS)
	Terrorist Screening Center (A division of the Federal Bureau of Investigation, DOJ)

Law Enforcement Cooperation Lead:	Assistant Secretary Immigration and Customs Enforcement (DHS)
	DOJ (responsible office unspecified)

Subgroups:

Removal issues	Shared Border Accord Can-US (Customs and Border Protection, DHS)
	US-Mexico Traveler & Cargo Security Working Group (Customs and Border Protection, DHS)
Repatriation	Customs and Border Protection (DHS)

Maritime Security and Transport	US Coast Guard (DHS)

Critical Infrastructure Protection Lead:	Under Secretary Information Analysis and Infrastructure Protection (DHS)

Sub-groups:

Energy	Electricity Delivery and Energy Reliability (An office of the Under Secretary, DOE)
Telecom	National Cyber Security Division (An office of Cybersecurity and Communications of the Under Secretary National Protection & Programs Directorate, DHS)
Transport	Transportation Security Administration (DHS)
	DOT (responsible office unspecified)
Water/Dams	International Boundary and Water Commission (Independent agency)
Cyber security	National Cyber Security Division (An office of Cybersecurity and Communications of the Under Secretary National Protection & Programs Directorate, DHS)
Public Health	DHHS (responsible office unspecified)
Food & Agriculture	USDA (responsible office unspecified)
	Food and Drug Administration (DHHS)
	Animal and Plant Health Inspection Service (USDA)
	Food Safety and Inspection Service (USDA)

Science and Technology
Cooperation
US-Canada: Under Secretary Science & Technology Directorate
(DHS)

US-Mexico: Customs and Border Protection (DHS)

Under Secretary Science & Technology Directorate (DHS)

Traveler Security
Lead: Customs and Border Protection (DHS)

Sub-groups:

Immigration & asylum	US Citizenship and Immigration Services (DHS)
Visa Policy	Assistant Secretary for Policy (DHS)
Document Fraud	Assistant Secretary Immigration and Customs Enforcement (DHS)
	DOS (responsible office unspecified)
Screening systems architecture	US VISIT – US Visitor and Immigrant Status Indicator Technology (Under Secretary National Protection & Programs Directorate, DHS)
Transportation worker ID	Assistant Secretary Transportation Security Administration (DHS)

Source: Author's compilation of data from: US Department of Commerce and Department of Homeland Security, Freedom of Information Act Request for Record Production by Judicial Watch, September 2006 and March 2007. Available at http://www.judicialwatch.org/SPP.

[a] Please refer to the list of acronyms at the end of Annex

Acronyms of US Departments involved in the SPP:

DHHS/HHS	Department of Health and Human Services
DHS	Department of Homeland Security
DOC	Department of Commerce
DOE	Department of Energy
DOJ	Department of Justice
DOS	Department of State
DOT	Department of Transportation
USDA	Department of Agriculture
USTR	Office of the United States Trade Representative

Annex 2 US departments and agencies with number and percentage of rules in 2005-2008

Departments and agencies in the SPP working groups (%)	Number of rules per Department/agency[1]	Percentage of rules relative to total[2]
DOT[a]	3,406	23.58
Environmental Protection Agency	1,898	13.14
DHS	1,540	10.66
Coast Guard	1,149	
Customs and Border Protection	34	
Immigration and Customs Enforcement Bureau	3	
Transportation Security Administration	27	
US Citizenship and Immigration Services	13	
DOC	1,282	8.88
International Trade Administration	17	
National Telecommunications and Information Administration	4	
USDA	932	6.45
Agricultural Marketing Service	334	
Animal and Plant Health Inspection Service	262	
Food Safety and Inspection Service	26	
Foreign Agricultural Service	0	
DHHS	674	4.67
Food and Drug Administration	454	
Department of Treasury	673	4.66
Federal Communications Commission	617	4.27
DOE	199	1.38
Nuclear Regulatory Commission	115	0.80
DOJ	112	0.78
Federal Bureau of Investigation	1	
DOS	83	0.57

Federal Trade Commission	35	0.24
USTR	1	0.01
International Boundary and Water Commission	1	0.01

Source: Author's compilation of data available on rules for different US departments and agencies, covering the period from January 1, 2005, the earliest date for which information on rules is available on Justia.com, to September 16, 2008, the day the research was conducted. Available at http://www.justia.com.

[1]The rules of agencies or bureaus of the departments are included in the total number of rules assigned to the specific department.

[2]The total number of rules for all departments and agencies of the US government, including those that were not members of the SPP working groups, for the covered period, is 14,445.

[a] Please refer to the list of acronyms at the end of Annex 1.

References

Abbott, F. M. 2000. NAFTA and the Legalization of World Politics: A Case Study, *International Organization* Vol. 54, No. 3: 519-547.

Abbott, K.W. and Snidal, D. 2003. Hard Law and Soft Law in International Governance. *International Organization* 54, No. 3: 421-56.

Ackerman, B.A. and Golove, D. 1995. *"Is NAFTA Constitutional?"* Cambridge, MA: Harvard University Press.

Ackleson, J. and Kastner, J. 2006. The Security and Prosperity Partnership of North America. *The American Review of Canadian Studies* 36 No. 2: 207-232.

Anderson, G. and Sands, C. 2007. Negotiating North America. The Security and Prosperity Partnership. White Paper Series. Washington, DC: The Hudson Institute.

Bélanger, L. 2007. "NAFTA: An Unsustainable Institutional Design". In *Governing the Americas: Assessing Multilateral Institutions*, eds. Gordon Mace, Jean-Philippe Thérien and Paul Haslam: 195-212. Boulder, CO: Lynne Rienner Publ.

Bélanger, L. and Ouellet R. Forthcoming. "Ruling the North American Market: NAFTA and its Extensions". In *Inter-American Cooperation at a Crossroads, 2010 Onwards*, eds. Gordon Mace, Andrew F. Cooper and Timothy M. Shaw. London: Palgrave Macmillan.

Bradley, C. A. 2006. Unratified Treaty Amendments and Constitutional Process. Unpublished manuscript prepared for the Duke Workshop on Delegating Sovereignty, February 6.

Bradley, C. A. 2003. International Delegations, the Structural Constitution, and Non-Self-Execution. *Stanford Law Review* 55: 1557-96.

Buergenthal, T. 1991. The CSCE Right System. *George Washington Journal of International Law and Economics* 25, No. 2: 333-86.

Bush, G. W. 2002. *Statement on signing H.R. 1646, the Foreign Relations Authorization Act, Fiscal Year 2003*, The White House, September 30.

Canada. 2001. Department of Foreign Affairs and International Trade, *Pettigrew Welcomes NAFTA Commission's Initiatives to Clarify Chapter 11 Provisions*, Ottawa: Department of Foreign Affairs and International Trade (Press Release No. 116), August 1.

Canada. 2004. *Canada-US Regulatory Co-operation: Charting a Path Forward.* Policy Research Initiative. Interim Report. December.

Canada-US Project. 2009. *Background Papers. From Correct to Inspired: Blueprint for Canada-US Engagement.* Ottawa: Carleton University, January 19. http://www.carleton.ca/ctpl/conferences/documents/BackgroundPapers-Final.pdf. Accessed December 14, 2009.

Chen, M. X. and Mattoo, A. 2004. *Regionalism in Standards: Good or Bad for Trade?* The World Bank, Policy Research Working Paper 3458.

Cinotti, D. N. 2003. The New Isolationism: Non-Self-Execution Declarations and Treaties as the Supreme Law of the Land. *Georgetown Law Journal* 91, No. 6: 1277-1301.

Congressional Research Service. 2005. *Committee System Rules Changes in the House, 109th Congress.* CRS Report for Congress RS22018, January 5.

Congressional Research Service. 2004. S.Res. 445: Senate Committee Reorganization for *Homeland Security and Intelligence Matters*. CRS Report for Congress RS21955, October 15.

CSIS-BENS. 2004. Task Force on Congressional Oversight of the Department of Homeland Security, *Untangling the Web: Congressional Oversight of the Department of Homeland Security*, Washington: Center for Strategic and International Studies, December 10.

Daalder, I. H. and Lindsay, J. 2005. America Unbound: The Bush Revolution in Foreign Policy. Hoboken, NJ: John Wiley & Sons, Inc.

Drezner, D. W. 2007. All Politics Is Global: Explaining International Regulatory Regimes. Princeton: Princeton University Press.

Eberlein, B. and Grande, E. 2005.Beyond Delegation: Transnational Regulatory Regimes and the EU Regulatory State. *Journal of European Public Policy* 12 (1): 89-112.

Epstein, D. and O'Halloran, S. 1999. *Delegating Powers. A Transaction Cost Politics Approach to Policy Making Under Separate Powers*. Cambridge, MA: Cambridge University Press.

Financial Stability Forum. 2009. *Financial Stability Forum Re-established as the Financial Stability Board*, Basel, April 2. http://www.financialstabilityboard. org/press/pr_090402b.pdf. Accessed December 14, 2009.

G-20. 2009. *Declaration on Strengthening the Financial System*, London, April 2.

Galey, M. E. 1985. Congress, Foreign Policy and Human Rights Ten Years after Helsinki. *Human Rights Quarterly* 7, No. 2 (May): 334-72.

Gattuso, J. L. (2008) *The Rulemaking Process and Unitary Executive Theory*, Testimony before the Subcommittee on Commercial and Administrative Law of the House Judiciary Committee, May 6 http://www.heritage.org/research/regulation/tst050708a.cfm Accessed February 5, 2010

Government Accountability Office (GAO). 2008. Various Issues Led to the Termination of the United States-Canada Shared Border Management Pilot Project (Report GAO-08-1038R).

Ghosh, M. and Rao, S. 2004. Possible Economic Impacts in Canada of a Canada-US Customs Union. *Horizons* 7, No. 1: 32-4.

Goldsmith, J. and Manning, J.F.. 2006. The President's Completion Power. *The Yale Law Journal* 115, No. 9: 2280-2312.

Guzman, A. T. and Landsidle, J. 2008.*The Myth of International Delegation*. Berkeley Program in Law & Economics. Working Paper Series 226.

Hart, M. 2006. *Steer or Drift? Taking Charge of Canada-US Regulatory Convergence*. C.D. Howe Institute. Commentary 229.

Hathaway, O. A. 2008. Treaties' End: The Past, Present, and Future of International Lawmaking in the United States. *The Yale Law Journal* 117, No. 7: 1236-1372

Hawkins, D, Lake, D. A., Nielson, D. and Tierney, M. J.. 2006. Delegation under Anarchy: States, International Organizations, and Principal-Agent Theory. In *Delegation and Agency in International Organizations*, eds. Darren Hawkins, David A. Lake, Daniel Nielson and Michael J. Tierney, 3-38. Cambridge, MA: Cambridge University Press.

Irish, M. 2009. Regulatory Convergence, Security and Global Administrative Law in Canada-United States Trade, *Journal of International Economic Law* 12, No. 2: 333-355.

Jockel, J. T. 2007. *Canada in NORAD (1957-2007): A History*. Montreal/Kingston: McGill-Queen's University Press.

Koh, H..H. 2006. Setting the World Right. *The Yale Law Journal* 115: 2350-79.

Koremenos, B. 2008. When, What, and Why Do States Choose to Delegate? *Law and Contemporary Problems* 71 (Winter): 151-92.

Moens, A. and Cust M.. 2008. *Saving the North American Security and Prosperity Partnership: The Case for a North American Standards and Regulatory Area*. Vancouver: Fraser Institute (Digital Publication), March. http://www.fraserinstitute.org/commerce.web/product_files/Security_Prosperity_Partnership.pdf. Accessed December 14, 2009.

North American Competitiveness Council. 2007. *Enhancing Competitiveness in Canada, Mexico, and the United States. Private-Sector Priorities for the Security and Prosperity Partnership of North America (SPP)*, February.

North American Free Trade Agreement (NAFTA). 1993. Ottawa, Acquisitions and Services Canada.

North American Free Trade Agreement Technical Working Group on Pesticides (NAFTA TWGP). 1997. *Terms of Reference for the NAFTA Technical Working*

Group on Pesticides, June 4. http://www.epa.gov/oppfead1/international/naftatwg/general/terms-of-reference.pdf. Accessed October 5, 2009.

North American Free Trade Agreement Technical Working Group on Pesticides (NAFTA TWGP). 2009. *Accomplishments Report for the Period of 2003-2008.*

Obama, B. 2009. *Statement on Signing the Omnibus Appropriations Act, 2009*, The White House, March 11.

Paquin Granier, J. 1980. Human Rights and the Helsinki Conference on Security and Cooperation in Europe: An Annotated Bibliography of United States Government Documents. *Vanderbilt Journal of Transnational Law* 13, No. 12-13 (Spring–Summer): 529-73.

Pope & Talbot [In the Matter of An Arbitration Under Chapter Eleven of the North American Free Trade Agreement Between Pope & Talbot Inc. and Government of Canada. Award in Respect of Damages, 2002. May 31.

Schwanen, D.. 2004. "Deeper, Broader: A Roadmap for a Treaty of North America." In *Thinking North America*, eds. Thomas J. Courchene, Donald J. Savoie, and Daniel Schwanen. The Art of the State, Vol. 2, No. 4. Montreal: Institute for Research on Public Policy.

Security and Prosperity Partnership (SPP). 2005. *Security and Prosperity Partnership of North America*. Report to Leaders, June 27.

Security and Prosperity Partnership (SPP). 2006. *Security and Prosperity Partnership of North America*. Report to Leaders, August.

Security and Prosperity Partnership (SPP). 2007. *Canada/United States/Mexico SPP Regulatory Cooperation Framework*, August 18. http://www.spp-psp.gc.ca/eic/site/spp-psp.nsf/eng/00095.html. Accessed December 14, 2009.

Shapiro, M. 1995. Changing the CSCE into the OSCE: Legal Aspects of a Political Transformation. *The American Journal of International Law* 89, No. 3: 631-37.

Softwood Lumber Agreement between the Government of Canada and the Government of the United States of America, 2006. September 12.

Stribe, L. H. 1995. Taking Text And Structure Seriously: Reflections on Free-Form Method in Constitutional Interpretation. *Harvard Law Review* 108, No. 6: 1221-1303.

Swaine, E. T. 2004. The Constitutionality of International Delegations. *Columbia Law Review* 104, No. 6 (October): 1492-1614.

US Congress. House. Committee on the Judiciary. 2008. *The Rulemaking Process and Unitary Executive Theory.* Hearing before the Subcommittee on Commercial and Administrative Law.110th Cong., 2nd sess. May 6.

US Congress. House. Committee on Energy and Commerce. 2004. *POPs, PIC, and LRTAP: The Role of the US and Draft Legislation to Implement These International Conventions.* Hearing before the Subcommittee on Environment and Hazardous Materials. 108th Cong., 2nd sess. July 13.

US Congress. House. 1993. *The North American Free Trade Agreement Implementation Act.* H.R. 3450. 103rd Cong., 1st sess. November 4.

VanAlstine, M. P. 2006. Executive Aggrandizement in Foreign Affairs Lawmaking. *UCLA Law Review* 54, No. 2 (December): 309-71.

Vogel, D. 1995. *Trading Up: Consumer and Environmental Regulation in a Global Economy*. Cambridge, MA: Harvard University Press.

White House. 2005. *Joint Statement by President Bush, President Fox, and Prime Minister Martin: Security and Prosperity Partnership*. Office of the Press Secretary, March 23.

Wilson-Forsberg, S. 2001. *Overcoming Obstacles on the Road to North American Integration: A View From Canada*. The Canadian Foundation for the Americas. Policy Paper FPP11-01.

WTO. 2009. The Importance of Regulatory Cooperation for Improving Governments' Ability to Fulfill Legitimate Policy Objectives While Facilitating Trade: The North American Experience. Committee on Technical Barriers to Trade. Document G/TBT/W/317, June 15.

Yoo, J. 2005. *The Powers of War and Peace: The Constitution and Foreign Affairs after 9/11*. Chicago: University of Chicago Press.

Chapter 3

The Governance of Mobility and Risk in a Post-NAFTA Rebordered North America

Isidro Morales

Introduction

Globalization, regionalization, technological change, and the setting of the North American Free Trade Agreement (NAFTA) has enhanced and expanded material and human mobility across the North American region, legal or not, and has impacted cross-border governance mechanisms prevailing in the region for dealing with transnational circulation. Most of the literature dealing with the emergence of regional blocs emphasizes the mobility aspects unleashed by regionalization and globalization. However, parallel to the enhanced mobility spurred by regionalization trends, regional blocs also witness a "thickening" of inner or outer borders, an overall retooling of strategies and technologies gearing to a redefinition of social distances, and the enhancement of deterrence and confinement. It is as though the more mobility is enhanced by the abatement of economic and technological barriers, the more state agencies and governments seek to reclassify and differentiate the capabilities of those people and material goods that are entitled to move from those who don't. A new social, economic, and political divide seems to emerge in the era of globalization and regionalization between strategies promoting material and human mobility and those enforcing entrapment and confinement. Is this a contradiction that regional blocs should overcome?

In this essay I argue that strategies enhancing mobility or deterrence are not a sign of an "anomaly"; rather, they complement one another and have become intimately intertwined. The two integrate a sort of circulation regime, the goal of which is to exacerbate those flows considered legal and beneficial for specific purposes according to states' policy and political preferences, while at the same time targeting undesirable, illegal, or risky movements that must be confined and quarantined. Within the North American space the mobility side of the circulation regime has been earmarked by NAFTA and the economic interdependence exacerbated by the regionalization trend, while the confinement side has been epitomized by the prosecution of "illegal" material transactions or "unauthorized" moving of people, and after September 11, by "suspicious" and "risky" flows of any kind. The governance of mobility in North America has become closely intertwined with the governance of risk. Though there seems to be a consensus among North American partners about enhancing mobility capabilities under the NAFTA rationale and mechanisms, mounting tensions and conflicts seem to dominate the different strategies pursued to enforce confinement. The essay explores the different models that are at the grounds of this circulation regime in the region and highlights flaws and tensions. The first part of the article attempts to theorize what is at stake in terms of circulation and governance in an era in which borders and social spaces are redrawn due to the pressures of globalization, regionalization, and information technologies. The second and third parts explain how NAFTA has become just one side of the circulation regime in North America, while the thickening of inner borders and a growing governmentality of risk have come to make up the other side. What is currently at stake in North America is not a further abatement of barriers of any sort for "deepening" integration. What is highly needed, however, is a reformulation of the scope of what must be included in the mobility field of the circulation regime, and how it should be managed; at the same time, North American governments should agree on what should be included or released from the deterrence and confinement side of the equation, and, most of all, how it should be governed.

The Governance of Mobility and Containment in the Global Era

The governance of circulation, of goods, people, risks, and diseases is at the core of the emergence of modern states. According to Michel Foucault, the emergence of urban spaces in the European space called for new forms of political intervention from public authorities for shaping and regulating the mobility of exchanges of all kinds. Cities became either the expression of political power exercised by powerful kings, disciplinary spaces for dealing with major crises such as plagues, scarcity, and starvation, or centers of multiple exchanges and constant mobility in which threats, risks, crime, and diseases were neutralized and tackled in their own circulation in order to keep them under a threshold of tolerance. From then on, to govern meant, among other things, to regulate the circulation of flows of any kind in its double form–mobility and containment–in order to attain specific outcomes, i.e. the health of the population (by confining and segregating ill people), the security of the city, or the wealth and power of the inhabitants (Foucault 2004b: 3-31).

The governance of circulation has remained a major target of modern politics, becoming more and more complex as power and authority became structured around nation-states. Until very recently territorial borderlines were the ultimate expression of this governance tool in the hands of states. Most territorial lines derive from war and geopolitical compromises. They are in some way the ultimate expression of the sovereign authority of a state. In the 20th century they became the frontier of citizenship and enfranchisement, vis-à-vis the foreigner, disenfranchised or "alien". In other words, as ultimate expressions of state power and citizenship, borders differentiated territorial-based circulation regimes from one another.

However, for the last two decades national-based mobility regimes have seemed to be challenged by the pressures of globalization. The Globalization primarily refers to a state of exacerbated mobility and interdependence in which some domestic processes, in the economic, political, financial, or cultural realms, interact with transnational processes as a means of reinforcement or rejection. The transnationalization of mobility not only has eroded state capabilities, but also has unleashed centrifugal pressures prompting governments and non-government actors to retool circulation regimes at the regional or cross-border levels. The best example of this pressing transformation is the European Union (EU), in which national or local rules have been redefined and crafted in order to build a "single enlarged market" for the mobility of commodities and people, a "eurozone" that has eliminated the sovereign authority of participating countries in monetary matters, and an enlarged security perimeter earmarked by the Shengen space. At the same time, the EU has become a new sort of "fortress" space in which new norms and governance practices are put in place in order to "filter", restrain, or deter the mobility of "disenfranchised" non-communitarian people and goods. The governance of circulation has ceased to be confined solely to statehood and its territoriality and is becoming more and more the target of cross-border regulation by state and non-state polities. Although the European case stands as the most radical example of these changing trends, other regions, including North America, do not remain aloof of these changing pressures.

According to Manuel Castells, globalization is the breakthrough of a new era, that of the "informational society", grounded in a new technological paradigm encompassing the following features: 1) electronically processed information has become the basic input of the overall economy; 2) the diffusion of information technologies has become generalized, impacting social processes and organizations; 3) the network system is becoming the organizational model not only of firms and other productive activities, but also of political, social, and cultural processes as they incorporate new informational technologies (Castells 1997: 61).

The "network enterprise", as Castells called it, is at the grounds of a complex functional integration of value chains impacting global sales and exchanges. This organizational model features a system of communications and functions, the goal of which is to be connected with other poles of autonomous organizational systems that pursue specific goals.[1] By so doing, networked firms, mainly led trough multinational companies (MNCs), have become the driving force of economic restructuring at the global level. MNCs organized under the network system have become agents *par excellence* of worldwide technology innovation and diffusion. By transforming their corporate strategies with the support of information technologies, MNCs have also transformed labor organization and spaces, i.e. from 'Fordist' labor organization patterns to Japanese-inspired, lean or flexible (Womack and Jones 1994).

---

1   According to Castells, social participation and agency as well as power and politics are being reorganized following the same model.

The growing and progressive internalization of market transactions has become another major trait of the reorganization of corporate strategies under networked corporations. Under their aegis, global markets have become a network of networks rather than the traditional arms-length competitive transactions involved in "free trade". At the end of the past century around two-thirds of global trade in merchandises and services was already in the hands of MNCs. If we take into account that most of MNCs sales are not done through foreign trade, but through direct sales within the markets they are located, it is easy to figure out how the global economy has become organized under the model of the network.[2]

The reorganization of economic processes and social activities under the model of the networked connectivity has also transformed the state-centered, territorial-based notions of space and time. In terms of space, the informational economy (and society) is fragmenting local spaces from those built around a network. Networks operate and interconnect in geographic and non-geographic spaces, which become enlarged or compressed according to the amount of interconnections and the complexities of nodes. In most cases the network system operates in what Jan Aart Scholte has called the "supraterritorial" space (Scholte 2000: 46-7), or the cyberspace, that is, interconnections linked by electronically processed information flows that are not territorialized. Castells has called these interconnections a "space of flows" through which digitalized data, images, sounds, and symbols are exchanged among fragmented units scattered on a world-wide basis.

By contrast, the space of place is attached to a specific territoriality and historical time. Local polities could maintain their particular features in spite of being cross-cut by global flows. They could even challenge the identities and power relations embedded in the space of flows. The latter operates in an ambiguous territoriality, and depending on the case, in a virtual supraterritoriality (i.e. financial markets, telecommunications, multimedia, and entertainment); at the same time, the exchange of information, signs, and symbols effectuated through this spatiality become ordered synchronically, that is, up-rooted from any narrative–either local or national–capable of referring them to the local memories to which they were attached. On the other hand, spaces of place are not only well defined geographically, but maintain or redefine the source of their own memories and historical narratives from which they construct their identities. (Castells 1997: 376-468). In that sense, and as some authors have suggested, globalization can be understood as a process or myriad of processes conveying a transformation of the spatial organization of social relations and exchanges from which transnational or interregional flows are unleashed, and networks of interaction, functions, and power are created. (Held and McGrew 1999: 483).

---

2   In 1994 exports of affiliated companies amounted to only 28 percent of their overall sales. (UNCTAD 1997: 17); that is, more than two-thirds of international transactions done by MNCs were channeled not through foreign trade, but by local sales done through their affiliates.

Acceleration of mobility and space and time differentiation beyond state-centered territorialities seem to be the major consequences of the raise of the informational society. This does not mean, however, that social hierarchies and distances have been suppressed. If globalization can be considered a circulation regime on its own–organized under the model of the network according to Castells–it also entails a reconfiguration of the technologies and practices of differentiation, deterrence, confinement, and entrapment. In other words, it seems that the informational society is also "globalizing" the technologies and social practices put in place by circulation regimes at the local or national levels, featuring what Foucault depicted in his genealogy around the rise of the modern state in Europe, i.e. the build up of a dual strategy of enhanced mobility and deterrence.

The reconfiguration of social hierarchies and consequently of social distances is being done, as Ronen Shamir asserts, between those populations who benefit from mobile credentials and capabilities and those who do not (Shamir 2005). The space of flows is conformed of the interconnection of fragmented spaces linked through information technologies. This very same space is interconnecting and accelerating the mobility of people. Hence, a first social differentiation in the era of globalization is between those who have access to a "mobility regime" and those who don't. However, to be part or to be connected to a flow spatiality does not homogenize the possibilities for mobility. Following Shamir's arguments, the retooling of ghettoes, gated communities, and quarantines, heavily used in the national models of circulation, is under way in the era of globalization. If the state-centered paradigm regulating international mobility differentiated between "authorized" and "unauthorized" migrants, between "citizens" and "aliens", the new paradigm for regulating "global mobility" is being used more and more, and especially after the September attacks on the US in 2001, in what Shamir calls the paradigm of "suspicion" (Shamir 2005).

A new social divide is being crafted at the global level between "low risk" and "high risk" flows. It also seems that the more global trends are challenging the state-centered paradigm of mobility, the more the new paradigm of "suspicion" is being reconfigured and retooled. This becomes evident with the governance of "unauthorized" migrants, which in the era of globalization became empowered by an emerging "global" regime of human rights. The more their mobility capabilities become empowered through that regime, challenging consequently the sovereignty paradigm built upon the notion of citizenship, the more they become criminalized and consequently stigmatized and confined under the new priorities of security, risk, and suspicion.[3]

---

3   This is precisely Shamir's thesis; he challenges the premise that globalization alone is accelerating the mobility of people and flows, a tenet held by some authors when they argue, for example, that the logic of "personhood" is superseding the logic of "national citizenship". Shamir argues that "We are witnessing the emergence of a global mobility, oriented to closure and to the blocking of access, premised not only on "old" national or

Social categories of differentiation such as ethnicity, race, gender, sexual preferences, and nationality–such as those attached to "rogue" or "unsafe" countries–among other labels, are being used and exploited in order to redraw the conditions and possibilities of circulation at the global level.[4] A new social global hierarchy is being construed around a differentiated ability to move in space, creating a sort of "mobility gap" (Shamir 2005: 200) whose logic is not so different from that operating at the national levels. Though Ronen Shamir argues that this global mobility gap is being articulated through a technology of "social profiling" (Shamir 2005: 200), modern Western states have traditionally used this technology of social differentiation since at least the implosion of the Industrial Revolution.

Michel Foucault studied social profiling around the concept of governmentality. The concept refers to the disciplinary and knowledge-intensive social practices and procedures through which Western societies have accomplished the steering and regulation of individual and social behavior. All technologies, knowledge, and social practices target the material and subjective identity of individuals or "populations" whose ultimate (political) goal is to modify, redress, normalize, stigmatize, or marginalize "social deviations" according to established standards and norms (Foucault 2004a and 2004b). Consequently, social and individual profiling is at the core of this technology. The body, time, and activity of individuals or specific populations are tactically intervened by a savvy technology of measurement and observation with the purpose of "intensifying" or "domesticating" their forces or attaching identities and subjectivities. However, the ultimate goal of what we could call the "modern" governmentality of body forces and social behavior is not social control, understanding by this the punishment of social deviations through violent coercive processes–normally undertaken by state authorities.

According to Foucault, technologies of governmentality do not express the power of a sovereign, or necessarily the disciplinary order of normative institutions–schools, factories, and hospitals. The ultimate goal of governmentality– as a technological and knowledge-intensive intervention of bodies and social behaviors–is to stabilize variations and fluctuations, but also deviations in the social performance of targeted populations (Foucault 2004b: 57-118 and 403-411). In contrast with disciplinary or sovereign-centered power technologies (such as prohibitions, prescriptions, repression, territorial control, physical extermination, quarantines, or confinements), governmentality aims at steering the range of possible behavior, resistance, and social outcome. It is in some way the regulation, calculation, and stabilization of social normalcy and deviation. In order to attain that goal, technologies of governmentality ought to be heavily embedded and legitimized across all levels of society, in the way space and mobility is organized and scattered or in the way science, knowledge, ideology, and law construe and

---

local grounds but on a principle of perceived universal dangerous personhoods" (Shamir, 2005, 199).

4   See Elaine Correa's chapter in this book collection.

sanction social norms and subjectivities. Once populations or social behavior become governmentalized in such a way, the governance of social misbehavior or "disorder" aims at stabilizing the range of social resistances and "anti-systemic" action.

The current emerging global circulation regime is not only accelerating mobility according to the network organizational model of connectivity, but also it has intensified sovereign concerns for enforcing disciplinary confinement and deterrence, normally by policing territorial borders, while at the time it is also deploying what we could call a "governmentality of risk" through which the spatial action and mobility of "suspicious", "threatening", "rogue" populations attempt to be scattered, fragmented, and neutralized. How is this being reflected in the North American case? The following section shall analyze how the two-way nature of the circulation regime is being adapted to the region: the model of disciplinary trade areas enhancing mobility throughout continentalized markets at the time that closure and confinement is being enforced at the territorial border under the banners of sovereignty and law enforcement. The governmentality of suspicious and risky populations as a means for regulating the spatiality and displacement of threat and risk emerged as an overlapping model after the September 11 attacks in the United States. This will be explored in the final section of this chapter. Mobility and risk, territorial confinement, and enhanced access to enlarged markets do not construe a "contradictory" model of circulation in North America. The governance of risk, through disciplinary, sovereign-based, or governmentality technologies is in some way a political mechanism for managing social legitimate liberties, distances, mobility of peoples and goods, as well as expected political and economic outcomes in any society or cross-border polity.

The Governance of Circulation in a Post-NAFTA North America

a) Enhancing mobility through market access governance.

Ideally the NAFTA regime in place since 1994 has aimed at building a sort of "borderless economy", the great metaphor dominating the ideology and narrative of global markets. This metaphor reflects well the spirit and backbone of the trade regime: to enhance and empower the circulation of goods and investment in the hands of firms and markets in order to boost wealth, productivity, and efficiency throughout North America, and to discipline state intervention in the economy. Nonetheless, the building of this circulation regime must come to terms with the reality of political enclosures and strategic imperatives of security. The creation of a borderless economic space has remained a metaphor since territorial and non-territorial borders were not barred nor banned by the NAFTA agreement. In fact it provoked the opposite, i.e. a progressive "securitizition" of the Mexico-United States border once unauthorized migration and illegal trafficking exacerbated.

Territorial borders remained untouched by NAFTA and even became redrawn by strategic imperatives, as we shall see in this and the following sections.

What NAFTA aimed at building was a sort of "business friendly" border throughout an enlarged "continentalized" market. The reality of this continentalization was already in the hands of larger exporter firms, or MNCs operating in the region and that progressively readapted their production and commercial chains according to the connectivity model of the network. Transnationalized industries such as automobile, food processing, chemical, electronics, and machinery emerged long before NAFTA as a way to reorganize operations by exploiting the location advantages of the continental space (See Morales 2008). What NAFTA provided was an institutional legalistic regime, with all its norms, values, principles, and disciplines covering specific issue-areas as well as its own enforcement mechanisms for facilitating the access and circulation of goods–either tangible or non-tangible–throughout the political enclosures of North America.

NAFTA was not only about trade, but also about a myriad of principles and disciplines whose goal is to govern legitimate trade mobility and circulation in North America by constraining state involvement in the economy. It is an institutional disciplinary device since NAFTA's normative goal is to contain state involvement in trade, finance, and economic activities, consistent with the ideological neoliberal wave that was crafted in Washington from the turn of the 1980s to the end of the George W. Bush era. The promotion of so-called "free trade", economic openness, the mobility of investments, and other market-oriented principles were the core values guiding this venture. These principles were explicitly stated in the foreword of the agreement and became the rationale for the foundation of an enhanced mobility area in commodities, services, and financial flows in order to increase efficiency, productivity, and welfare in the economy of each participating country.

A corollary of these principles was the protection and empowerment of corporate and private property rights from intrusive or abusive state intervention. The removal of non-tariff barriers, mainly through the use of countervailing duties (CVDs) or antidumping (AD) as protectionist devices, aimed to reduce transaction costs as a means for strengthening more efficient markets. All these values were embedded in the principles of neoclassical economics suggesting that wealth creation must be in the hands of markets rather than states. NAFTA aimed to enhance material and financial mobility as a means to strengthen the positioning and competitiveness of market actors, mainly MNCs already operating in the North American space and whose production and trade activities were already continentalized.

Though we may consider NAFTA as a "hard law" trade regime gearing to the mobility of capital, it remains grounded on a sovereign-based model of governance. Since the beginning of negotiations, party members made manifest the idea of not emulating the European model of integration. There was no interest in creating institutional organisms, staffed with their own bureaucracies, similar to what in Europe became the European Commission. In fact, the idea of creating supranational institutions has permanently been anathema in the official parlance and rhetoric. Though Canadians and Mexicans perceived NAFTA as a first step gearing towards a deeper "integration" in the region, Washington officials have traditionally conceived it as a foreign policy tool for enhancing export markets and impacting trade negotiations at the hemispheric–as was the case of the so-called Free Trade Agreement of the Americas (FTAA)–and global levels–at the World Trade Organization (WTO) round negotiations (See Morales 2008). Washington trade commitments were not exclusive to the region, but became part of an evolving trade diplomacy whose limits were reached with the financial crisis witnessed by the US economy at the end of the past decade.

Though still anchored on state interests, NAFTA's legalistic delegation model was successful in abating tariff barriers, enhancing intraregional trade and investments, and incepting a mechanism of communication among the three leaders of the party members.[5] What was innovative for the region was the introduction of disciplinary legalistic mechanisms in order to induce actors to play by the rules. Within the new enlarged economic space openness is being provided, overseen and enforced by the work and supervision of arbitrated panels, the so-called alternative dispute resolution mechanisms (ADRMs). They do not precisely work as law enforcers, but rather as facilitators in government to government negotiations when dealing with conflicts stemming from most of the areas covered by NAFTA. However, disputes and conflicts arising from the infringement or interpretation of trade remedy laws, those prescribing the rights and mobility of investments, are being solved by ad hoc ADRMs, which are entitled to award "quasi-adjudicative" decisions, that is, decisions taken by neutral panels and that are mandatory. However, state agencies have the final decision in any conflict.

Through NAFTA arbitral panels became a new judicial figure mediating between states and between firms and states (in the case of investment disputes). Arbitral panels are entitled to assess whether a breach of the agreement or a threat to comply with it has been committed by one party. The fact that panel determinations are not politically motivated, but rather technically based and rules-framed, entitles them to build the general framework under which confidence building and conflict resolution is implemented among partners. Even in those areas in which state-to-state negotiations remain important to the maintenance of the regime, the role of NAFTA's normative institutions and dispute resolution is no less important, provided it facilitates policy options and the mutual adjustment of state's preferences. The NAFTA mobility regime encloses a level of authority delegation from state agencies to arbitral institutions. At the same time that delegation was clearly constrained and limited by state members. Panels have no authority for creating new legislation of any kind, nor are they entitled to give new interpretations to the rules and laws of any party state. Their decisions do

---

5   For a balance of the strengths and flaws of this mobility regime see Hufbauer and Schott 2005, Pastor 2001, and Morales 2008.

not create any juridical precedent for dealing with similar cases. NAFTA is very clear throughout all its normative architecture that current and future national legislation remains solely the domain of states. States also remain as the ultimate authority able to enforce the mechanism, since they are entitled to use retaliatory measures to compensate the breach or impairment of the agreement. Retaliatory measures range from simple trade sanctions to those more politically sensitive such as fines or the denouncing of the overall agreement. Arbitral panels have no role in defining or suggesting these sanctions. States hold the final decision to gauge the consequences for imposing any type of sanction.

Although civil society groups alleging the narrow and biased scope of the mobility regime have challenged NAFTA, and in spite of the pitfalls, NAFTA's normative framework seems to benefit from the support and consensus of North American economic and political elites. With the Obama administration in the midst of a major financial crisis, that consensus seemed to erode in 2009 due to domestic pressures calling for protectionist measures.[6] In spite of that, material mobility across member parties will remain regulated according to the N AFTA rationale in the years to come. What has become contentious, by contrast, is how confinement and risk have been handled since the very inception of the NAFTA regime.

b) The governance of enclosure and deterrence. The functionality of the barricaded border

Mobility and confinement do not comprise a contradictory model of circulation in North America. European societies have debated and acknowledged since the 17th century that the more freedom of movement is enhanced for attaining either economic or political purposes, the more territorial challenges, threat, and risks proliferate. Mobility and threat are the two faces that any modern circulation regime must confront in order to achieve specific outcomes. In the case of North America illegal migration and the activities of organized crime were, before the September attacks on New York and the Pentagon, the major challenges to deal with in the new era of enhanced mobility.

i) Barricading and deflecting migratory flows

Unauthorized migration coming from Mexico, though tolerated for decades, has traditionally been perceived in the United States establishment as a breach to its own migratory laws and hence a violation to its sovereign right to decide who enters and circulates within its territory (Torpey 1997). Though the crafting of NAFTA was nested in a trilateral debate stressing the complementarities and interdependence of the three economies, migratory issues remained a strictly

---

6   See Wise's contribution in this book.

sovereignty-centered policy for the three countries. In this sense, Washington never felt obliged to discuss or consult migratory issues with its two neighbors.

The enforcement of this sovereignty-based right was already manifested along the Mexico-United States border before and after the signing of NAFTA. While NAFTA set the possibilities of building a business-friendly border between the two countries, the growth of illegal trade–mainly illicit drugs–and unauthorized migration, fueled in part by the burgeoning of a "borderless economy", have reinforced the need in the United States to police its border more severely since the inception of NAFTA.

It was in 1994, when NAFTA came into ruling, that the US Immigration and Naturalization Service (INS)–now absorbed under the Department of Homeland Security (DHS)–launched an aggressive multi-year strategy called the National Strategic Plan (NSP), aimed at enforcing migratory laws at the southwest border, that is, along more than 3,500 km. with Mexico. The NSP materialized in a strategy known as "Prevention Through Deterrence", whose goal was to deploy a massive buildup of agents and resources on the front line in order to deter the entry of illegal aliens instead of arresting them once they had entered the country. This massive concentration of human and material resources, which included the buildup of physical barriers at specific points of entry, focused on the policing of major border urban settlements through which the highest levels of illegal migration and drug trafficking took place (Seghetti *et al.* 2005: 21-2).

The emergence of a barricaded border at the turn of the century followed the principle that the United States maintains a "state monopoly" in deciding who is entitled to enter and circulate in its own territory. This sovereignty-centered principle highlighting the monopoly of states for deciding the modalities of circulation of "aliens" and illicit goods, and that highly contrasts with the mobility regime enforced by NAFTA, ensuring trade, investment, and corporate rights, was at the grounds of a historical political divide of the United States-Mexico economic space until recently. It was the shock of the terrorist attack of 2001 that prompted Washington to a geopolitical rebordering of the whole region under the principles of risk and security. This emerging approach will be analyzed in the final section of this essay.

The barricading of the southwest border became a "politically successful policy failure", as Peter Andreas stated (Andreas 2003:4). It became a policy failure because it failed to deter illegal migrants to trespass the border. It was from the second half of the 1990s that the amount of unauthorized migrants accelerated its growth. Strategies such as Gate Keeper deployed at the San Diego border or Hold the Line, implemented in Ciudad Juárez-El Paso, just rerouted migrants and smugglers to more hostile or sophisticated roads, such as the Arizona desert, sea routes, tunnels, etc. Migrants became more vulnerable when trespassing the line, increasing their risks for losing their lives, but they were not deterred from finding a higher-paid job in the United States. Although the US Border Patrol (USBP) argues that this "preventive" strategy reduced the criminality in major urban centers such as San Diego or El Paso, the numbers show that the massive buildup did not fulfill its main goal.

While NAFTA promised in the 1990s to create job opportunities as a means of curbing mid- to long-term illegal migration, the statistical estimates show the opposite effect. It instead provoked the acceleration of cross-border human mobility within North America. Since the last migratory amnesty granted by the US government in 1986, illegal Mexican migration sharply increased during the 1990s–that is, during the years when most tariffs were phased out by NAFTA–and jumped once again to the top of the bilateral agenda when Mexican President Fox (2000-2006) asked for a new guest worker program as a means to formalize the de facto labor market between the two countries. As of the end of 2008, the overall unauthorized population in the United States was estimated at between 11.5 and 12 million people, most of Mexican origin, i.e. 6.2 million. Sixteen percent of this population arrived in the United States in the late 1980s, and an additional 18 percent from 1990 to 1994. Rates of growth were progressively increasing across periods; while the number of unauthorized workers grew on average by 180,000 yearly during the 1980s, this number jumped to 400,000 yearly during the following period. Rates of growth jumped to 570,000 yearly from 1995 to 1999 and to 850,000 yearly from 2000 to 2005. In other words, 66 percent of the overall illegal population estimated in the United States arrived after 1994. (Passel and Cohn 2008:ii, and Passel 2006:2)

By contrast, this migratory deterrence strategy was a political success for domestic purposes: USBP became better funded and reinforced, borderline populations perceived their cities becoming more secure, and the federal government sent the symbolic message that it was concerned and doing something to curb the entry of illegal aliens, which raised the support of specific constituencies.[7]

The fact that border politics is intended to reap political gains domestically, rather than to effectively deter illegal migration (which specific industries in the United Sates highly demand), or drugs (also highly demanded by US consumers), was reinforced during the second term of the George W. Bush administration. In parallel to the discussion in the upper and lower houses of Congress of an eventual regularization of unauthorized workers in the country, and the possibility of creating a guest worker program for Mexicans, President Bush and the lower house voted at the end of 2006 for the buildup of a border fence 1,500 kilometers long. Though the funding and feasibility of this "Berlin-like wall" (as Mexicans perceived it) are yet to be ensured, the reinforcement of the barricades on the southwest line conveys exactly the same message as the "Prevention Through Deterrence" project initiated in the aftermath of NAFTA: It will certainly make it more difficult and dangerous for smugglers and illegal human flows to trespass the line, but it probably will not deter or curb their entrance, and it has reinforced the sovereignty-centered rhetoric, supported by nationalistic constituencies, that

---

7   For an interesting background on Mexico-US border politics, see Andreas, 2000.

the United States is still capable of deciding on the mobility of "aliens" and illicit commodities in its own territory.

Besides the political domestic gains triggered by the deterrence of illegal mobility, the barricaded border also has yielded economic gains and "rents" for "market" or "private" actors operating on both sides of the line. The most evident of these gains is in the labor side of "illicit markets". It is well established that unauthorized workers are not only overexploited in the United States, but also provide for a sort of "subsidy" in specific US industries and activities. Wage differentials and the dynamism of the US economy continue to attract and assimilate the new cohorts of illegal migrants–the so-called "pull factors". Irrespective of their labor background in Mexico, around two-thirds of illegal workers who entered the United States over the past 15 years are employed in four industries: agriculture, construction, manufacturing, and hospitality (restaurants, hotels, etc), and are settling in new areas beyond the traditional ones (in California or Texas), such as Atlanta, Georgia or Raleigh, North Carolina, where there is a steady labor demand from the construction industry, or New York City, where hospitality industries employ newcomers. The job concentration in these four industries is higher for unauthorized migrants than for the average legal resident in the United States, suggesting that Mexican migrants are not necessarily competing with US citizens in the job market.

Besides being concentrated in these specific industries, illegal labor continues to be the cheapest labor force available in the United States. The mid point or median of the earnings distribution of new unauthorized migrants is $300 per week, well below the median wage of $360 per week for all foreign-born Mexican workers and $384 per week for all foreign-born Hispanic workers in the United States (Kochhar 2005:22). Consequently, the US economy is benefiting from a burgeoning labor force coming from Mexico and that is better educated than the average Mexican[8] and is paid below the bottom of formal wages.[9] These figures show how Mexican migration is not only providing for a sort of "subsidy" to specific industries in the United States, but how the reserve of cheap labor coming from Mexico operates at the cross-border level.

---

8   The new cohort of Mexican illegal migrants does not come from the edges of Mexican society. Most of them were not unemployed in Mexico when they took the decision to migrate, although certainly many of them were underemployed. Their level of education is in general terms above the average currently prevailing in the country, they come from the core of Mexico's labor force (i.e. agriculture, construction, manufacturing, and retail), and more and more are from states other than those located in Mexico's Central West, such as Guerrero, Oaxaca, Puebla, and Veracruz (Kochhar 2005:3-9 and 29).

9   In 2005 the US poverty line for a family of three was $16,090 a year. The median weekly wage of a migrant amounts to $15,000 a year, which means that many of them are automatically located below that line. Thanks to their networks of family and friends, which allow them to abate the costs of housing and living, most of these workers can afford to live with these low wages and even transfer money to their families and relatives located south of the border (Kochhar 2005:22-5).

There is evidence that a *de facto* labor market is already operating between the United States and Mexico, a market that former President Vicente Fox attempted to formalize by putting on the table of negotiations the legalization of unauthorized workers in the United States and the launching of a guest worker program between the two countries. Since a borderless economic space was set by NAFTA, it made sense to take the first steps toward formalizing the integration of labor markets. To regularize labor flows into the market mechanism–and consequently to pool them out from the deterrence-sovereign-centered dispositive–made sense also since the structuring of this cross-border market is grounded on the functionality of social networks, ensuring, as in the space of commodity flows, the mobility of workers.

In fact, the structuring of this informal labor market rests on the different social networks supporting and nourishing it. This social network has at its origin a community base supporting the diaspora (either financially or by providing information about job opportunities in the United States through kinship or friendship). At the destination the network is led by "established migrants"[10] and by people who often have the same geographic origin as the trans-migrants (Munshi 2003). In some way social networks feeding informal labor markets between the two countries could be considered polities, in the sense that they are anchored in social communities and have a constituency; they certainly have a leadership, the "established" or "senior" migrants who may provide contacts, information, and sometimes job opportunities at the migrants' destinations. Most important, these networks provide great utility or value to the participants: reductions in transaction costs for migrants (job opportunities, location possibilities, sometimes housing or funding, and sometimes better paid jobs in the hospitality and construction sectors) and for employers in the United States, since Mexicans are ready to enter into sectors where job turnover is high and uncertain, and to earn less than equivalent authorized workers (Munshi 2003.). Trans-migrant communities form different types of polities that structure the informal labor markets and a sort of informal mobility regime, similar to that prevailing in the space of manufacturing flows articulated around MNCs, at least between the United States and Mexico. The fact that these migrants are still entrapped in the confinement side of the circulation regime has made current national-based migratory policies in North America highly contentious.

---

10   Established migrants are not necessarily people possessing permanent residence in the United States. They could have spent from four to 15 years living in the United States (and not necessarily in the same place), with occasional trips back to their place of origin in Mexico. Eventually they return definitely to Mexico (see Munshi 2003). This suggests that many Mexicans participating in this seasonal circulation do not migrate to the United States because they're pursuing the "American dream"–that is, they don't intend to remain there and pursue a social mobility there. They want to earn the money they cannot find in their place of origin and to return eventually to their original communities.

ii) The confinement of illicit goods.

The sovereign-centered border-deterrence regime works in a similar way in drug trafficking, though in this case the "informal" or illegal mobility regime supporting the market activities of organized crime is much more complex than the one enhancing migratory flows. The entrance of narcotics and illegal drugs into the United States is organized under a networked economy of production, distribution, and consumption that parallels well the space of flows built upon the global legal activities of MNCs depicted in the first session of this essay. In other words, organized crime activities function at the global level under the mechanism of the network connectivity. Since they operate against sanctioned legal architectures, and since government authorities–either at the subnational or national level–still maintain the monopoly of prohibition and consequently of law enforcement, "criminalized" global markets become heavily distorted by opaque, fragmented, "unveiled" or secret-strategic information scattered among participants and by the type of policies and instruments used by state authorities to enforce the law. The result is a serious perverse effect in the operation of these markets: The better government authorities become "law enforcers", the higher the incentives in the supply chain for relocating production, substitution, and distribution networks. This is so because for almost a century, that is, since the United States began to criminalize the commerce and consumption of narcotic substances in 1914, law enforcement in this country has failed to cope with increased domestic consumption and rather focused on abating illegal trade at the border (Astorga 2003).

Similar to what prevails in informal labor markets, US authorities have prioritized a sovereign-centered law enforcement approach at the points of entry in order to confine or deflect the flows of narcotics; flows whose mobility is heavily anchored in a networked economy organized at the global level. However, the rationality for keeping unauthorized migrants at bay has both political and economic domestic payoffs. Fragmenting regional or global migratory markets by criminalizing unauthorized flows deepens the mobility gap between those entitled with circulation privileges and those not,[11] and keeps "illegal" or informal wages low, extracting a subsidy from criminalized workers. By contrast, effectively keeping the entrance to narcotics shut has the perverse effect of increasing the rents of illegal trafficking, making the incentives for new entrants and the restructuring

---

11   As a consequence of the inception of "smart borders" in the region after September 11, the United States established expedite lanes for those persons and goods that were previously registered and screened by border authorities. The myriad of programs ranges from the NEXUS and CENTRI, targeting drivers and travelling people, to the FAST program including commodities and goods. Though facilitating traffic within borders, these programs deepen the mobility gap across the region, between the so-called "NAFTA people"–those entitled to move expeditiously–and normal travelers who may be stopped, yet refused entrance at a border point, and the myriad of unauthorized and suspicious moving people.

of the supply and distribution chains skyrocket. The rent-seeking behavior of drug traffickers explains why specialized literature compares the organizational and behavioral structure of organized crime to that of firms, tribes, and cartels (Frey 1997, Friman 2004, and Williams 2008). However, while firms in cartelized markets have the power to set prices, in illegal markets state authorities, depending on how effectively they dislocate the value chain of the narcotics industry, become price setters. This explains the paradox that the better the government deflects the different chains of the narcotics industry, the better the incentives for rent seekers and new entrants in this business.

This paradox has prevailed for almost a century at the US-Mexico border, and was politically managed through what Peter Andres called "border games"; that is, through changing tactics whose ultimate goal was not the suppression of the mobility of drugs, but the political staging, dramatization, and exploitation of major "victories", i.e. seizures of major drug cargoes or the capture or fall and incarceration–or physical elimination–of drug barons (Andreas 2000). However, as long as illegal drug consumption kept growing, the business remained sound–though risky–and with strong incentives to new entrants each time government agencies accomplished major seizures controlled by powerful transnational criminal organizations (TCOs), or captured a warlord or drug baron.

From the 1960s to the present this border game has been called bilateral cooperation in the "War on Drugs". Although not properly a "conventional war", because the strategy was not to eliminate the circulation of narcotic substances but to permanently fragment markets and dislocate supply and distribution chains, the cooperative game was built under the following commitment: US antinarcotics agencies were satisfied with their Mexican counterparts as long as they demonstrated major quantitative seizures of illicit drugs and, from time to time, the arrest of a drug czar. Success and cooperation in this "common war" was never assessed against the evolution of US domestic demand, or global demand, and the ratio of seizures in relation to the total amount of drugs entering the US market (See Astorga 2003, Andreas 2000). The tactical positions in this war remained scattered within the bureaucratic labyrinth of US agencies, provoking sometimes tensions and clashes between the State Department and border authorities, unleashing periods of "crisis" in the bilateral cooperative mood, i.e. Operation Interception in 1968–through which border traffic was severely interrupted for inspections–or the warnings of a possible "decertification" during the 1990s when the US government judged Mexico's cooperation in this war as insufficient. In spite of these tensions in the tactics of the border game, cooperation was always exploited on both sides of the line and subordinated to the overall strategic interests shared by the two nations.

This was evident during the NAFTA negotiations. Although members of Congress warned the White House and trade negotiators of a possible acceleration of drug flows if a free trade area was established with Mexico, the State Department deliberately made the frontline of the war on drugs a low-priority issue. This was perfectly understood by the Salinas administration (1988-2004), which doubled the seizure of major amounts of drugs and made the capture of the drug baron of the time, Miguel Ángel Felix Gallardo, proof of goodwill and cooperation with the United States. At the time the priority between the two governments was to pave the road for NAFTA and consequently to avoid any crisis in the border game (Andreas 2000: 56-65). The road to NAFTA not only increased the geopolitical importance of Mexico, but also highlighted once more the need for Washington to count on a stable, reliable, and predictable neighbor, regardless of the political and economic pacts pursued by its political class in order to hold government. Since the Second World War, and during the Cold War, Mexico functioned as a sort of "buffer space" for US interests, either for avoiding or repelling a military attack coming from the southwest border, or for filtering social and political unrest coming from revolutionary waves in Latin America (See Chacón 2008, and Ojeda 1976). The War on Drugs was part of this overarching deterrence policy pursued by the United States in facing illicit markets.

Border games remained functional once NAFTA was put into place and trade and investment flows began to increase in parallel with the illegal flow of people and drugs. The filtering properties of borderlines became refined in order to accelerate the transit of "NAFTA people" and commodities while fragmenting and dislocating the mobility of unauthorized, undesirable, illicit, or banned people and goods. This double mechanism of accelerating the mobility of those who are entitled to move and deterring and dislocating those who are not accelerated the barricading of the US-Mexico frontline. In the past two decades, when mobility was accelerated due to NAFTA and the pressures of globalization, the US-Mexico border became "thickened" by the erection of walls of all kinds, including electronic and "cyber walls"; the increase in staff and budget of border operations, surveillance mechanisms and patrolling; and the growing militarization of policing activities. Military equipment and deterrence tactics used by the US army in the Gulf War of 1990 were transferred and adapted to the US-Mexico frontline. The rationale for a growing militarization of the border was not to prepare the US army for an eventual attack against smugglers or warlords, but to assist border authorities in the accomplishment of their multiple duties of surveillance, policing, deterrence, and confinement. (Andreas 2003)

Since the rationale of the War on Drugs was not to suppress mobility (which depends on drug consumption), but to displace and disrupt the entrance of illicit goods, the perverse effect of this strategy became rapidly amplified, provoking dangerous externalities that nullified the benefits of the border game. At the turn of the century Mexico was the major exporter of marijuana to the United States and had become the target and platform of major drug producers of cocaine and other illicit drugs from Colombia. Since US antinarcotics agencies were successful in shutting down the entrance of drugs coming from the Caribbean and the Gulf of Mexico route, drug traffickers opened the road through the Pacific, making the Pacific side of Mexico, mainly the states of Michoacán, Sinaloa, and Baja California, platforms for re-exporting or substituting cocaine, amphetamines, and other chemical precursors for drugs. Since rents became higher as circuits were relocated from the Caribbean to the Pacific, and thereafter were concentrated more in Mexico due to the weakening and fragmentation of the Medellín Cartel, drug barons and their warlords had the resources to infiltrate and corrupt border agents on both sides of the border, Mexican law enforcement authorities, and all levels of the Mexican political class, including the army.[12]

The corruption surrounding the Salinas administration was scandalously unveiled once NAFTA was put into force, and with the start of the Zedillo administration, when Salinas' brother, Raúl, was arrested and formally accused of murdering the former president of the Partido Revolucionario Institucional (PRI), Francisco Ruiz Massieu, and of embezzlement. The incarceration of Raúl Salinas started a saga of political scandals in Mexico in which the complicity between its political class, drug trafficking, and money laundering was set in the spotlight.[13] Different levels of law enforcement authorities managed illegal drug markets in Mexico as de facto taxation resources. People involved in production, mobility, and transit were bribed as part of the functionality of the supply chain. During the Zedillo administration the same antinarcotics czar, General Jesús Gutiérrez Rebollo, was also prosecuted and put in jail, accused of working for the drug cartels. In parallel with these political scandals of mounting bribes and corruption, drug barons also injected liquidity to Mexico's prison system in order to regain their freedom. The most scandalous case was when Joaquín Guzmán, alias "El Chapo", capo of the powerful Sinaloa Cartel and considered by Forbes magazine to be one of the most powerful men in the world in its survey published at the end of 2009, escaped from prison of at the beginning of 2001, (CNNExpansión.com 2009).

All this happened when the attacks against the twin towers, in New York, and against the Pentagon were perpetrated, in September 2001. The attacks were a breakthrough for the world and for US interests, policies, and politics. A new sense of physical vulnerability spread throughout US society and was rapidly exploited by the George W. Bush administration so he could launch his War on Terror. In this new edition of the war, territorial borders became a fragile front, since the new notion of the enemy was not a specific state or a specific population, and since the very notion of threat changed, being not nuclear or military imbalances, but terrorism. Once the threat of terror and terrorists became associated with the challenges managed under the mechanisms of border games, US authorities recognized the need to move to a more comprehensive strategy for dealing with the new notions of risks and threat. Consequently, the War on Drugs was subsumed into the War on Terror. While the first one had as its main goal the deterrence

---

12   For a comprehensive analysis of the role played by Mexico and Mexican-based TCOs see US Department of Justice, 2008, Manwaring 2009, and Cook 2008.

13   In a recent interview–perhaps the last one–between former president Miguel De la Madrid (1982-1988) and highly respected independent journalist Carmen Aristegui, the former president acknowledges the corruption during the Salinas years as well as Salinas' brother's contacts with drug barons. See Aristegui and Trabulsi 2009: 96-104

of illegal flows, the second one is betting on prevention, on keeping the risk of terrorist attacks at bay, or on recurring to preemptive action. While the goals are different, as is the overall strategy, the two have made war a never-ending game, since the first does not tackle the problem of consumption, nor does the second tackle the current sources of terrorism.

3. Towards a governmentality of risk in a rebordered North America

After September 11 US border politics seemed to shift from the sovereignty-centered border game of protecting and exercising the monopoly of the state in deciding on the legal transit of "aliens" and goods in its territory, to a rather war-centered paradigm in which protection of the homeland, not only its borders and territory, but also its population, resources, and all their interconnections with the "outside world", is at stake. This "war-centered" paradigm does not substitute the "sovereignty-based" one; they overlap and reinforce each other. The "historically embedded" territorial border is still to be protected against "illegal aliens", but the focus is being shifted to those criminal aliens potentially linked to or exploited by terrorist purposes. In this sense, the War on Terrorism is anchored in a generalized "politics of fear" re-launched by the US government after the attacks of September 11, 2001.[14] That fatal date provoked the shutting of US territorial borders, causing serious and costly disruptions in all production chains supplied or demanded by its two NAFTA neighbors.[15] The closure of the north and southwest frontlines, although done for extreme and critical reasons, showed the limits and flaws of the territorial border game of barricading and policing lines. It seems that the terrorists who perpetrated the attacks entered the country legally and overstayed their visas in order to prepare their criminal activities. Although isolationism and quarantine were extreme sovereign options for the United States to protect its territory and space, it was clear that it was not a suitable strategy for dealing with the new nature of threat and enemies that the country confronted. The attacks not only initiated a new endless state of war based on preventive and preemptive attacks–a state of war that has been pursued as well by the current Obama administration, although with a less muscular tactic–but also created a new sense of vulnerability, fear, and insecurity in US public opinion that urged Washington to revisit its security paradigms for the new "Era of Terror".

---

14   According to Noam Chomsky, The US government has traditionally controlled social and individual behavior in US space by articulating a politics (I would say a governmentality) of fear through which the notion of the enemy and insecurity is being construed and socialized. After September 11 this politics of fear has been renovated through a narrative on the "War on Terror" (Chomsky 2005: 18-41).

15   Canadians estimated that a one-hour assembly line shutdown cost around US$1.5 million. A 10 percent increase in border costs could reduce Canada-US volumes by 25 percent. (The Senate 2003: 7 and 9).

It is in this context that "smart borders" were conceived, as moving and changing checkpoints whose technology and knowledge-intensive mechanism for screening and profiling suspicious or risky people aims at building a threat assessment for the homeland. According to Washington, "smart borders" and transport are intertwined, in the sense that every community in the United States, be it small or large, is interconnected with a worldwide transport infrastructure. Harbors, railroads, airports, highways, energy grids, virtual networks, and any flow conveying people or commodities are currently considered to be part of that "world-wide transportation infrastructure" (White House 2002, Bush 2002). That is, smart borders were not devised for deterring and confining peoples or goods, a task accomplished by barricaded lines. The tactical goal of these moving, flexible supervision checkpoints is not to interrupt or dislocate, but to enhance mobility by helping to differentiate risky movements from those that are not.[16] Smart borders have thus the goal to promote, by using modern screening technology–digital analysis of fingerprints, irises and other biometrics–the "efficient" and "safe" transit of people, goods, and services across the homeland and its interconnections. Framed in those terms, Canada and Mexico became a de facto extension of the US homeland and were suddenly urged to cooperate with Washington in their respective territories to ensure the security of the North American transport and conveying belt networks.

Canadians were the first to make this cooperative move in the new geopolitical rebordering of North America. Fearing that security would became a costly barrier in its productive chains integrated with US industries, and fearing a sort of "thickening" or "Mexicanization" of their own border, Canadians were the first to propose the establishment of intelligent checkpoints in order to avert US security priorities from trumping the legal mobility of people and goods. Similar to what happened in the design and inception of the trade regime, Mexicans joined as followers in this geopolitical redrawing. Smart borders became a trilateral device and were the grounds of the emergence of a new continental security regime, which under the George W. Bush era was labeled as North American Security and Prosperity Partnership (SPP).[17]

Conceived not as a military alliance, SPP aimed at its origins to reinforce intergovernmental policy cooperation for the protection of North America as a common territorial unit. The original bulk of initiatives and scheduled targets aimed at preempting the entrance (legal or illegal) of presumed terrorists and criminals to the overall region. The "prosperity" side of the equation was not rhetorical, and obeys both Canadian and Mexican concerns for keeping security priorities from

---

16   In contrast with territorial borders embedded in historical national narratives and identities, smart borders are constantly moving and changing; they could be an embassy or consular premise; they function at customs clearance or preclearance; they could be activated when a cargo in a container is being registered in advance; they are in airports and aircrafts, in shipping routes and pipelines.

17   See Belanger's and Ramos' articles in this volume.

becoming a new entry and costly barrier in the continentalized economic space that could eventually affect the competitiveness of integrated networked industries. As Canadians have claimed since the setting up of SPP, the new security regime must strive for protection without increasing protectionism. It was Corporate Canada that originally advocated a comprehensive approach to security with the United States with the goal of reducing possible harm to trade and production links with US firms (See Morales 2008: 164-168). Pursuing "protection without protectionism" as a common goal for the emerging security regime in North America summarizes what is at stake for the region. Instead of beefing up a strategy of barricades and quarantines, which at the same time increases the costliness of mobility, it became more convenient for corporate interests and all partners involved in the NAFTA space of flows to increase cooperation in risk assessment capabilities in order to ensure the safe mobility of goods and services that are supposed to be at the heart of North American competitiveness. In other words, SPP, in contrast with the NAFTA regime, was grounded at the core of the rationale of any circulation regime, i.e. to ensure the governance of both mobility and risk in order to obtain specific or attended results, in this case, a so-called North American "prosperity" and competitiveness fueled by networked firms and market actors. A thickening of borders–according to the Canadian jargon–or worse, the "Mexicanization" of the Canada-US divide would have risked the cancelation of the advantages of mobility.

This explains why the emerging and crafting of SPP ran parallel with the geopolitical rebordering of North America and the inception of establishment of checkpoints. The first goal of this overall redrawing was to "enlarge" the mobility gap across the region. This was done through the inception of expeditious lanes at clearance or pre-clearance customs points for pre-registered people and goods which proved to be "safe". The NEXUS, CENTRI and FAST programs, all currently expanding and working at points of entrance north and south of the US territorial borders, aim to pre-screen and profile people and goods in order to afford them mobility privileges and access to expeditious lanes. US Visit Program also aims at screening and profiling all temporary visitors arriving to the United States by ritually taking their fingerprints, taking iris metrics, and checking their ports of exit.

Once SPP was established its goal was to coordinate, through summitry mechanisms and the creation of ad hoc working groups, the internalization of the costliness of security and safety in key fields such as energy, critical infrastructure, automobile, natural resources, and public health, among others. At the intergovernmental level SPP sent the message that the leaders of the three NAFTA countries were working in common to build a safer region while keeping mobility expeditious for the "prosperity" and "competitiveness" of the overall region. Threat assessment and cooperation in intelligence and security became reinforced between the United States and Canada within the North American Aerospace Command (NORAD), a bilateral Cold War mechanism targeting air warning and control between the two countries, and the creation in 2002 of the US Northern

Command (USNORTHCOM), whose mission is to deter, prevent, and defeat aggressions menacing the US homeland and its extensions, that is, the continental United States, Alaska, Canada, and Mexico. The creation and strategic functions of USNORTHCOM made a de facto enlargement of the perimeter of security of North America, comprising not only its territory and space, but surrounding waters of circa 500 nautical miles (www.northcom.mil). The command is led by a US Air Force four-star general who at the same time commands NORAD, proof of the close intertwining between the two commands and the nature of military cooperation between the United States and Canada.

Mexico-US security cooperation became much more complex and delicate. Once the United States launched the War on Terror on the global front, barricaded and smart borders became tools of the domestic front of the war on the US-Mexico line. While on the global front the war against terror is profiling rogue populations and territories, on the domestic front barricaded and smart borders attempt to detect and target risky people and devise "inner" spaces of vulnerability. In other words, the new politics of borders became another means of conducting the War on Terror within the homeland, this time between the inner line separating US and Mexican territories.[18] In contrast with the deterrence approach followed before September 11, which highlighted the legal and sovereign dimension of the territorial border, the "smart borders" and new security approaches rely heavily on a technology of governmentality of human mobility and the type of risks they convey.

While the barricaded border is targeting the trespassing of the "illegal alien" or the illegal commodity (narcotics), the smart border aims at profiling, in priority, the terrorists, the would be terrorists, and their weapons–either weapons of mass destruction (WMD) or others–that they eventually may convey. Within this new hierarchy of risk, the unauthorized migrant is still a risk, but not a priority target. Illegal flows such as narcotics are still a risk because they need an interface to enter the "wider" (North American) or the "core" (the US) homeland: the smuggler. Smuggling has become a high-risk activity since terrorists may use them as conveying belts for penetrating the homeland. As a Patrol agent warned, the new concern is that "...terrorists and violent criminals may exploit smuggling routes to illegally enter the United States" (Committee on the Judiciary 2005:21). This is why the new approach is targeting and profiling risky people or flows not only before they enter the homeland, but also once they are at home. The DHS has

---

18   A representative on Capitol Hill from the State of Texas highlighted very well this double front of the "War on Terror" during a congressional hearing: "No more serious of an issue could exist before this Congress, this Nation–than the WAR (sic) that is being waged on our southern border. While most of the country knows that we are actively fighting the War on Terrorism–only a small fraction of the American public is aware of the battle our local law enforcement officers are waging on our border with Mexico" (Committee on the Judiciary 2006:54). Indeed, "law enforcement" to combat crime and terrorist-related activities, either at US territorial borders or within the homeland has become the "inner face" of the War on Terror.

conferred the first task to the Customs and Border Protection (CBP) agency, and the second one to Immigration and Customs Enforcement (ICE). They coordinate with each other to detect a risk before it enters the homeland or once it develops at home (See Siskin 2006: 24-30).

These new agencies, in coordination with local and federal authorities and intelligence services, attempt to define, classify, and modify the new priorities for targeting and detaining people under suspicion according to the circumstances. According to a memorandum sent by the Under Secretary for Border and Transportation Security to both CBP and ICE, the rationale is as follows: Apart from those cases requiring mandatory detention for breaching the Immigration and Naturalization Act (INA),[19] "(a)liens who exhibit specific, articuable intelligence-based risk factors for terrorism or national security concern not solely based on the alien's race, ethnicity, nationality or religion" are among those who must be detained on a "high priority" basis. "Suspected alien and narcotics smugglers" were classified (so far) on the "Medium Priority" list, while those arrested in worksite enforcement or other aliens not subject to required detention were put on a "Lower Priority" category. (DHS 2006: Appendix D).

This new hierarchy of risk clearly differentiates criminal and terrorist-related populations from unauthorized labor populations, since illegal aliens are not required by current federal legislation to be under detention. However, this list clearly establishes the link between the illegal (the unauthorized workers), the criminal (the smugglers), and the priority target (the terrorists). Smugglers are the interface between illegal and all kinds of criminal populations. By differentiating populations according to their level of risk and the way they relate to other types of populations, the new strategy devises security policies that attempt to become more efficient in their results. Agents and agencies linked to DHS are asking for more staff and space to increase the number of detainees, according to the changing priorities crafted by the security of the homeland (See DHS 2006). Priorities are being framed according to what those agencies understand by "intelligence-based" or "terrorist-based" risk. New risky populations are being crafted by a combination of ethnicity, nationality, religion, and other cultural factors stigmatized by the evolving War on Terror. New typologies are constantly

---

19   INA warrants the detention of any alien who has committed a felony or an aggravated felony. This law contains many definitions of aggravated felony, including terrorist activities. The fact that the memorandum includes intelligence-based terrorist-related factors as a "high priority" reason for detention highlights the nature and priority of screening operations. So far, trespassing the border illegally is not a felony, but a civil violation, which allows for expeditious or voluntary deportation with no prosecution. However, this is rapidly changing since at the state level unauthorized migration is being criminalized more and more, i.e. SB1070 approved in the state of Arizona in April 2010, by which police and border authorities could detain in public spaces people suspected of being in the state illegally. In this case, social profiling of "suspicious" people is being carried out by phenotypic traits and social appearance. See Hussain's article in this book collection.

emerging for being part of the mandatory or "high priority" list, and changing according to the circumstances.

Circumstances are changing rapidly south of the Mexican border. The growing "securitization" of the US-Mexico line is targeting not only illegal flows and the activities of smugglers and would-be terrorists, but also more and more the violence triggered by organized crime embedded in all kinds of illegal trade. The emergence of uncontrolled violence and "lawless spaces" in Mexico has become a major security concern for the United States, especially when current President Calderón decided, at the beginning of his administration, to combat TCOs operating in the country with military means. This has unleashed violence, the creation of private armies, and the emergence of "zones of impunity" throughout the country. If civil government fails to rule those lawless spaces, then the governance falls into the hands of organized crime. This explains the perception, coming from corporate interests and strategic analyses commanded by the Department of Defense, that Mexico could eventually become a "failed state" (see USJFC 2008).

According to the terms used by current Secretary of the DHS, Janet Napolitano, Mexico's violence and security problems have become "intermestic" for the United States; that is, Mexico's security problems are both an international and a domestic threat to US security standards. Mexico's current violence has become a homeland security problem of such magnitude that the Department of Justice (DOJ) has considered Mexican drug TCOs activities as the "the greatest organized crime threat to the United States" (DHS 2009a).

Since Mexico's drug-related violence has been perceived as "intermestic" by the United States, the Obama administration has decided to go beyond a muscular-barricaded approach on border issues to a rather "shared-governance" strategy. Some of the mechanisms already in place along the Canadian borderline have also been transplanted to the southwest line, as witnessed by the "border enforcement security teams" (BEST) already functioning and whose goal is to produce and share information between federal agencies that are responsible for border security and state and local law enforcement agencies in order to trace the violence linked to TCOs; they also devise strategies for attacking human and smuggling organizations that contribute or are linked to that violence. Their goal is to build up "calculated spaces" of risk by tracing and monitoring criminal or illegal behavior, their connection with illicit flows–either human or material–and their eventual link with "homeland security" or "intermestic" concerns.

This does not mean that the US-Mexico border will move into a thinner Canadian-type regime; just the opposite, in fact: Shared and intelligent mechanisms will reinforce the barricaded line in order to make it more efficient and functional. Shared governance mechanisms also will function differently than they do at the northern borderline since Mexico's army and intelligence agencies lack the institutional strength that Canadian forces possess. Since Mexican security agencies witness corruption and infiltration within their structures–in some cases connected to the drug dealers they are pursuing– security concerns along the southwest border are evolving differently than those prevailing on the US-Canada line. The US security strategy toward Mexico is a combined effort of strengthening and modernizing Mexican military and police forces with a myriad of shared counternarcotics and intelligence operations involving many specialized agencies on both sides of the border. The first task is being implemented through the Merida Initiative (MI); the second one through a myriad of multiagency operations involving Mexican organizations at various levels.

The MI was supported by the US Congress through its funding of US$1.6 billion for a three-year term, 1998 to 2010. It is worth noting that the MI encompasses Mexico as well as Belize, Costa Rica, the Dominican Republic, El Salvador, Guatemala, Haiti, Honduras, Nicaragua, and Panama. From 1998 to 2010 appropriations for Mexico under this security mechanism amounted to US$1,330.3 million, of which 32 percent funded military equipment and 65 percent drug trafficking control and law enforcement.[20] Though most of the funding for the first three years of this initiative was used for buying sophisticated military equipment and military training, the US Congress appropriated US$75 million for what they labeled "judicial reform, institution building, anti-corruption, and rule of law activities" (Seelke 2010:4). The latter could be considered a euphemism for Washington's interests in combating corruption embedded in some key intelligence and law enforcement agencies of Mexico. Since MI is under the umbrella of the Department of State, Hillary Clinton, currently at the head of the office, has already made two visits to Mexico in order to highlight this new phase of shared governance and shared responsibility for combating DTOs and organized crime. Similarly to what Jane Napolitano has recognized at DHS, Mrs. Clinton also has acknowledged that the mobility of drugs is dependent on burgeoning US consumption and illegal trafficking of guns.

As for the multiagency operations involving Mexican organizations, I will mention the most relevant ones. Through Operation *Armas Cruzadas*, US and Mexican agencies are joining efforts to detect and prevent the smuggling of illegal arms into Mexico. By putting this joint operation in place, the United States finally has recognized a point raised for the first time by the Calderón administration–that illegal drug markets operate both northbound and southbound.[21] It is presumed that 90 percent of the guns and ammunition used by Mexican-based cartels are smuggled from the United States (Seelke 2010: 16). Through Operation Firewall, the US Treasury Department has been attempting to prosecute money laundering from Mexican-based criminal organizations in the United States. Thorough Operation Stonegarden the DHS is increasing funding for enhancing current state, local, and tribal law enforcement staff and operations all along the southern

---

20   See John Bailey's contribution in this book collection.

21   Illicit drug trade between Mexico and the United States forms part of both a regional and global market, openly recognized by the DOJ (See DOJ 2008). Efforts for combating or abating illegal flows must include the reduction of illegal narcotic consumption in the United States, a major health and security problem already recognized, albeit belatedly, by the US government.

border. Through Operation Accelerator and Project Reckoning, both multiagency and multinational efforts led by the DOJ, the government's mandate is to seize and confiscate illegal funding to Mexican-based criminal organizations (for a summary of all these operations see DHS 2009b).

What policy goal is pursued with these measures? The goal is not to suppress the activities of organized crime, but to weaken them, to relocate them outside of North America, the Caribbean, and Central America. Such policies aim to avoid making Mexican political elites the hostages of these TCOs and seek to restore the stability and predictability of Mexico's political system. Mexico had functioned in geopolitical terms as a sort of "buffer state" since the end of the Second World War. Political stability, predictability, and continuity provided by the then vigorous Mexican political system, whose centerpieces were a strong Presidency and a hegemonic political party–the PRI–proved to be beneficial for Washington's geopolitical interests. Mexico's political continuity ended with the burgeoning pressures for democratizing the political system, provoking Vicente Fox's victory to the presidency in 2000, and earmarking the end of PRI's hegemony after more than 70 years. Mexico's political predictability and stability are currently challenged by the confrontations among TCOs and their warlords and the violence unleashed by the War on Drugs, fueled and backed by the MI.

A balance sheet of the military combat against TCOs by the Calderón administration looks pessimistic. Government figures currently recognize more than 22,000 people killed since the Calderón administration launched its military confrontation against drug barons. Key cities such as Ciudad Juárez, located on the borderline with the United States, have literally collapsed, .i.e. have been seized by the army but are unable to stop violence and strengthen civil authority. Though key leaders of private armies and of TCOs have been killed, captured, or extradited to the United States, they have proved to have an extended network of operations, sophisticated guns and arms, and especially a dear amount of financial resources. Although President Calderón praised his war as a success, more and more voices are being raised on both sides of the border challenging this perception, and calling for a new approach or paradigm for dealing with the problem.

New proposals seem to privilege more a further governmentality of drug trafficking under the figures of risk and suspicion, rather than the reinforcement of the sovereignty-based strategy of defending borders and regaining territorial control through armed forces. In the years to come most probably the War on Drugs will be more and more governmentalized under a myriad of overlapping sectoral policies ranging from a possible de-penalization or legalization of some drugs that prove not to be so harmful or addictive, such as marijuana, to social intervention policies targeting "populations at risk" in order to change their incentives for being recruited by TCOs.

Conclusions

National policies and interests dominated cross-border flows of any kind among North American partners until very recently. NAFTA did not move this inward-looking governance practice at the supranational level, as it was case in the EU. It rather inaugurated a sort of shared-governance mechanism earmarked within the principles and values of NAFTA. At the same time, NAFTA set the basis for building a model of continental mobility across borders. The model, however, did not compensate for the strong asymmetries prevailing among parties, and the scope remained biased towards corporate and United States interests. Key issues such as cross-border migration, border security, and development of lagging regions remained outside the mobility model. The governance of illicit or non-authorized flows remained barred and stigmatized according to national policies, preferences, and prejudices.

It was after the attacks of September 11 on American soil, and with the establishment of SPP, that for the first time North America moved to a cross-border circulation regime in which mobility–though still circumscribed to corporate and Unites States interests–became intertwined with a sort of continental security approach. Although barricaded lines were not suppressed, the instauration of intelligent borders moved from the confinement and rerouting approach to the build-up of calculated spaces and the notions of threat assessment and social profiling. At the core of the strategy was the enhancement of material and human mobility–according to the NAFTA scope and values– in parallel to the intensification of social distances and the establishment of new hierarchies according to the notions of risk and suspicion. Though SPP reflected the concerns and fears of the master player in North America, it created the umbrella from which a continental circulation regime could evolve in the region.

Though Washington and corporate interests still have the strong hand for setting the agenda of what is being "authorized" or banned to circulate across borders, the pressures of economic integration–either formal or informal–, the complex interdependence connecting the three countries, the reconfiguration of borders, and the impact of the information revolution in social organization are empowering more and more polities, government agencies and principled networks to move beyond the status quo. Since the mid-1990s and up to the present, Mexico has strongly voiced the de-penalization of unauthorized migration, claimed the protection of human rights of migrants, and the formalization of the de facto continental labor market. At present more voices are being raised for de-penalizing or liberalizing the circulation of some banned drugs, such as marijuana. Shared governance operations also have been accepted for enhancing continental mobility while ensuring security. What has become strongly contested in the region is the divide between what is allowed and what is banned to circulate. In the years and decades to come, moving this divide will become the major issue of debates and intensive negotiations among key actors able to impact the North American agenda. Though SPP attempted to become the umbrella for such a debate, it remained constrained to the interests of the previous George W. Bush administration. A new paradigm is needed to recast the governance of cross-border circulation throughout North America.

Meanwhile, the choreography of sovereign-based border games is losing ground and legitimacy, as witnessed by the parochial and discriminatory legislation enacted in some US border states and the growing death toll of transmigrants in their way to find new jobs. The more the sovereign model of cross-border governance is challenged–in terms of its effectiveness and legitimacy–the more the need to shift the divide between what is allowed and banned to move, and to change the approach from deterrence and confinement to that of prevention and social profiling. Moving from the status quo will not necessarily be a result of a rational adjustment process–or rational choices as some have argued for the European experience–among North American partners. It won't be either the natural consequence of a spill-over effect started by NAFTA or the SPP, as neofunctionalist integration theories would probably argue. As witnessed by the North American experience, to craft a shared-governance circulation regime will most probably be the byproduct of exacerbating conflicts and crises among partners from which Washington elites will realize the advantages to move to a more govermentalized security regime. The state of border surveillance will not be removed, but it will be retooled as a more sophisticated mechanism for intensifying social differentiation, space fragmentation, and for portraying risk and threat hierarchies in order to tactically intervene the mobility capabilities of all sorts of flows across North America. By tactically fragmenting and pervasively differentiating the mobility capabilities of material, intangible and human flows, the permanent war against all sorts of risks and enemies prevailing in the region –whatever the matrix used for defining them–will be continued by less muscular means.

References

Andreas, Peter. 2000. *Border Games. Policing the US-Mexico Divide*, Ithaca, N.Y. Cornell University Press.

Andreas, Peter. 2003. "Redrawing the Line. Borders and Security in the Twenty-first Century", *International Security*, Vol. 28. No. 2. Fall. pp. 76-111.

Aristegui, Carmen and Trabulsi, Carlos, 2009, *Transición. Conversaciones y retratos de lo que se hizo y se dejó de hacer por la democracia en México*, México, D.F., Grijalbo.

Astorga, Luis. 2003, *Drogas sin fronteras. Los expedientes de una guerra permanente*, México, D.F. Editorial Grijalbo.

Bush, George W., 2002. The Department of Homeland Security, The White House, June, http://www.whitehouse.gov/homeland/ (accessed April 15, 2006).

Castells, Manuel, 1997, *The Rise of the Network Society*. Malden Massachusetts: Blackwell Publishers Ltd.

Chacón Susana, 2008, *La relación entre México y los Estados Unidos. Entre el Conflicto y la Cooperación (1940-1955)*. México. D.F., Tecnológico de Monterrey and Fondo de Cultura Económica.

Chomsky, Noam, 2005, *Imperial Ambitions. Conversations on the Post-9/11 World.* New York: Metropolitan Books.

CNNExpansión.com, "El Chapo repite en Forbes", http://www.cnnexpansion.com/ negocios/2009/12/14/el-chapo-repite-en-forbes, accessed on April 12th, 2010

Committee on the Judiciary. House of Representatives, 2005, "Weak Bilateral Law Enforcement Presence at the US-Mexico Border: Territorial Integrity and Safety Issues for American Citizens", Joint hearing, Serial No. 109-90, Washington D.C., November, http://judiciary.house.gov.

Cook, Collen W., 2008, "Mexico's Drug Cartels", CRS Report for Congress, February.

Department of Homeland Security (DHS), 2006, *Detention and Removal of Illegal Aliens.* Washington D.C., April.

Department of Homeland Security (DHS). 2009a. Testimony of Secretary Janet Napolitano before Senate Homeland Security and Governmental *Affairs* Committee. Southern Border Violence: Homeland Security Threats, Vulnerabilities, and Responsibilities [online]. Available at: www.dhs.gov/ [accessed 30 March 2009].

_____2009b. Press Briefing by Secretary of Homeland Security Janet Napolitano; Deputy Secretary of State Jim Steinberg; and Deputy Attorney General David Ogden on US-Mexico Border Security Policy [online]. Available at: www.dhs. gov/ [accessed 30 March 2009].

Department of Justice (DOJ). 2008. *National Drug Threat Assessment, 2009.* Washington, DC (December).

Foucault, Michel. *Naissance de la biopolitique.* 2004a, Paris : Gallimard/Seuil.

Foucault, Michel. *Sécurité, Territoire, Population.* 2004b, Paris, Gallimard/Seuil.

Friman, Richard H.,2004, "The great escape? Globalization, immigrant entrepreneurship and the criminal economy", 2004, *Review of International Political Economy*; Vol. 11, No. 1, February, pp. 98-131

Frey, Bruno S., 1997, "Drugs, Economics and Policy", *Economic Policy*, Vol. 12, No. 2, October, pp. 389-398

Held, David and McGrew, Anthony., 1999, "Globalization" *Global Governance* Vol. 5, No. 4 (October-December): 483-96.

Hufbauer, Clyde, y Schott, Jeffrey, 2005, *NAFTA Revisited. Achievements and Challenges,* Washington DC, Institute for International Economics.

Kochhar, Rakesh, 2005, "Survey of Mexican Migrants. The Economic Transition to America." *Pew Hispanic Center Research Report.* 6 December. http://www. pewhispanic.org (accessed September 5, 2006).

Manwaring, Max G., 2009, "A New Dynamic in the Western Hemisphere Security Environment: the Mexican Setas and other Private Armies", Strategic Studies Institute, www.StrategicStudiesInstitute.army.mil/ (accessed March 20, 2009.

Morales, Isidro, 2008, *Post-NAFTA North America: Reshaping the Economic and Political Governance of a Changing Region.* New York: Palgrave-Macmillan.

Munshi, K. 2003. Networks in the Modern Economy: Mexican Migrants in the US Labor Market. *The Quarterly Journal of Economics*, 118(2) (May): 549-599.

Ojeda, Mario, 1976, *Alcances y Límites de la Política Exterior de México*, México, D.F., El Colegio de México.

Passel, Jeffrey S, 2006, "The Size and Characteristics of the Unauthorized Migrant Population in the US" *Pew Hispanic Center Research Report,* 7 March, http://www.pewhispanic.org (accessed September 5, 2006).

Passel, Jeffrey, S. and Cohn, D'Vera, 2008, *Trends in Unauthorized Immigration: Undocumented Inflow now Trails Legal Inflow*, Washington, D.C., Pew Hispanic Center, October.

Pastor, Robert, 2001, *Toward a North American Community*, Washington, D.C., Institute for International Economics.

Scholte, Jan Aart, 2000, *Globalization. A Critical Introduction*. New York: St. Martin's Press, Inc.

Seelke, Clare Ribando. 2010, "Mérida Initiative for Mexico and Central America: Funding and Policy Issues", Washington, D.C., CRS Report for Congress (R40135)

Seghetti, Lisa M. (coordinator) and others, 2005, "Border Security and the Sotuwest Border: Background, Legislation, and Issues." *CRS Report for Congress* Washington D.C., Congressional Research Service, The Library of Congress, 18, 28 September.

Shamir, Ronen, 2005, "Without Borders? Notes on Globalization as a Mobility Regime", *Sociological Theory*, 23:2, June.

Siskin, Alison (coordinator), 2006, "Immigration Enforcement Within the United Status." *CRS Report for Congress* Washington D.C., Congressional Research Service, The Library of Congress, 6 April.

Torpey, John, 1997, "Coming and Going: On the State Monopolization of the 'Legitimate Means' of Moving", *Sociological Theory*, Vol. 16 No.3, pp. 239-59.

The Senate, 2003, *Uncertain Access: The Consequences of US Security and Trade Actions for Canadian Trade Policy* (Volume 1), Report of the Standing Senate Committee on Foreign Affairs, June.

UNCTAD, 1997, *Transnational Corporations, Market Structure and Competition Policy*. New York: World Investment Report.

United States Joint Forces Command (USJFC). 2008. *The Joint Operating Environment.* Suffolk, Virginia [online]. Available at: www.jfcom.mil/newslink/storyarchive/2008/JOE2008.pdf [accessed March 20, 2009].

White House, 2002, "Estrategia nacional para la seguridad del territorio nacional. Resumen ejecutivo." Office of the Press Secretary, 16 July, http://www.whitehouse.gov/news/releases/2002/07/200207-16.es.html (accessed October 13, 2006).

Williams, Phil, 2008, "From the New Middle Ages to a New Dark Age: The Decline of the State and US Strategy", Strategic Studies Institute, www.StrategicStudiesInstitute.army.mil/ (accessed March 20, 2009).

Womack, James and Daniel T. Jones, 1994, "From lean production to the lean enterprise." *Harvard Business Review* (March-April): 93-103.

PART 2
The Governance of Continental Security: Is it Possible to Move to a Common Approach?

PART 2

Chapter 4

Is There an Integrated Electricity Market in North America? Institutional Challenges in Mexico

Alejandro Ibarra-Yunez

Introduction

When Canada, Mexico, and the United States signed the North American Free Trade Agreement (NAFTA), chapter VI presented two opposing conditions for deep energy integration. On the one hand, the principles of National Treatment shielded Mexico's protected energy sector from an expected swift liberalization and upgrading. On the other, and given newly passed domestic laws, the agreement allows for investment and trade in electricity and gas if not to be sold to the final consumers. Minimum and maximum energy prices were explicitly banned under the agreement to provide for non-distortionary conditions and to enhance trade and market access for the sector. However, after 9/11, when security was made a forefront condition of other economic integration plans, and after the failure of the California energy de-regulation (Joskow 2001), the efforts to increase international integration in the electricity market in the region were slowed. In the new administration of President Calderón, Mexico faces the challenges of regulatory reform as key to improving its infrastructure, becoming more aligned as a competitive North American partner, and moving towards a more competitive national market.

Integration of trade and projects between national electricity markets requires interconnections, technical arrangements, convergent price structures, aligned investments, and convergent institutional arrangements. In the semi-liberalized electricity market in Mexico, generation is open for private participants that share the market with the state-run Comisión Federal de Electricidad (CFE), namely independent power producers, co-generators, auto-generators, and traders, while transmission and distribution continue to be monopolized in the hands of CFE, which owns the transmission grid through the subsidiary Consejo Nacional de Control de Energía (CENACE). Moreover, for generators to invest in power plants and be able to access the national grid there must be a coordinated investment between generation and transmission that extends to trans-border projects.

As for demand, the Northern Mexico border and Southern US communities have faced consumer growth rates higher than the rest of their respective economies, and trend demand for energy will need increasing infrastructure efforts. The Mexican Energy Commissioner Pérez-Jácome (2002) has acknowledged such pressure in various bilateral meetings since 2000, but due to the world economic crisis and recession growth rates have been revised downward, at least for the short term. When economic growth resumes, electricity demand is expected to grow at 4.5 percent in Mexico, 2.5 percent for the United States, and 2 percent for Canada in 2010, but there is no projection for the following ten years.

Of the three partner countries, Canada is an exporter with a market structure and governance that has worked for Canadian firms opening trading subsidiaries in US states (see below), while Mexico and the US are importers. This tradable good has been rather ignored after 15 years of NAFTA. This scenario contrasts with that of some European countries that are heavy traders (Jamasb and Pollitt 2005). The main causes of the low trade and integration from Mexico's perspective seem to be the insufficiency in a) liberalization of the sector; b) heterogeneity in vertical and horizontal unbundling between partners, mainly transmission; c) uncertainty in Mexican policies that affect attraction of private investors; d) the structure of the North American markets and connections; and e) the Mexican legal compact related to electricity and gas.

The present analysis reviews the state of the Mexican electricity sector and the institutional challenges to increasingly integrate and interconnect with the North American energy market, given the restrictions in industry structure and governance. It defines key restrictions and opportunities for the emerging business of electricity generation, trade, trans-border integration, and security after fifteen years of NAFTA operation.

Brief Historical Policy Objectives, Regulatory changes, Theoretical Approaches, and Results

Efforts to restructure the electricity sector date back to the Zedillo administration in 1997, but the Mexican congress banned efforts to unbundle and liberalize the state-owned Comisión Federal de Electricidad (CFE) and Luz y Fuerza del Centro: LFC (the latter serviced the central part of the country and its capital city until the end of 2009 when it was liquidated by a presidential decree and merged into CFE).

Another presidential proposal not including vertical disintegration by the Fox administration also received a setback from the Mexican congress in 2002. However, the laws establishing an independent regulator in 1995, and opening up of private investment in 1993 for self-supply, cogeneration, small-scale production, and independent power producers (IPP) now account for around 20 percent of electricity production (CFE 2007, SENER 2001). Moreover, special treatment under the so-called "Open Season [Temporada Abierta]" began in 2007 to promote renewable energy projects and permits (CRE 2008) that have opened up wind projects, mainly in Southern Mexico. In short, a *de facto* liberalization in generation has occurred, but with policy uncertainties, at the same time that the incumbent CFE still manages the national transmission grid. Moreover, President Calderón sent a law proposal to Congress in 2008 that concentrates on a restructuring and corporatization of the oil producer Pemex, but after a long period of congressional review, a set of rules was passed by congress that excludes electricity in general, but promotes conditions for generation in renewable resources maintaining the *status quo*.

Literature on an integrated North American market related to Mexico is scarce. Rosellón and Halpern (2001) analyse the Mexican gas and electricity industries and conclude in favour of liberalization and decentralization (not necessarily privatization), mainly proposing an independent transmission operator and marketer or Transco. Also, Rosellón (2006) focuses on a transmission clearing price mechanism in risk sharing contracts to mitigate market uncertainty. Ibarra-Yunez (2004) argues that the state-run CFE acts as the market regulatory mechanism determining wholesale and retail prices in a semi-monopoly sector, as it sets threats of capacity and transmission to private generators. Carreón and Jiménez (2003) refer to regulatory capture in the Mexican electricity sector. Little or no treatment to an integrated Mexico-US market has been produced. Finally, the Country Analysis Brief of the Energy Information Administration (2005) emphasizes that the upstream oil monopoly PEMEX makes double marginalization in its sale of natural gas and final gasoline prices (two monopolies 'in tandem') a problem to consumers, but opens the door for Mexican industries to increase imports of gas and electricity with complex contracts, mainly in border states, and also forces private industrials to form co-generation and auto-generation projects. The present framework sets the inquiry of how deeper integration of trans-border electricity transmission and trade could be accomplished as an emerging challenge of the North American cross-border governance architecture.

State of Electricity across North American Partners

Electricity liberalization needs a long range of policy changes and time, but includes at least the following: a) sector restructuring, mainly regarding open access and pricing rules; b) separation between generation and transmission; c) competition in trading and generation, and transparent rules for wholesale trade under a regulatory regime that tackles the externality characteristics of the sector (qualified users); d) incentive mechanisms for investment and reliability (Jamasb and Pollitt 2005, Joskow 2001, Newberry and Pollit 2002). For example, Argentina has experienced with public-private investment projects in transmission. In 2006, the Calderón administration sent a proposal to congress to separate CENACE from CFE, but legislative decisions are pending. Newberry and Pollit (1997), and Jamasb and Pollit (2005) address the challenge to a European integrated market, and present proposals for a market design in Europe, stressing the need to separate transmission (and trans-border trade) from generation to achieve competition in wholesale electricity markets, at the same time that third party access is guaranteed through qualified users. For this to happen, investment, a long-term strategic variable, is endogenous to prices (access or wholesale, as well as final prices) in the short run that form signals for participation under clear rules of the game in the long run, regarding transmission (Bushnell and Ishii 2007, Willems 2000).

In the case of NAFTA and the trilateral and then bilateral efforts for integrated energy, a vehicle called the Security and Prosperity Partnership for North America, SPP was implemented as a forum of discussion of emerging issues not addressed explicitly by NAFTA. Mexico faces the most pressing challenges for its electricity and upstream gas and fuel market design, and allocation of budgets and funds to modernize infrastructure are daunting. According to Mexico's official energy prospects, an estimated US$50-70 billion is needed to update infrastructure to satisfy national demand, where trans-border trade appears as a marginal objective. New issues related to climate change projects, cap-and-trade mechanisms in the US, and multilateral projects under the Clean Development Mechanism applied to Mexico under the Kyoto protocol make the political economy of the present sector a complex topic that needs commitment from the three partner countries and governments, but a substitute to the SPP has not been proposed.

The Mexican Utilities Law (called Ley del Servicio Público de Energía Eléctrica or LSPEE) passed in 1993, right before NAFTA, allows private generation participation of Independent Power Producers (IPPs), as complement to the CFE, as well as more than 800 licenses for private generators (co-generation, auto-generation, and renewable) to form private partnership agreements to supply their own energy, with sales of residual power to the state-run entity under power purchasing agreements (PPAs). However, proposed models to expand infrastructure, via transmission auctioned rights or a model of an independent Transco that allocates infrastructure plans of all participants in a regulated way, have yet to become a reality (Rosellón 2006).

Another critical aspect is how clearance of trade prices takes place. Paredes and Sagap (2001) propose an electricity market liberalization similar to that of the United Kingdon, but via an energy bourse (bolsa de energía), where transactions take place between suppliers, traders, and consumers every day at an array of prices. One question is how financial derivatives, or a stepwise model of financial transmission rights (FTRs), overseen by the regulator, share the risk. These FTRs exist for some of Canada-US trade, but still not for Mexico. Price alignment seems to be evident in an increasingly integrated market, subject to market design differences and regulatory instruments.

Prices increased beginning in 2003, and Mexico has faced the highest hiking prices due to restrictions in supply, problems in market balance, and subsidies to households but not to industrials, which seems at odds with other subsidy packages elsewhere and can become distortionary signals for private generator plans. In 1998 and 1999 prices were similar across the three countries, which call for price mechanisms across borders, but this makes governments less prone to cooperate.

Canada's Interlinks

In the case of Canada, the federal government regulates energy through the National Energy Board (NEB), following national and international agreements such as NAFTA. NEB is an independent agency that operates under public interest and issues electric power export permits. Initiatives have been passed to restructure the sector at provincial levels, both at wholesale and retail competition. Most electricity companies are private, such as Ontario Power Generation, Hydro-Quebec, and B.C.Hydro (EIA 2009). Companies in Alberta or British Columbia have embarked on infrastructure projects in partner US states. Imports are not regulated and under NAFTA national treatment projects among these partners are protected. Prices in some provinces are still regulated, so the market is semi-liberalized while private companies promise that competition will eventually eliminate price caps (EIA 2009).

According to the Energy Information Administration (EIA), Canada is a strong electricity trader, with integrated transmission infrastructure and sales, mainly with the northeast United States and recently, Montana and the Cascadia region in the northwest United States. After the US blackout of 2003, efforts have been increased to coordinate and cooperate towards a more integrated trans-border market. In 2003, Canada exported 33 bKWh to the United States (5.8% of total production), similar to many European economies, and imported around 22 bKWh or 4.2 percent of its domestic consumption, although trade varies by province. Except for Alberta, all Canadian provinces have transmission links with the US grid. Projections in 2009 after the world economic crisis show that trade will increase slightly between Canada and the US, and will show a stronger increase between Mexico and the US, with more weight on renewables.

The US Electricity Sector

Since its origins the sector has been private. The Federal Energy Regulatory Commission (FERC) regulates interstate transmission of electricity, gas, and wholesale fuel. It also administers finances and accounting. A private-driven sector since the early 1920s, generation and transmission grew hand-in-hand, giving rise to oversight mechanisms that entail local governments and state public utility commissions (PUCs), then federal regulators, and nowadays, a profuse involvement of more than 15 agencies and commissions. The United States continues to be the largest world consumer, but both consumption and generation show highest increases in non-OECD Asia, according to Synapse (2005). A deeper integration would arguably reduce prices while a massive and efficient integration market would emerge at both North American borders where demand needs are more dramatic. Canada and the United States have similar agencies and market-oriented sectors. For example, the North American Electricity Reliability Council NERC has operated since 1968 to coordinate 140 control areas between Canada, the United States and the Mexican state of Baja California. CENACE, with the oversight of the Secretary of Energy (Sener) has bi-national plans to increase trade and transmission connections, but Mexico faces the biggest challenges to restructure, modernise, set regulated prices more aligned with cost and market structures, and update the legal codes to promote investment to supply border communities and implement upgrading of the international grid.

Mexico's Electricity Structure

The Energy Regulatory Commission (CRE) was established in 1995 as an autonomous, although not necessarily independent agency, since it only oversees operative and technical aspects, as well as licenses and contracts between private generators and the now integrated state-run CFE. CRE oversees the CENACE expansion plans but, as it is part of CFE, information is proprietary within CFE that reduces the agency's ability to expand transmission and distribution. Moreover, CRE depends on the Secretary of Finance (Hacienda) to set electricity prices (and subsidies) to industries and the public, more according to budgetary plans rather than according to congestion and market aspects (EIA 2009). For increasing integration, subsidies will have to be adjusted. Installed capacity is a limiting factor in the electricity plant and in the use of gas and fuel, controlled by the other state-run entity, PEMEX, and so price distortions prevail in the national market.

Challenges in Interconnection Infrastructure

Transmission at high voltages (higher than 345 kV) with asynchronous direct current connection is critical for the development of the entire electricity industry, because capacity shortages limit generation and increase prices to final users. Traders seek electrical flow close to congestion in the short run, but mechanisms to expand capacity in the long run, and mainly trans-border capacity, are complex. Hence a combination of traditional regulation along with auctions for long-term transmission rights have been used in Australia, Europe, the northeast United States, and Argentina. Energy costs are not independent from transmission costs (Hogan 2002). In this market the investor has to cover the negative externalities that are created at the same time that transmission rights are abundant either in a futures market or in the hands of an independent dispatcher. Alternatively, the transmission company is regulated through incentives for investment, but needs to determine production and costs of transmission. Generators then depend on so-called loop-flow constraints and incentives to use actual or expanded capacity. Interconnection agreements are bilateral between provincial companies in Canada, with regional markets in the United States. For Mexico, two submarkets are active but marginal: the Mexican northwest with Sempra in California, and the northeast with Texas independent company ERCOT.

In Mexico the regulator CRE, along with incumbent CFE and the Secretary of Energy, have made efforts to grant rights to independent generators (IPPs), and CFE to increase investments in the power grid, following the vision of a more integrated North American market. However, financial needs to upgrade the grid are daunting and subject to the market design. Between 1998 and 2006, Baja California was a member of the National Energy Reliability Council (NERC), and the northeast firms and state governments of Nuevo León and Tamaulipas negotiated to increase interconnections with Texas at high-needed voltage that depends on the state of border transmission capacities. According to CFE, Mexico has high-voltage grids with capacities of 69 to 138 kV with XLP, covering the low end of the required US Department of Energy ranges of between 138-775 kV. International connections exist between Mexicali-San Diego with 408 MW; Ciudad Juarez- El Paso with 200 MW, and Reynosa-Matamoros- Texas Lower Valley. The above contrasts with high voltage connections in Canada and the United States by each Canadian province, at 230 kV and higher. Mexico's CRE has granted permits to four private electricity trading companies on the border with Texas with exports of around 12.1 bKWh. Oversight mechanisms of CRE now extend beyond the domestic market and into promoting competition and bilateral trade with the United States (Carreón and Jiménez 2003).

Regarding final tariffs, changes between 2000 and 2005 are +33.3% and 32.1% for Canada (industrial and household, respectively); + 23.9% and 15.9% for the USA; and + 72.6% and 42.7% for Mexico (again, industrial and household), which has depended on input price changes faced by CFE (mainly natural gas and fuel) at less than minimum efficient scale capacities of generators, depending of the *status quo* of the transmission infrastructure. Moreover, from a peak in electricity trade between 1997 and 1999, both imports and exports have declined mainly since 2001, along with a rather static installed capacity (INEGI BIE 2007). In sum, Mexico faces non-competitive markets in generation, transmission, trading, and investment that condition integration into a strong North American regional market. However, private investors (co-generation, auto-generation for own needs, and independent power producers for CFE) now account for around 20 percent of Mexico's generation and trade and are projected to increase their participation. Moreover, Sener expects that 65 percent of infrastructure investment in 2013 will originate from private interests.

The Northwest increased capacity to sell to the national grid (mainly to south and central Mexico), but also to export to California, while the Northeast, as mainly an importing region, would cover part of the pent-demand and imports from the Texas market. This sub-region seems to have been the most active in the recent past. The central part of generation basically attends to inter-exchanges with the grid to service the capital city and the central valley of Mexico. Regarding transmission investment, 62 percent was subcontracted with the private sector, with about US$6.7 billion (Mx$ 75.3 billion), against about US$5.6 billion (about Mx$69 billion) in generation (Hartley and Martínez-Chombo 2002). However, planned and realized investments seem to consider a closed market with basically no consideration of market potential for international trade. Moreover, project subcontracts seem to be at the edge of the Mexican constitution that bans private participation in utilities.

Modelling Approaches to Trade Expansion Subject to Transmission Capacity Constraints

There is debate about how to attract investment for long-run expansion, given an optimal return in a close to congested node in the short run, but with insufficient incentives for capacity expansion in the long run (Rosellón 2003). Energy costs and transmission costs are simultaneously determined in the spot market. Models can be divided into three groupings. First, some models concentrate on optimal generation in games of capacity constraints set by either the transmission authority or a systems operator. To model these types of games, one needs to spell out production and cost functions with capacity constraints, such as is done by Borenstein, Bushnell, and Wollak (2002), and Ibarra-Yunez (2004). If the model is expanded to bilateral trade flows and integration of transmission capacities, the effects would imply expanded opportunities for power generation on the one hand, and cost allocation, input prices, and transaction costs on the other, that limit those opportunities.

A second approach focuses on how an incumbent state-run entity shares the market with private independent producers in a mixed market, where given market power, the incumbent displaces the regulator in setting prices and access rights to a vertically integrated market with the consequence that a) the incumbent becomes the self-centred regulator; b) generators could be subject to discrimination in access to the grid or through excessive access charges; and c) infrastructure projects are subject to risk uncertainty. Works by Cremer, Marchand, and Thisse (1989) on the superiority of the incumbent in volumes but at high prices and low quality, as well as De Fraja and Del Bono (1989) on regulatory capture by the state-run entity on the system operator, Joskow and Tirole (2000), Hogan (2002), and Willems (2000) on transmission constraints with many entrants, are seminal in focusing on the institutional market settings. No model in this aspect has been produced on bilateral trade in energy and transmission connections.

Finally, as is shown by Rosellón (2003), and Woolf (2003), it is impossible to model marginal costs when facing the flow-loop problem. The key variable is an informant price schedule to clear short-run and long-run access and investment, and propose models of bidding long-term financial transmission rights (LTFRs). With such an approach, problems of infrastructure, bilateral asymmetric regulations (and regulators), and other market design aspects can be reflected in a well-designed auction market for transmission rights, but where a well-established dispatcher is required, and that does not exist at present between North American partners.

The above can be described with a game theoretical approach following Laffont and Martimort (2005) in a stylized way. Assume that the problem is whether to build a bi-national infrastructure between a rich and a poor country (The United States and Mexico, respectively) to share the long-term benefits and also the costs of the project, and where there are governments involved, as well as consumers gaining from the project on both sides of the border. Pricing then can take a cooperative joint form of determination or a non-cooperative, independent form. One can assume that governments are welfare maximisers, to simplify the case of governments that have a private agenda. However, the government of the poor country might decide not to disclose information of the net benefits of the project in order to extract rent from the rich in the financing (the free-rider problem). Since a joint project is costly, a joint source of financing would be required. Commitment is then key.

In transnational transmission projects, a clear sharing rule for costing and funding is required. In the recent past, the Mexican CFE and ERCOT in Texas, and CFE with Sempra in California have begun to explore joint projects. Additionally, industrial licensed importers, mainly in the states of Chihuahua, Nuevo León and Tamaulipas, have also invested in transmission within Mexico to buy electricity that is not considered utilities (a required "wheeling" of CFE electricity of 15% of consumption by auto-generators and co-generators is set by the Mexican law). With the above, the extent of cross-border trade is largely a function of:

1. Available interconnection capacity, which depends on incentive regulations at governmental and private agent levels. Homogeneous standards, mainly in asynchronous flows of DC interchanges, are needed.
2. Generation capacity on both sides of the border, which in the case of Mexico also depends on legal and regulatory definitions of non-utilities for private generation in a mixed market (co-generation and auto-generation).
3. Cost structures on both sides of the border, with asymmetric scales of production. Mexico, as can be inferred, faces higher costs.
4. Load price differences between Mexican and US partners such that flows will depend on where the lowest net prices originate.
5. Resource (input) mixes, which seem to be similar between the United States and Mexico (not between Canada and the US that favour Canada in their cost allocation of hydropower).
6. Endowments of regulators, and the use of their assets and institutional assets, as well as sources of budgetary funds.

Some of the above conditions are interrelated. A critical aspect is the separation of generation and transmission in legal, accounting, and administrative and real terms. Regarding CFE, it continues to be vertically integrated and no clear plans exist for any administrative or real unbundling, but only on accounting terms. Transmission and distribution expansions require approval by the Secretary of Energy, the Secretary of the Treasury (allocated funding from the federal budget), and the Secretary of the Environment. This creates a double decision window that can cause regulatory uncertainty in bilateral projects. Contracts are covered in risks by merchant transmission firms, under "build-operate-transfer" forms, at least in Mexico, where some of the building costs are not known, and where asymmetric information on node prices, given short- versus long-term loop flow problems, have affected projects.

Liquefied natural gas (LNG) has become a complement to the growing consumption, with specialized sea ports' investments in the Gulf of Mexico (Altamira) and the Pacific (Baja California), and also re-gasification plants by private firms or contracted under build-own-operate-transfer. In sum, conditions for a full-blown integration seem to be suboptimal and challenges abound at the market design level and at the convergent regulatory levels.

Role of the Security and Prosperity Partnership of North America and the Future

Originally formed in 2001, the North American Energy Working Group (NAEWG) was established to promote energy efficiency, increase connections and bring the three North American partners to the policy table toward an integrated vision of a regional energy market. The NAEGW was merged to the Security and Prosperity Partnership of North America (SPP), established in 2005 by the governments of Canada, the United States, and Mexico, as an outgrowth of NAFTA, to address coordination and bilateral and trilateral cooperation to a) enhance security mainly from a US point of view, and extend the security border around the NAFTA region; and b) improve cooperation in aspects that were not subject to NAFTA, such as migration, security and law enforcement, norms and standards not addressed before (such as against bio-terrorism), secure but facilitate transport of traded merchandise in this leading market, and finally, integrate energy (not totally separating oil, gas, and electricity). Additionally, the US State Department has begun to coordinate actions of both the Department of Homeland Security and the Department of Commerce. Mexico formed parallel working teams under the coordination of the Secretary of the Interior (Gobernación), and the Secretary of Economy. On the energy front, the Secretary of Economy delegates cooperative efforts to the Secretary of Energy and CRE (Ibarra-Yunez 2008).

As opposed to NAFTA, which has an institutional architecture arising from business interests and where all are involved, the SPP arose mainly from top-down, 'hub-and-spoke' manner lead by the United States at its highest levels (Anderson 2006). Pastor (2001) argues that while the European Union seems to deal with too many institutions, the NAFTA area has not enough. For example, Laffont and Martimort (2005) argue in favour of an independent agency to oversee grid integration. After the SPP was closed with the incoming Obama administration, no outgrowth of a trilateral agency has been proposed to address emerging issues of the three North American partners. During the three years of operation of the SPP, the following was accomplished related to energy (electricity):

1. Work plan to cooperate in metrology, on track at the trilateral level.
2. Border Information Flow Architecture to determine economic and social needs at US-Mexico borders (BIFA), at a bilateral level.
3. Vehicle fuel efficiency programs, ongoing at a trilateral level.
4. By June 2005, a trilateral regulators' group was formed to integrate information, to improve practices by regulated firms and regulators, to improve cross border energy projects (even in the US, the National Council on Electricity Policy has called for a more integral data integration effort since 2004).
5. Funding of Science and Technology research in energy began in 2005 and is ongoing although political positions regarding climate change under the Kyoto Protocol vary.
6. A council was established in January 2006 as a discussion forum to explore renewable and other green sources of energy. A vision centred on domestic agendas makes cooperation in this aspect rather difficult.
7. Cooperation at a trilateral level on research and policy proposals, on the market implications of oil sands production and impact on refineries, as well as CO_2 from oil sands operations for oil recovery.
8. As for Mexico's participation in NERC, it has been as an observer since 2005, with no plans to become involved in reliability harmonization.

Missing aspects, critical to integration, are measures at the transmission and interconnection submarket, as stressed by EIA (2009), Carreón and Jiménez (2003), and Jamasb and Pollitt (2005), and Hogan (2002) for Europe. Additionally, regulators need to converge in their span of activities and promotion of trans-national integration and market design.

The role of the regulator, its granted incentives, and the design of the regulator competence and endowments and its governance design has been the weakest part of modelling this complex market for developing countries, as stressed by Beato and Laffont (2002). It is important to note that part of the insufficient dynamism of this sector in Mexico and North America derives from weak regulators. Jordana and Levy-Faur (2005) have analysed regulatory dynamics, which first depend on international convergence. Then they analyse similarities and differences of regulatory design across network sectors within the same country, such as energy, telecommunications, or banking. According to Wallsten, Clarke, *et al.* (2004) regulators can be approached by a set of endowments that can be separated into governance, meaning legal, policy design, and administrative or decision making frameworks; and content, meaning the legal, procedural, and judicial attributes or arms towards pricing, competition, entry conditions, access, or investment.

The Comisión Reguladora de Energía (CRE) was created in 1995 by a decree and then a federal law. With operative, administrative, and technical autonomy from the Secretary of Energy, its role was defined to encompass electricity and gas in: a) issuance of permits to private participants of non-utilities, including cross-border trade; b) approval of methodologies for wheeling and surplus energy acquisitions by CFE under power purchasing agreements; c) oversight of technical standards of all operators in the market; d) giving opinion; e) promotion of private investment and projects via permits to develop the sector; f) promotion of private participation in electricity generation with renewable resources; and g) mediation and penalties for non compliance of permits.

As a federal entity, it participates in other policy decisions with the Secretary of Energy, with the incumbents PEMEX, CFE and LFC, and with the international sections of the Secretary of Economy. CRE does not intervene in the administration and expansion plans of the national transmission grid and the distribution networks that concentrate in the incumbent utility CFE, so it plays a somewhat passive role in international integration processes of its competence (Pérez- Jácome 2002). Additionally, expansion energy plans are not part of CRE's obligations, but of the Secretary of Energy. In short, CRE might oversee a vertically integrated sector with state-run entities with fragmented competences (Kessides 2003).

Given the *status quo* of governance design of the regulator, achieving an integrated North American regional market calls for action at various levels and at the highest levels of government with counterparts in the United States and Canada. But then, what is it for the regulator? CRE is weak in both governance and content. Moreover, the SPP initiative and the trilateral groups on energy put CRE at a disadvantage in committing itself to integration plans, mainly because other orders of the Mexican government need to be involved: a problem of coordination, not only of endowments.

The history of regulatory change in the United States transited from a pragmatic reaction to increasing deployment of power plants and transmission interests in the 1920s at higher voltages and distances (the state public utilities commissions), so as to accommodate increasing interstate (regional) integration, both from public utilities and private non-utilities, to deregulation in the seventies. Noteworthy is the passage in 1978 of the Public Utility Regulatory Policies Act (PURPA) that promoted non-utility operators. It was an important part of the complex regulation because it directly faced the need to grant non-discriminatory access to an increasing and powerful grid market. In 1992, the Energy Policy Act was passed, after competitive generation had been proven to grow and the market for access had matured. It emphasized free, non-discriminatory access to the grid by any non-utilities generator. It also set the basis for a wholesale market with regulated prices and incipient unbundling (Brown and Sidano 2004).

In recent times the Federal Regulatory Council (FERC) passed Orders 888 for unbundling and administrative separation rules for participants of the market, and corporate conduct obligations; 889 related to day-ahead, and day-to-day market of tradable market capacities; order 2000 for transmission interests to form regional organizations (RTOs); and Order 2003-A of 2004 on sharing rules for allocating costs of transmission upgrades. All these are necessary for increasing investor certainty (Brown and Sidano 2004, *op cit.*). In Europe and elsewhere, qualified users are a key signal towards competition and market discipline, and competition via import liberalisation is happening, but an integrated and competitive market is not yet a reality. For the case of Mexico and the United States, price alignment and forward-looking cost structures on both sides of the border need to move forward as a condition for deeper integration.

Conclusions

Given the present market structure and design, along with a weak regulator, there are challenges. A first implication of the above analysis is that prices, given the size of the Mexican grid, and double marginalization by the incumbent, will continue to be misaligned with the other North American partners. High margins and insufficient allocated resources to grid expansion and interconnection would reduce the attractiveness of private investors in this sector with high potential but unclear market discipline. Also, a shadow market of co-generators and self-generators of non-utilities will pressure the transmission infrastructure within the country and through exports and imports of electricity.

A second implication for the Mexican market and its need for higher international integration is related to the size and quality of transmission infrastructure at higher voltages and energy output. The need to modernize them has been calculated at between US$50 and US$70 billion for the next ten years. Demand at the Northern Mexican border and Southern US border is predicted to resume growth at higher than 3 percent per year between 2010 and 2020. It is impossible to depend only on government funding for infrastructure upgrading, so improving certainty for private investors, even at build-operate-transfer forms could call for new formulas of risk sharing, such as deduced from the analysis. However, in order to develop models such as long-term financial transmission rights, a derivatives market would need to be developed, as well as the operation of a Transco, affected by the recent downward economic cycle. Moreover, short of a developed transmission rights market, insufficient data on costing procedures and allocation or sharing of access rights versus transmission investment coverage by non-utility players is a restriction to expanding the market, both domestically and at transborder levels.

Third, generation and transmission governance seems not to be a problem in a domestic integrated market, but for IPPs the costing rights for access to the transmission grid should be lower than the final price to consumers in order for the generation market to remain sustainable, so the role of the regulator is important in preventing price squeezes or access discrimination. In international integration, even if CFE is vertically integrated, the market becomes *de facto* liberalized.

A weak regulator CRE with little or no power to a) open up trans-national transmission contracting via new governance forms; and b) set price regulation can do little to reform the market. There is a need to upgrade the CRE secondary laws and regulations to which CRE would adhere. Both international regulation benchmarks and other sector regulators' design would become inputs and guiding lines towards regulatory improvement, such as the separation of CENACE as the key player in internalizing project costs and efficiency matters. For this to happen, executive orders must be swift and visionary for Mexico. Regulatory convergence depends on commitment by all key players in the sector.

Reality shows that divergent objectives between efficiency and redistribution of a bilateral project could be private information for which a free-rider problem could emerge. This fact would put on the discussion table whether both governments should work independently (with low commitment), or under the coordination of a bilateral or independent agency, with the typical mentioned free-rider problem.

Fourth, it seems clear that integration will be ensued in steps. A sub-regional integrated market could work. The above analysis shows three main connection points in Mexico's northern border: one on the Baja California Peninsula (the most developed one); another in the northern centre between Ciudad Juarez and El Paso, Texas; and finally the northeast with Southern Texas. Additionally, LNG investments both in the Gulf of Mexico and Mexico's Pacific coasts for regasification and transport will improve the energy balance for the high demands in the sub-regional market, hence opening up opportunities for transnational trade. The SPP's working groups moved on various fronts that include metrology, fuel efficiency and green sources of energy, and determination of energy needs on both sides of the border, but interconnection efforts are, until now, of secondary priority and not addressed by the Obama administration, nor by Mexico, as opposed to Canada. For convergence and integration, price convergence at sub-regional levels and common market rules should be planned. At present all policy making has concentrated on national markets, although CFE and Sempra, and CFE with ERCOT, have both rendered joint grid investment projects in the recent past.

Finally, for capacity to be increased, there are key investment and environmental issues to be solved, and transmission systems require careful cost-benefit analysis for day-ahead and balancing market development. Similar to many European markets, incentive-based regulation is still developing in electricity and gas, versus other networked industries such as telecommunications, ports, or financial markets.

The SPP or the substitute organization under the new US administration, and domestically driven efforts in the Calderón administration might lead the progress made in the foreseeable future. As a corollary, the future seems to be toward more, rather than less, international integration in energy markets.

References

Anderson, G. J., 2006. North American economic integration and the challenges wrought by 9/11. *Journal of Homeland Security and Emergency Management*, 3(2), 1-30.

Beato, P., Laffont, J.J. Eds., 2002. *Competition Policy in Regulated Industries; Approaches for Emerging Economies*, Washington, DC: Inter American Development Bank.

Borenstein, S., Bushnell, J.B., Wollak, F., 2002. Measuring market inefficiencies in California's deregulated wholesale electricity market. *American Economic Revie*, 92(5), 1376-1405.

Brown, M. H., Sidano. R. P., 2004. Electricity Transmission: A Primer. Washington DC, *National Council on Electricity Policy*, June.

Bushnell, J., Ishii, J., 2007. An equilibrium model of investment in restructured electricity markets. Center for the Study of Energy Markets WP 164, January.

Carreon, V., Jiménez, A., 2003. Mexican electricity sector: economic, legal, and political issues. Program on Energy and Sustainable Development Working Paper #5, available at <http://iis-db.stanford.edu>

Cremer, H., Marchand, M., Thisse, J.F. 1989. The public firm as an instrument for regulating an oligopolistic market. *Oxford Economic Papers*, 41, 283-301.

Comisión Federal de Electricidad. CFE. 2007. *Desarrollo del Mercado Eléctrico 1996-2010*. CFE, Mexico City.

Comision Reguladora de Energia. CRE, 2000. *Mexico's Future Energy Regulatory Agenda*, Mexico City, CRE, May.

De Fraja G., Del Bono, F., 1989. Alternative strategies of a public enterprise in oligopoly. *Oxford Economic Papers*, 41(1), 302-311.

Energy Information Administration EIA, 2009. Official Energy Statistics from the US Government, at <http://www.eia.doe.gov.>, accessed in June 2008 and update in December 2009.

Hartley, P., Martinez- Chombo, E., 2002. Electricity demand and supply in Mexico. *mimeo*, Rice University.

Hogan, W., 2002. Electricity market restructuring: reform of reforms. *Journal of Regulatory Economics*, 21, 103-132

Ibarra-Yunez, A., 2004. Strategic conduct and access discrimination, in the semi-liberalized electricity sector in Mexico. *Frontiers in Finance and Economics*, 1(1), June, 57-69.

Ibarra-Yunez, A., 2008. Fronteras seguras y facilitación de comercio: análisis de economía institucional. *Gestión y Política Pública*. México CIDE, XVII(1), 3-33

INEGI- BIE, 2007. Banco de Información Económica Mexico, INEGI online, accessed on May 1, 2007 at <www.inegi.gob.mx>

Jamasb, T., Pollitt. M., 2005. Electricity market reform in the European Union: review of progress toward liberalization and integration. Center for Energy and Environmental Policy Research 05-003 WP, University of Cambridge.

Jordana J., Levy-Faur, D., 2005. The diffusion of regulatory capitalism in Latin America: sectoral and national channels in the making of the new order. Annals APPS #598, 102-124

Joskow, P. L., 2001. California's electricity crisis. Cambridge, MA. *National Bureau of Economic Research*

Joskow, P., Tirole, J., 2000. Transmission rights and market power on electric power networks. *Rand Journal of Economics*, 31, 450-487

Kessides, I.N., 2003. *Reforming Infrastructure: Privatization, Regulation, and Competition.* Washington, D.C., The World Bank.

Laffont, J.J., Martimort, D. 2005. The design of transnational public good mechanisms for developing countries. *Journal of Public Economics,* 89, 159-196.

Newberry, D., Pollitt, M.G. 1997. The restructuring and privatization of Britain's CEGB- was it worth It? *Journal of Industrial Economics,* 45, 269-303.

Newberry, D., Pollitt, M.G., 2002. *Public policy for the private sector: the restructuring and privatization of the U.K. electricity supply-was it worth it?* The World Bank Group.

Pastor, R. A., 2001. *Toward a North American Community: Lessons from the Old World for the New.* Washington D.C. Institute for International Economics.

Pérez– Jácome, D., 2002. North American electricity regulatory overview. Comisión Reguladora de Energía (CRE) presentation, November.

Rosellón, J. 2003. Different approaches towards electricity transmission expansion. *Review of Network Economics,* 2(3), September, 238-268.

Rosellón, J., 2006. Merchant mechanism for electricity transmission expansion. *Journal of Regulatory Economics,* 29(2) March, 167-193.

Rosellon, J., Halpern, J., 2001. Regulatory reform in Mexico's natural gas industry: liberalization in the context of a dominant upstream incumbent. World Bank Policy Research Working Paper No. 2537.

Secretaría de Energía SENER, 2001. Statistics on energy in Mexico, accessed on May 2007 at <www.sener.gob.mx>

Security and Prosperity Partnership for North America SPP, 2007. Report to Leaders, accessed on April 12, 2007, available at <www.spp.gov>

Synapse, 2005. Database and discussion list on long term power contracts, accessed on March 29, 2007 at <www.synapse-energy.com>

US International Trade Commission, 2000. *Electric Power Services: Recent Reforms in Selected Foreign Markets,* Washington, DC. USITC.

Walsten, S., Clarke, G., Haggarty, L., Kaneshiro, R., Noll, R., Shirley, M., Colin Xu, L., 2004. New tools for studying network industry reforms in developing countries: the telecommunications and electricity regulation database. *Review of Network Economics,* 3(3), September, 248-289.

Willems, B., 2000. Cournot competition in the electricity market with transmission constraints. Working Paper Series No. 2000-4. Leuven, Katholieke Universiteit Leuven.

Woolf F., 2003. Global Transmission Expansion: Recipes for Success. Pen Well, Tulsa, OK.

Chapter 5

Continental Borders and National Security: A Logical Diagnosis

Stephen Clarkson

Introduction

This volume's mandate to investigate more innovative architectures of regional governance by empowering citizens and civil society participation and widening the social legitimacy of public management of North America's transborder problems by promoting a continental agenda of shared sensitive issues, which exceed the simple scope and capabilities of national policies and intergovernmental cooperation is an eminently worthy but disconcertingly tall order. It is worthy because many policies with transboundary effects that are produced by the individual federal, state, and provincial governments on the continent are sub-optimal, even self-defeating. But it is a tall order because North American borders themselves have become sites of complex, historically determined contradictions that, in the name of national security, actually generate considerable insecurity for both the nation itself and its two bordering countries.

Because borders demarcate boundaries between the Us and the Them, they are prone to generate sensitivities that are often expressed in a discourse that blames the Other for whatever is wrong with a given situation (Tsoukala 2008: 137-152). Since the basic continental discourse shifted after September 11, 2001, from economic integration and border disarmament to national security and border rearmament, North America's boundary problems have become ever more intellectually and politically intractable. The policy debate gets so enmeshed in questions of detail (what kind of biometric indicators should be required in identity cards) and outcome measures (what is the trend in truck crossings since 2001) that the big picture tends to disappear from sight and the debate over a specific policy proposal degenerates into haggling over its minutiae, worrying about its funding, and flailing stereotyped enemies (Ackleson 2005: 165-84).

In the hope of sketching the kind of change that would be required to produce more lasting solutions than the incrementally tightened measures typically proposed in the US Congress and implemented by the Department of Homeland Security, this chapter attempts to present a broader analysis of North America's continuing border crisis. It will do this by stepping back from the immediate fray to comprehend the pattern of counter-productive consequences that are often inadvertently generated by policies designed to achieve a specific political objective.

Because buttressing a nation state's defenses against various threats generally involves some measures that affect another state, we can understand that, in trying to generate security for itself, a country may cause other countries to feel either more secure or more insecure. These countries' reactions may then boomerang, causing the first mover ultimately to feel more insecure as well. In promoting its own security, a state may also promote another state's security, generating a positive-sum relationship. But in building what it thinks is its security, a state may become the author of another state's insecurity, generating a zero-sum relationship. These reactions may further increase the first state's insecurity.

The first part of this chapter will elaborate this schema by examining half a dozen different security logics in North America. It will become clear that, to some extent, the United States is the author of its own insecurity. It will also emerge that, in several crucial respects, elements of Mexico's and Canada's civil society constitute the United States' worst security threat–a situation that paradoxically makes the Mexican and Canadian governments Washington's most indispensable allies. In order to reach my concluding reflection I will propose how the continent needs to re-institutionalize its trilateral relationship in order to resolve its border crises.

North America's Six Security Logics

Every set of intergovernmental problems has its own policy logic. While each could be elaborated in book-length detail, the following sketches will simply suggest their major features.

1. The Logic of Continental Expansion

A root cause of insecurity in the North American continent derives from the long-term impacts of US military preponderance over its neighbours.

In the 18th and 19th centuries, the messianic expansionism of the burgeoning young Republic generated several–albeit failed–invasions of Great Britain's colonial territories to the north. While military aggression and territorial annexation by the United States is no longer considered a credible threat by its neighbors, its huge superiority in military force creates a subliminal psychosis, which causes Canadian politicians occasionally to depart from their default tendency of fully supporting US security policies.

To the south, the independent United States of Mexico's disastrous defeat by US troops and their subsequent occupation of its capital city led it to surrender one half of its territory. The annexation at the end of the Mexican-American war in 1848 of what now comprise the states of California, Nevada, and Utah and portions of Texas, Arizona, New Mexico, and Wyoming helped produce enormous mineral, agricultural, and industrial wealth for the emerging colossus. This prosperity generated unprecedented economic and military power, a power that should have guaranteed the country's security. At the same time, defeat, humiliation, and the constant threat of further armed intervention by American forces entrenched a deep distrust of Uncle Sam in Mexico, an animus which in several respects constrained US foreign-policy efforts in the hemisphere after World War II.

The perverse logic of the United States in pursuing its own interests through aggression can be seen in the economic consequences for Mexico of losing the resources of Texas and the fertile lands of California, which would have allowed it to develop as a first-world economy. In other words, US expansionism condemned Mexico to a poverty that has turned its unemployable citizens into a demographic security threat for the United States–a phenomenon that, in turn, has its own complex logic.

2. The Logic of Demographic Exports

At face value, the vigorously growing US economy's demand for labour that could be satisfied by a global supply of willing and eager immigrants is a clear case of the United States generating its own economic security. Geographical propinquity and historically open borders made Canada and Mexico the two leading suppliers of both trained and unskilled labor to the United States. Having failed to develop equally prosperous and attractive economies, Canada and Mexico were in this regard the authors of their own economic insecurity because they lost large cohorts of their most productive workers, a brain and brawn drain that further increased the disparity between themselves and their economically unchallengeable neighbour.

In one societal and cultural respect, the easy assimilation of large numbers of Canadians generated security for the United States because multiple cross-border kinship ties helped spread the goodwill that is characteristic of the attitudes of US citizens and Canadians towards each other. The same positive result cannot be ascribed to Mexican immigration, particularly in the last two decades, when it reached massive proportions. The assimilation barriers faced by Spanish-speaking laborers make "Hispanics" more visible and more problematic in the United States than were Canadian immigrants. US entrepreneurs in the service sector, farmers, and well-off families may enjoy paying undocumented immigrants less than the minimum wage. Cultural nationalists warning of the threat to Anglo-Saxon values (Huntington 2004), low-income US citizens competing for the same bad jobs, and recent immigrants wanting to close the door behind them experience a social insecurity that fans the flames of an anti-Mexican nativism whose amplification by the Mexican media , in turn, aggravates Mexicans' anti-Americanism. The resulting intolerance for the Other produces actions such as US border vigilantism and border-wall construction, which make the constructive solution of mutual problems politically unachievable (Navarro 2008, Doty 2007, Dechaine 2009, Gilchrist 2006).

Another perverse facet of North America's border security logic can be seen in the way the United States increased its demographic insecurity by pursuing its own economic well-being. In the light of the American corn industry's having lost its market in the Soviet Union, the US government pushed Mexico hard during its trade liberalization negotiations in the early 1990s to liberalize its corn market (Ackerman, et al). But "free" trade did not necessarily mean fair trade. Since nothing in the North American Free Trade Agreement (NAFTA) prevented Washington from massively subsidizing its industrialized and already highly productive corn industry, Mexico was soon flooded with US imports priced so low that vast numbers of *campesinos* were forced off their land in the next decade, exacerbating the flow of manpower across the US-Mexico border (Nadal 2000). In this way the neoconservative model of continental integration that ruled out the solidaristic notion that the two rich members should help their poorer partner in order to raise its level of well-being proved socially and politically disastrous. NAFTA's contribution to increasing economic disparity between and within its three members thus increased, rather than mitigated, the demographic insecurity along both sides of the United States' southern border.

3. The Logic of Economic (In)security

The US economy–the world's greatest success story for capitalism–showed the United States in the first instance as author of its own security through the development of a massive, self-expanding internal market. At the same time, through trade and foreign investment, the US economic motor proved to be the author of economic development in other countries. Specifically in the North American periphery, jobs were created by US investment in Canada and Mexico where revenue grew from the extraction and export of raw materials to the United States.

But there was a darker side to this narrative. The US economy's overwhelming dynamism also generated insecurity in the economies next door. Unbalanced economies characterized by staple-led exports, branch-plant industrialization, and a weak domestic entrepreneurial class were condemned to polarize around which national development strategy to pursue. Keynesian nationalists in both Canada and Mexico had some success after World War II advocating an import substitution industrialization that increased national economic security at some cost to some US economic interests (Gutiérrez-Haces 2002). Neoconservative elites in the three countries subsequently reversed the periphery's search for autonomy by triumphantly negotiating and implementing global and continental integration agreements that re-constituted a North American trade and investment space.

The resulting increased integration had contradictory security implications. US energy security was enhanced by guarantees that prevented Canadian governments from turning off the tap of its oil exports, and the US economy benefited from increased direct investment from Canada. On the other hand, US workers were made more insecure by the "giant sucking sound" of outsourcing that 1992 US presidential candidate Ross Perot maintained would bleed jobs to the low-wage *maquiladora* operations just south of the US-Mexico border. Canada's and Mexico's exports to the United States increased, but so did large-scale job losses in small and medium enterprises that were bought out or displaced by more powerful US transnational corporations. At the macro level, the periphery's deeper continental integration also increased its vulnerability to the negative impacts of such a US economic crisis as that of 2007-10, which highlighted the perils of an open border between a highly industrialized and a poor, developing economy.[1]

4. The Logic of Military (In)security

When its continental dominance had stabilized by the mid-19th century, the United States only needed a navy to provide defense against attack from overseas and to support its gunboat diplomacy, once it had put on Spain's imperial mantle and expanded its sphere of dominance in Latin America and Asia.

With the development of industrialized warfare in the first half of the 20th century, the United States ' two land borders became a new security threat to the extent that Canada and Mexico's territories might have provided a terrestrial conduit for possible German or Japanese attacking forces. Washington addressed this constraint on its security by an implicit threat to take over the defense of its neighbors' territories. Faced by a potential major incursion on their sovereignty, Ottawa and Mexico City negotiated cooperation agreements with the US government. While each peripheral government undertook to deny the military forces of their common enemies the capacity to pass through its territory en route to the United States, Washington promised to secure both its neighbours from attack.

In the Cold War, long-range bombers and ground-launched intercontinental missiles created a new vulnerability for the United States to transpolar air attacks, a scenario which also put Canada at risk of Soviet nuclear weapons. The Pentagon turned Canada from conduit of air borne insecurity into a buffer against Soviet attacks by integrating Canadian forces under the North American Air Defense Command (NORAD). Rather than passively accept the complete loss of sovereignty inherent in a US security guarantee, Canada invested heavily in its own military forces. In a sovereignty-maintaining doctrine labeled "Defense against Help," Ottawa financed its own air, sea, and land forces which, in practice, were placed under Pentagon command through NORAD or the North Atlantic Treaty Organization . This subordination was not total: The residual autonomous strain in their political culture caused Canadian leaders to reject participation in the Pentagon's anti-ballistic missile defense program.

---

1   As Sidney Weintraub commented, "The big loser in Latin America was Mexico, where GDP in 2009 declined by more than 7 percent... Mexico's improved economic policies during the good years were overwhelmed by what happened in its northern neighbour in 2008-2009."

In stark contrast with Canada's general conformity with US military strategy, Mexicans generally resisted the United States' foreign policy in Latin America which they deemed to threaten their own security by encouraging US intervention in the domestic affairs of Hispanic states. Mexico City blocked the United State's attempt to use the Organization of American States to legitimize intervention in revolutionary Cuba in the 1960s and, in the 1980s, defied the Reagan administration's military support of right-wing "contra" forces in Central America's civil wars by leading the Contadora peace process (Pellicer de Brody: 33-4).

These examples underline how subjectively any logic of (in)security is constructed. From the point of view of the relentlessly anti-communist definition that Washington gave to US security during the Cold War, Mexico's foreign policy increased US insecurity. A less ideological position could understand Mexico's actions as promoting greater stability in the hemisphere and thus actually enhancing the United States' best long-term interests there (Ojeda 2006). Both views found common ground in Mexico's support for declaring Latin America to be a nuclear-free zone. Having no reason to fear a nuclear attack from its south made the United States more secure.

5. *The Logic of Anti-Narcotic (In)security*

Narcotics provide a dark version of empowering citizens and civil society participation because the citizens that the drug industry empowers are outlaws and the society in which they participate is not what most analysts mean by "civil."

As with its territorial expansionism, the United States has paradoxically been the author of its own drug insecurity. Because of the costly crime, societal damage, and the wrenching individual tragedies caused by narcotics addiction,[2] the United States–along with most industrialized countries–criminalized the manufacture, distribution, and even consumption of non-prescription narcotics. This prohibition did not stop US domestic demand from growing, but it did push criminal networks to integrate their supply chains at home with foreign producers' cartels abroad in order to satisfy the world's largest market.

Drugs flow southwards from the United State's industrialized and wealthy neighbor, but narcotics and firearms also flow north to Canada. As a result, there is a tendency in both countries to blame the other for abetting crime at home. Given the relatively symmetrical nature of these mutual threats, the US and Canadian governments work cooperatively on common programs to interdict the relentless operations of their narcotics industries.[3]

The United States has also been the author of its Mexico-centered insecurity thanks to measures it took to answer its immediate security needs. It was Washington that first stimulated a Mexican narcotics production capacity during World War II when the US medical industry required a substitute for the painkiller heroin

---

2   http://whitehousedrugpolicy.gov/publications/economic_costs/.
3   http://www.publicsafety.gc.ca/prg/le/oc/_fl/us-canadian-report-drugs-eng.pdf.

it had previously acquired from Asia. Later, high levels of distrust for Mexican authorities' ability or even desire to suppress their narcotics entrepreneurs led Washington to take frequent unilateral steps in its loudly proclaimed "War on Drugs". These measures, which included kidnapping suspected Mexican dealers and spiriting them across the border for incarceration in American jails, aggravated anti-gringo feelings in Mexico. Later still, the United States' success in reducing the flow of narcotics from Colombia by sea turned Central America into a supply route by land and, as a consequence, made Mexico a key territory that then became the business domain of new and ever more powerful cartels.

Together, Mexican and Canadian drug cartels, which have developed strong working relationships with each other, are the primary narcotics suppliers for the illicit US drug market. Of the top five main narcotics types entering the United States–cocaine, methamphetamine, marijuana, heroin, and ecstasy–four are produced primarily in these two countries[4] and have led to the creation of the principal criminal organizations within the United States, exerting unrivaled control over the drug trade there. In sum, as the largest sources of prohibited narcotics for the US market, criminal organizations in Canada and Mexico comprise American society's greatest external threat. Ironically, the United States manages to aggravate this threat through its domestic hands-off policy on firearms (Dooley, et al 2009, US Committee on Foreign Relations 2007) . Mexican cartels and Canadian gangs' capacity to undermine US American security is enhanced by the fact that the US market supplies them with high-power small arms that they smuggle across the US borders. This enhanced firepower increases violence among the Mexican drug cartels and spills back across the border into the United States.

As with US military security, the transborder logic of the narcotics trade constructs the continental periphery simultaneously as both a security threat and a security ally. The physical contiguity of Mexico and Canada, which turns these territories into the main drug trafficking conduits into the United States, also makes the periphery's governments the most important actors–for better or for worse–in the construction of American drug security. For better: US narcotics security depends greatly on the ability of these neighbours to detect and then prevent illegal narcotics from entering the country. Since the Cold War, Washington has launched numerous cross-border security initiatives with Mexico and Canada to increase bilateral anti-drug cooperation. When harmonized, the policies implemented in the periphery also help to legitimize US/ counter-narcotics policies. For worse: if the Mexican and Canadian governments' domestic drug regulations are more liberal, or if their enforcement capabilities are weaker, they can have a significant impact on the volume of drug flows across the US border. When Mexican officials have been corrupted by the cartels they undermine the American approach's integrity. Presently, a more enlightened awareness of its dependence on its Mexican counterpart has led the US government to make significant efforts to boost Mexico's capacity to support its own drug interdiction strategy. Most

---

4   http://www.usdoj.gov/ndic/pubs31/31379/31379p.pdf

recently the Mérida Initiative promised hundreds of millions of dollars in aid to that effect, although the US Congress has authorized only a tiny fraction of the money. For its part, Canada's pilot projects for safe heroin injection sites and its decriminalization of the possession of small amounts of marijuana in the 2000s were deemed threatening by the US government.

6. The Logic of Anti-Terrorist (In)security

The fundamental paradox of the US terrorist problem is that Washington's policies were the root cause of its own insecurity. Had the United States believed its own rhetoric about the efficiency of free markets, it would not have felt the need to establish military control over the Middle East's oil reserves (Hamilton).[5] Without US bases in Saudi Arabia, Osama bin Laden would not have been provoked to launch al-Qaeda's *intifada* against the United States, and Islamic terrorism would not have emerged for American politicians to demonize. As it is, self-reinforcing vicious circles of policy over-reactions inadvertently promote recruitment to al-Qaeda's cause. The US-induced military engagement by NATO members in Afghanistan, the American invasion of Iraq, and, worst of all, Washington's practice of torture of suspected al-Qaeda members all fostered recruitment to Bin Laden's *jihad*.

Whatever the might-have-beens of US history, Islamic terrorism is no longer simply a threat to US embassies, barracks, and personnel overseas. Since Bin Laden's September 11 coup, an adroitly manipulated security paranoia has transformed the US governmental paradigm both domestically and internationally in ways that generate contradictory oscillations between heightened insecurity and security at both land borders. United States' efforts to enhance its own security created insecurity for its neighbours. Only indirectly connected to the *jihad* threat, Canada and Mexico experience overwhelming US pressure to ramp up their anti-terrorist capabilities on pain of facing greater export barriers at their land borders.[6] As with all its allies, the United States insisted on their adopting tighter measures with respect to issuing visas, vetting passengers embarking on planes destined either for the United States or flying over it, and investigating shipments leaving from their ports for American destinations.

In parallel with US narcotics insecurity, Mexico and Canada are unique among the United States' international counterparts because their geographical contiguity makes them immediate possible conduits for terrorists, along with any weapons of mass destruction they might obtain. Still, the same contiguity turns these neighbours into Washington's most important partners in its "war" against this

---

5   Hamilton, L.H., Upon the United States (the "9/11 Commission"). Interview 30 March 30, 2005.

6   These negotiations culminated in the Canada-US Smart Border Declaration and Action Plan of December 2001 and the Mexico-US Border Partnership Agreement of March 2002.

threat. Canada (somewhat reluctantly) and Mexico (very reluctantly) have had to accept their incorporation in the United States' anti-terrorist security zone. With their deeply ingested "Defence against Help" understanding that if they do not protect themselves from what the United States determines to be its foreign threat, Washington will take over directly; with their police and intelligence institutions happy to have their budgets, staff, and high-tech equipment expanded; and with their continuing concern about US harassment of their exports, Canadian governments have complied, raising Ottawa's security spending by large increments.

With its far weaker governmental capacity to control human traffic and with no shared commitment to global security norms, Mexico's ability to deliver border security to the United States is so limited that Washington has to devote its own resources to strengthening its southern neighbor's ability to act as a buffer against infiltration by al-Qaeda.

North America's Re-Institutionalization as a Security System

The policy utility of this broad-gauged analysis can be to suggest broad-gauge solutions, but it raises the question of how to bridge the gap between the ideal and the possible: while root solutions to root causes are conceivable, they cannot be expected to materialize fully-formed for any of the six logics just presented any time soon.

1. Overcoming the gross economic disparity between an impoverished Mexico and a victorious United States will not happen by relying on the magic of the market place's invisible hand. A North American equivalent to the post-World War II Marshall Plan is conceivable but unlikely absent some overriding and Mexico-specific threat equivalent to the post-World War II fear of a Soviet takeover of Western Europe.
2. Achieving historical justice would also tackle the root cause of North America's perverse demographic logic, since a prosperous Mexico would generate jobs for its own citizens who would no longer have to seek work across their northern frontier.
3. It was a delusion of neoconservatism to maintain that undermining the Canadian and Mexican states' regulatory powers with free trade agreements would benefit the weak more than the strong, particularly when these economic integration agreements did not cause the US government to give up its own protectionist powers.
4. With the passing of the Soviet threat, resolving the military tension between Mexico and the United States is a relatively easy task that is already being addressed quietly.
5. Since the war on drugs has patently failed, border violence and the social upheaval resulting from massive addiction in society will unlikely be

mitigated until the narcotics industry is decriminalized and US arms sales are regulated.

6. If the root cause of Islamic terrorism is the US attempt to dominate the Arab world with its military power, the solution is strategic withdrawal from the Middle East and the United States' concomitant abandonment of its self-reinforcing messianism and siege mentality.

Making a leap to such long-term solutions appears dauntingly unfeasible given the short term realities of the Mexican cartels' growing power, the incapacity of the Mexican government's incapacity to achieve its goals, and Mexican civil society's political weakness. Prospects for continent-wide solutions are not helped by Ottawa's determination to re-establish its old special bilateral relationship with Washington by extracting itself from trilateral relations with Mexico. For its part, the US political system's chronic gridlock requires almost inconceivable levels of bipartisan consensus to transcend the vicious circles that perpetuate self-destructive policy patterns.

It is nevertheless possible to imagine a new trilateralism in which Canada and Mexico reject their traditional passivity vis-à-vis the United States, change their self-consciousness from objects to subjects, and together address the big policy picture. If they were to help each other and take their outlaw cartels in hand by strictly regulating their decriminalized businesses, they could develop as a bilateral powerhouse. If Canada were to engage in a determined struggle to save the continent from collapse, it could work toward long-term solutions in which the periphery took back its power and the United States-realizing it was no longer invincible or all-powerful–recognized its dependence on its neighbors for its own well-being and security.

North America 's six logics of insecurity may be distinguishable by analysts who work out regulations in their respective institutional silos, but they merge and bounce off one another in practice for citizens hoping to visit relatives across the border, for exporters getting their product to market, or for workers trying to find jobs in the neighboring country.

Conclusions

This chapter has argued that

–Security is not always a collective good; it is sometimes a zero-sum commodity, as when the US drive for security begets its insecurity, which is rooted in a dangerously weak Mexico still obsessed by a historical memory of mistreatment.

–What is security for some (employers of cheap labor or the US corn industry) is insecurity for others (fired American workers or dislocated Mexican *campesinos*).

–Policy knots become difficult to disentangle. Because the periphery's greatest security threat is the economic loss of its access to the US market, it complies with measures demanded by Washington to deal with the United States' military security threat.

–Integral to most of the continent's security logics is the periphery's contradictory role as both the chief conduit of military, narcotics, and terrorist threats and the principal buffer against them.

In considering how to bridge the gap between the dysfunctional present and the root solutions that are desirable in the long term, it becomes clear that North America's informal institutionalization as two dependencies chronically responding to Washington-generated policies needs to change. Rather than policies in the periphery being determined by the outcomes of domestic struggles within Washington's Beltway, North America needs a new governance culture that cooperatively develops security. A continental solidarity that created substantive equality and social harmony among its three member states would help reconstitute North American security as a collective good.

Relating this analysis to the volume's mandate to find more innovative architectures of regional governance suggests three final considerations. First, there is a need to incorporate Canadian and Mexican interests in the development and execution of US policies so that a continental agenda of shared sensitive issues can exceed the simple scope and capabilities of national policies.

Second, no such continental agenda can be developed at the expense of intergovernmental cooperation. Promoting a program that will engender citizens and civil society participation but widen the social legitimacy of public management requires that leadership remain as the responsibility of governments–federal, provincial or state, and municipal.

Third, even though North America can barely be said to exist as a coherent governance region,[7] the extensive institutionalized and ad hoc federal, provincial or state, and municipal cooperative links across the United States' two borders can be reinforced to build less counter-productive, more positive-sum practices to bring an ideal future closer to a lived reality. Otherwise, North American borders promise to remain lines demarcating self-contradicting security and insecurity logics.

---

7   This issue was examined in systematic detail in my *Does North America Exist? Governing the Continent after NAFTA and 9/1.*

References

Ackerman, F, Wise, T.A., Gallagher, K, Ney, L. and Flores, R. "Free Trade, Corn, and the Environment: Environmental Impacts of US – Mexico Corn Trade Under NAFTA," *Free Trade, Corn, and the Environment* Washington, DC: G-DAE Working Paper No. 03-06.

Ackleson, J. Constructing Security on the US-Mexico Border. *Political Geography* 24:1 (2005), 165-84.

Borderscapes: Hidden Geographies and Politics at Territory's Edge. (Minneapolis: University of Minnesota Press, 2007), x.

Canada-US Cross-Border Crime Forum, *United States – Canada Border Drug Threat Assessment 2007* (March 2008). Available at: http://www.publicsafety.gc.ca/prg/le/oc/_fl/us-canadian-report-drugs-eng.pdf.

Dechaine, D.R. 2009. Bordering the Civic Imaginary: Alienization, Fence Logic, and the Minuteman Civil Defense Corps. *Quarterly Journal of Speech* 95:1, 43-65.

Clarkson, Stephen. *Does North America Exist? Governing the Continent after NAFTA and 9/11* (Toronto: University of Toronto Press and Washington: Woodrow Wilson Press, 2008).

Dooley, C.R. and Medler, A. A. 2008. Farewell to Arms: Managing Cross-Border Weapons Trafficking. *Hemisphere Focus.* Center for Strategic and International Studies Americas Program. 16:2 9 September Available at: http://csis.org/files/media/csis/pubs/hf_v16_02.pdf; United States Committee on Foreign Relations, "The Merida Initiative: 'Guns, Drugs, and Friends'," S. Prt. 110-35 (December 21, 2007): 9-10.

Doty, R.L. States of Exception on the Mexico–US Border: Security, Decisions, and Civilian Border Patrols. *International Political Sociology* 1:2 (June 2007), 113-37.

Gilchrist, J and Corsi, J.R. 2006. *Minutemen: The Battle to Secure America's Borders.* Los Angeles: World Ahead Publishing.

Gutiérrez-Haces, M.T. 2002. *Procesos de integración económica en México y Canadá: una perspectiva histórica comparada* México: Universidad Nacional Autónoma de México, 1–152.

Hamilton, L.H. President and Director of the Woodrow Wilson International Center for Scholars and Vice-Chair of the National Commission on Terrorist Attacks Upon the United States (the "9/11 Commission"). Interview 30 March 30, 2005.

Huntington, S.P. The Hispanic Challenge. *Foreign Policy* no. 141 (March/April 2004), 30-45.

Nadal, A. 2000. *The Environmental and Social Impacts of Economic Liberalization on Corn Production in Mexico.* Washington, DC: Oxfam GB and WWF International, September.

National Drug Intelligence Center, National Drug Threat Assessment 2009 (Dec. 2008), United States Department of Justice, http://www.usdoj.gov/ndic/pubs31/31379/31379p.pdf (Accessed on Dec 28 2008).

Navarro. A. 2008. *The Immigration Crisis: Nativism, Armed Vigilantism, and the Rise of a Countervailing Movement.* New York: Altamira Press.

Ojeda, M. 2006. *Alcances y límites de la política exterior de México* México, D.F.: El Colegio de México.

Pellicer de Brody, O. 1972. *México y la revolución cubana.* México D.F.: Centro de Estudios Internacionales, El Colegio de México, 33-4.

Tsoukala, A. Boundary-Creating Processes and the Social Construction of Threat. *Alternatives* vol. 33 iss. 2 (2008): 137-152; Prem Kumar Rajaram and Carl Grundy-Warr.

Weintraub, S. 2009. Situation in Latin America – Year-end 2009. *Issues in International Political Economy* No. 120, Center for Strategic and International Studies. December.

White House Office of National Drug Control Policy, "The Economic Costs of Drug Abuse in the United States, 1992-2002," (December 2004), available at: http://whitehousedrugpolicy.gov/publications/economic_costs/.

Chapter 6

The North American Partnership for Security and Prosperity (SPP) and the Development of the Northern Border Region of Mexico

José M. Ramos

Introduction

In an age marked by globalization the challenges of international crises must be overcome jointly. It is important to maintain dialogue, trust, and cooperation among Mexico, the United States, and Canada, countries whose values were founded upon democracy, freedom, justice, respect of human rights, and sovereignty.

The North American Partnership for Security and Prosperity (SPP) is a government initiative developed by Mexico, the United States, and Canada to facilitate communication and cooperation across several key policy areas of mutual interest, but because it is not a signed agreement or treaty, it contains no legally binding commitments or obligations. More recently a new plan, the Merida Initiative, grew out of the extension of NAFTA into security areas and followed the lines of the SPP.

Also called Plan Mexico, the Merida Initiative is a three-year regional security cooperation plan (2007-2010) that the former Bush administration presented in October 2007 and that the new Obama Administration widely supports. It proposes a package of US counterdrug and anticrime assistance for Mexico and Central America. The intent was that it would be a new kind of regional security partnership between the United States, Mexico, and Central America.

Originally the Merida Initiative was to be announced in the context of the SPP trinational summit, but it was delayed and in spite of its announcement in 2007 and not 2005, it is also considered as part of the same strategy (Whitney 2010).

This chapter analyzes SPP's impact on promoting regional security and development along the northern Mexican border. First, it describes US policy on border security and if such policy has a positive impact on the flow of labor and material goods at the US-Mexico border. Second, it examines future prospects of development given current US government policy.

An agenda based on SPP poses limitations. Since 2001 the US federal government has paid more and more attention to border security issues (CMAI 2006), but the Federal Government of Mexico has not matched these measures.

In spite of the lack of response from the Mexican side, several measures supported by the US government under the SPP framework have fostered investments and have developed competition in Mexico.

Towards a New Paradigm in Security and Development

Since the 2001 terrorist attacks, the US government has redefined its view on national security at an international level and in respect to its relationship with Mexico (Maira 2002). In this context, the relationship between security and development is supported by four arguments.

First, the Strategy of National Security of the United States (2002) promotes economic development in strategic countries like Mexico:

> "In the Western Hemisphere we have established flexible coalitions with
> countries that share our principal interests, in particular Mexico, Brazil, Canada,
> Chile and Colombia. Together a hemisphere that is genuinely democratic will
> be built, with our integration of boosting security, prosperity, opportunities and
> hope" (http://usinfo.state.gov/espanol/)

According to the Strategy of National Security, a policy for development represents an option for legitimizing a security policy in a bilateral and international context. Some governmental actors in the United States have indicated that democracy, economic growth, free trade, and sovereignty are priority domains that need reinforcement so that global insecurity may abate. One of the main challenges for the US is to create development policies compatible with the reduction of global insecurity. John Merrill, Director, Western Hemisphere Affairs, International Security Affairs, Department of Defence, Pentagon, Washington, DC presented the idea on 30 January 2004. It was part of the Program of International Visitors, State Department, *The Fight Against Terrorism and International Crime.*

The US Congress took such measures by funding the Merida Initiative, appropriating over $1.1 billion of the 1.4 billion in the plan to Mexico. Mexican President Felipe Calderón asked the US for the funds to help in the war on drugs. These funds currently provide technical expertise and assistance to Mexico for police professionalization, judicial and prison reform, information technology enhancement, infrastructure development, border security, and the promotion of a culture of lawfulness (Ribando 2010).

Are required 15% of funds dedicated for low enforcement and military assistance to be spent on human rights related aspects.

Second, the security policy can promote development if the US government conceives a comprehensive and global vision that is relevant to the current economy, commerce, migration and development. Mexico will benefit from such policies which are promoting bilateral exchange and are encouraging employment.

NAFTA has been a framework for invigorating a commercial relationship with the United States, but it has not had an impact on development. This is no surprise, since development was not its essential goal.[1] Proposals for expanding commercial initiatives have been proposed to support the implementation of structural reforms with greater social impact.[2] Yet sustained policy coordination among the states and between their respective federal governments has historically been lacking, leaving unilateral decision-making in the hands of state governments rather than at the local or regional level both in Mexico and in the United States. For this reason a new paradigm is needed, one that leverages the region's synergies and improves regional security and thus enhances the quality of lives of residents on both sides (*Rethinking the US-Mexico Border* 2009). This change depends on a new bi-national border management, focused on enhancing cross-border trade, environmental issues, and security collaboration. Short and long-term projects need to arise in the principal areas of security, trade facilitation, economic development, the environment, water, and migration. To secure the border and maintain trade, processes and technologies need to be continually improved, with the complementary goals of security and prosperity in mind.

Third, the notion of security associated with development must be translated into comprehensive public policies. The US also must focus on dependencies associated with security and development. A comprehensive, intergovernmental focus should be shared by the principal US federal agencies associated with national security policy and development to generate greater impact. Nevertheless, in practice this focus is difficult to demonstrate because of bureaucratic interests and other priorities that have generally characterized the national security policy of the United States (Wise 2002, GAO 2007). This new paradigm makes a distinction between bilateral foreign policy and border policy. Authorities in both countries need to be able to respond quickly to changes in their way of operating. Instead of waiting for bilateral foreign policies that are unencumbered by time-consuming bureaucratic processes, it's better to work on policies at a local and regional cooperation level.

Other federal agencies, such as the State Department, the Commerce Department, the Environmental Protection Agency (EPA), and the US Agency for International Development (USAID) (Arcos 2006), all would be responsible for promoting the development foreseen by SPP. In the case of the security agenda, the Department of Homeland Security (DHS) has played a fundamental role. Hence, it may be suggested that there are two agendas: one on the matter of security, and the other on the matter of development, and that they are not being managed with an intergovernmental focus.

---

1   See an evaluation of the commercial and political impact of NAFTA in Sydney Weintraub 2004. *NAFTA's Impact on North America: The First Decade*, CSIS.

2   A critique of the limitations of commercial policy in the government of president Ernesto Zedillo, which determined a lesser commercial impact, and that of Mexican economic growth is put forth by Salinas 2004.

These two agendas open the possibility for Mexico to strengthen its program with bureaucratic actors from both agendas and to promote a greater articulation of these actions in a policy of regional development.[3] The impact of a greater interdependency under the SPP may diminish some of the causes of migration toward the United States. But in order for this to occur, it is indispensable that a development policy be one of the priorities of current president Felipe Calderón (Consejo Mexicano de Asuntos Internacionales 2006, CMAI 2005).

On the Mexican side solid institutions, reforms, and policies that can be articulated with those implemented on the US side are needed. We shall further analyze one concept, undertaking reforms to both modernize and improve police effectiveness to make good use of the US aid stipulated in Plan Mexico. The effectiveness of such reforms may take a while, but significant steps are being taken to modernize Mexico's police forces and to improve their crime fighting ability. Several major reforms and reorganizations of the federal police have been attempted: the creation of the Federal Preventive Police in 1999 (Policia Federal Preventiva - PFP), a federal agency with centralized control; the creation of the Agencía Federal de Investigación (AFI) in 2001 with investigative capacity of law enforcement under the control of the Federal Attorney General (PGR); the creation of a separate and independent Secretariat for Public Security (Secretaría de Seguridad Pública - SSP) by separating the police from the Internal Affairs Secretariat (Secretaria de Gobernación – Segob) (2006); the signing into law of a series of constitutional reforms by Calderón's Administration in 2008 for improving the justice system and the code of criminal procedures (An important aspect of this reform was the adoption of a "presumption of innocence" standard in criminal cases, and the change to an accusatorial system that includes oral trials); and the creation of the Federal Police (Policia Federal - PF) in 2009.

Building strong, modern, and accountable police forces at the local, state, and federal level in Mexico will take time and a lot of government resources, and also will require an important commitment to institution-building both in Mexico and the United States.

Finally, security implies development, because the policy of border security proposes a greater improvement in the flow of people, automobiles, and goods at the US-Mexico border.

One of the priorities in border security policy with the United States is that there is a balance between security and crossings. To achieve this purpose the US government designed the initiative of an *intelligent border*. The history of this proposal goes back to the creation of a Partnership for Prosperity between Mexico and the US in 2001.[4] This initiative was brought up at the meeting between the US and Mexican presidents in Guanajuato (February 2001); it was reaffirmed at

---

3   For the importance of regional development in Mexico in the framework of national US security policy see Barajas 2006.
4   See Partnership for Prosperity 2002

the next presidential meeting of both governments in Washington D.C. in early September 2001.

The objective of the initiative was to encourage private investment in areas of low economic growth in Mexico by way of an alliance between the public and private sectors of both countries.[5] Additionally, other professional actors and businesses in both countries would participate in the creation of a plan of action.[6] The subject of security played no part because the terrorist attacks of September 2001 had not yet occurred.

A second context in analyzing the policy of border security was referred to at the international meeting for Development Funding (Monterrey, NL 21 March 2002), in which the concrete actions of the Partnership for Prosperity in the matter of economic development and the 22 point strategy of the initiative of the *intelligent border* with Mexico were recognized.[7]

The Monterrey meeting was important because it brought about an integration of initiatives for technological strengthening and also cooperation in security by promoting a safe and efficient flow of people and goods along the length of the border.[8] For the first time the bases were established to achieve a balance between border security and the agility of commercial operations between Mexico and the United States.[9]

Some consider that the creation of the 22 points initiative of *intelligent border* was brought up by the US government to get Mexico to commit its support to a joint initiative for security and economic development from a long-range perspective.[10]

The priority of achieving a balance between security and border crossings was reinforced with the Joint Declaration of 2005 of the SPP, which was conceived of as the next phase of a common security strategy to better protect North America and assure efficient traffic of travelers and legal merchandise through the common borders. It is hoped that Mexico, Canada, and the United States will work together to guarantee the instrumentation of the highest standards of regional security and to speed up border processes.[11]

---

5   To identify the actions effected by said Alliance in the years of 2003 to 2004 Available at: www.sociedadparalaprosperidad.gob.mx

6   The White House 2001.

7   An analysis of the initiative of border security appears in CSIS and ITAM 2004. *US Mexico Border Security and the Evolving Security Relationship*. April.

8   The White House 2002. *Joint Statement by the Presidents of the United States and Mexico*, March 22, Monterrey, Mexico.

9   To appreciate the importance of such a reunion in the framework of an international policy in matters concerning the encouragement of development see Amartya Sen 2003.

10   To identify the achievement of the policy of the *intelligent border* see Homeland Security and Secretaria de Gobernación 2005.

11   See Agenda for Security. SPP 2005. This chapter does not attempt to analyze the ensemble of actions in security matters foreseen by the SPP. For a closer analysis and some of its results see SPP 2005. *Report to the Heads of State*. Annex. June.

A preliminary analysis of governmental interest in achieving a balance between greater security and border crossings leads us to affirm that such a balance has not been achieved, because security has been prioritized. Nonetheless, a few advances have taken place in hopes of reducing delays in arriving to the US through border ports of entry.[12]

The policy of speeding up vehicle and pedestrian crossings on behalf of the United States government has presented important limitations, fundamentally associated with management.[13]

The four previous arguments reflect the complexity and challenges implied in a greater advancement of the SPP in the Mexico-United States relationship, with a focus on development and on the framework of global insecurity.

From the Strategy of Border Security to SPP: Scope and Limitations

In the United States the policies of Homeland Security began with the broadcasting of the Patriot Act in October 2001 (US Congress 2001).

US strategies toward Mexico have been fundamentally characterized by the of *intelligent border* initiative.

The *intelligent border* initiative intended to create a "border of the future" in which distinct dimensions in terms of land, maritime, and air crossings would be considered by way of a border inspection system of vehicles, articles, and people entering the United States (The Office of Homeland Security, op. cit.).

With the later creation of the SPP in 2005 the *intelligent border* policy was reinforced under the security agenda. United States, Canada and Mexico committed to working on strategies to improve border security, air security, and maritime security, as well as on creating a common model for facing emergencies.

The central question is whether the actions of the *intelligent border* initiative have effectively reduced the delays at border crossings between Mexico and the United States, and whether they have promoted commercial border transactions. The analysis of the earlier question is based on the following:

a) To date (early March 2010) the delays for autos attempting to enter the US have not been substantially reduced at the principal border entries.[14]

The border between San Diego, California, and the state of Baja California is one of the most important because of the number of crossings. Every day 136,000

---

12   See the proposal of Commissioner Robert C. Bonner, in conference before the US Chamber of Commerce Washington, D.C., 18 November 2005.

13   For a more in-depth analysis of the problem of management in the policy of border security see GAO 2006.

14   See South County Economic Development Council, San Diego Dialogue, Tijuana Trabaja, 2001. *Who Crosses the Border-2001*, Project Overview. Preliminary Information, October, San Diego Association of Governments (SANDAG) and California Department of Transportation (CALTRANS) 2006.

autos, 6,200 trucks, and close to 340,000 people cross this border through the ports of San Ysidro, Otay Mesa and Tecate (SANDAG and CALTRANS 2006).

These delays are caused by a closer border inspection by US authorities, an increase in the flow of people and autos attempting to enter the neighboring country, and the fact that the infrastructure in the ports of entry has not been updated.[15]

In other words, even though the policy of border security has been the principal factor in decreased speed at the border crossings between Mexico and the United States,[16] there are other factors that also have contributed to the delays.

b) Border inspection technology, which is considered one way of achieving a balance between security and speed at border crossings, has experienced some management and implementation problems, and so its use has not become widespread at all border ports of entry. For example, one of the principal strategies of the security policy of the United States for speeding up the traffic of people and merchandise is through an inspection system called US-VISIT (US Visitor and Immigrant Status Indicator Technology). However, its implementation has had some management problems.[17]

Another strategic program of the border security policy is that of SENTRI line–a rapid crossing card equipped with an intelligent system. The problem with this program is that at the times of greatest vehicular traffic, from 5 a.m. until 9 a.m., the principal ports of entry between Mexico and the US become saturated (Tijuana and Ciudad Juárez). Despite the increase in demand for this card, vehicular bottlenecking in the rest of the crossing lanes has not been substantially reduced. In these lanes, crossing time is estimated to be from 1.5 to 2 hours between 5a.m. and 9a.m., which is the period of greatest vehicular access toward the United States. During the rest of the day the average crossing time is approximately one hour, and it worsens on weekends, when the average crossing time into the United States, especially at the port of San Ysidro, California–one of the most important in the border with the United States–is from 1.5 to 2 hours on average.[18]

In the last three years the number of people and vehicles attempting to enter the United States has increased by nearly 10 percent in comparison to that of 2002.[19] This has not been met by a parallel increase of the infrastructure in the principal border crossings such as Tijuana, Ciudad Juárez and Nuevo Laredo.[20]

---

15   See California Department of Transportation 2004.

16   See SPP 2006. *Joint Declaration*, March and SPP 2005.

17   See GAO 2006. *Border Security: US-VISIT Program Faces Strategic, Operational and Technological Challenges at Land Ports of Entry.*

18   See wait times at the borders of Mexico and Canada Available at: http://apps.cbp.gov/bwt/

19   See US Department of Transportation and Mexico Secretariat of Communications and Transportation 2004. *Binational Border Transportation Infrastructure: Needs Assessment Study*, July.

20   See US Department of Transportation and Mexico Secretariat of Communications and Transportation 2004. ibid.

Border inspections by the US government face a variety of challenges: increasing their efficiency diminishing delays, reducing urban bottlenecks, diminishing environmental pollution at the border, and fundamentally attending to economic impacts. Here one can appreciate the interrelation of the policy of border security with the problems of urban development, environment, and economic development.

Technology is still one of the best options to achieving a balance between security and speed at border crossings.[21] The increase in infrastructure to create other border crossings is difficult, because at most of the border ports of crossing the urban areas have practically been integrated,[22] reflecting a deficiency in urban and trans-border planning. There is also the problem of high cost.[23]

c) Another manifestation of the current policy of border security in the United States is an increase in the seizure of drugs entering from Mexico, in comparison to 2002.[24] Nonetheless, the drug trade has not been reduced, because criminal groups have reoriented their strategies for getting drugs into the United States; furthermore, the supply and demand for illegal drugs is still maintained in the bi-national market.

According to the State Department, the Mérida Initiative has four primary goals: to break the power and impunity of criminal organizations; to assist the Mexican and Central American governments in strengthening border, air, and maritime controls; to improve the capacity of justice systems in the region; and to diminish the demand for drugs in the region. In late 2009, due to drug-related violence in Mexico and the potential threat of a spillover along the Southwest border, concern increased in Congress to speed up the Mérida Initiative.[25]

By the end of September 2009, the State Department had given $830 million of the $1.3 billion in Mérida funds appropriated for Mexico and Central America, but only $26 million of the funds had been spent (Ribando 2010). In December 2009, the Obama Administration requested $450 million in Mérida funding for Mexico. According to a recent report, $77.2 million worth of equipment was delivered to Mexico at the end of December 2009, including 30 ion scanners and five Bell helicopters for the Mexican Army (Ribando 2010). Advances in programs involving police professionalization and continuing education, prison reform, prosecutorial capacity building, and human rights training programs were also reported. There were further changes regarding what equipment is actually

---

21   On this problem see GAO 2006. *Information Technology: Customs has made progress on Automated Commercial Environment System, but it faces long standing management challenges and new risks.*

22   About this problem see US Department of Transportation and Mexico Secretariat of Communications and Transportation 2004.

23   See GAO 2007. *Homeland Security: US-VISIT.*

24   See *Testimony of John S. Comer, Assistant Special Agent in Charge, Phoenix Field Division DEA 2006.*

25   Ribando Seelke, C. 2010.

needed, the difficulty of delivering an aid package that involves so many actors, administrative procedures, and the need to enhance institutional capacity on the part of both recipient countries and the United States to implement the assistance.

The program will be a success only if all the participants fulfill their domestic obligations under the Mérida Initiative. Congress is expected to monitor how Mérida funds have been used, check progress to date, revise any planned adjustments in the uses of funds, and design post-Mérida security cooperation, under the Obama Administration budget request.

The post-Mérida bilateral security cooperation strategy will focus on disrupting the operational capacity of organized crime, institutionalizing Mexico's police force capacity and judicial reform, creating a border structure, and building strong communities.

d) The impact of border security is not homogeneous in all the cities bordering Mexico and the United States. The impact is subject to the size of the population with a border visa, the importance of the local-regional economy, the influence and role of local governmental and non-governmental actors in both countries in proposing flexibility in the processes of inspection, and border vigilance by US authorities.

e) Border security police has not seen an increase in the number of detentions of people attempting to enter the United States illegally at border ports of entry and other areas of crossing. However, border security has demonstrated some efficiency in other fundamental problems at the border, such as drug trafficking (SPP 2006. *Joint Declaration)* and labor migration toward the United States (GAO 2007). The United States policy of border security has reduced the possibility of terrorists entering through borders with Mexico (GAO 2006, GAO 2007).

However, the central goal of the policy of border security is to achieve a balance between security and border crossings. This issue has not been totally addressed (GAO 2006).

In summary, in the short term (2009-2010) it will be difficult to achieve such a balance between security and trade issues (SANDAG and CALTRANS 2009) because the subject will continue to be dominated by the policy of border security.

The border communities of both sides have been affected by the delays in crossings through fewer sales at border businesses in the United States and less tourism in Mexican border cities.

The speeding up of the border crossings and a redirection toward options of border development will depend on the level of influence of Mexican and US local and trans-border actors, and on their alliance with the Departments of State and Commerce. These agencies have generally adopted less rigid postures in matters of security and trade policies.

Flexibility in the US border security policy could be feasible if one considers that close to 90 percent of those who cross into the United States are people who live in neighboring border communities.[26] Those in this flow do not have the profile of terrorists (sic), which means that stricter inspection could be applied to the 10 percent of the population that does not reside in the cities bordering Mexico and the United States (SPP 2005, ASPAN, 2006). However, flexible programs have not been established because of perceived risks on behalf of the Department of Internal Security of the United States. Nonetheless, there is a low risk profile among the populations of the border communities on both sides (SANDAG and CALTRANS 2006). The central goal of the security policy of the US government is to achieve a balance between security and border crossings.

Some Gains and Limitations of SPP from the Perspective of Border Development: A New Proposal toward Economic Integration

The SPP offers some opportunities for the promotion of growth, competition, and quality of life. For the first time in the recent history of Mexico-US relations, the US government has proposed a focus on development to promote greater cooperation with Mexico, sustained within the context of security.

The importance of the SPP for Mexico lies in, among other aspects: a) an option for linking security and development, b) an alternative for obtaining financing for strategic areas of development and border security, c) the possibility of rethinking border development within the framework of security, d) an opportunity to promote the planning of border development based on two strategic areas: security and development, which are associated with the environment and social development. These opportunities may appear limited if Mexican actors lack vision and the ability to base border development on the new problems that characterize it; similarly, there is a predominance of ineffective management and intergovernmental cooperation in Mexico in the matter of border management.

In the framework of the SPP, important interest groups driving the focus on security and development have arisen in Canada, Mexico and United States. The central purpose of the Independent Work Group (2005)[27] indicates:

> (...) the creation in 2010 of a North American community that increases security, prosperity and opportunity. (...) Its parameters are defined by an external tariff in common, and an external security perimeter, within which the movement of people, products and money should be legal, organized and secure. Its goal is to guarantee a North America that is free, safe, just and prosperous" (Council on Foreign Relations, et. al., op. cit., 2005: 127)

---

26   See South County Economic Development Council, San Diego Dialogue, Tijuana Trabaja, 2001 .*Who Crossers the Border-2001*, Project Overview. Preliminary Information. October.

27   A parallel proposal was in the report of the WWICS, CMAI and ITAM 2005.

North America faces three types of challenges: "the menaces shared by our security, the shared challenges of our growth and economic development and the shared challenge of unequal economic development" (*Council on Foreign Relations 2005*).

In contrast to the SPP, the initiatives of the Group are more general and seek to spread benefits toward economic development. It notes that, "*Mexico also requires significant and energetic reforms in its fiscal policy, with the aim that it be able to use its own resources with greater efficiency and improve its economic development*" (Council on Foreign Relations 2005).

This type of proposal is important because it reopens the debate on advances in the process of integration between Mexico and the United States and because it places emphasis on the need for a greater cooperation in security matters and calls for a reinforcement of a development policy. It reiterates the argument in respect to the SPP: this project will have a greater social impact, in the measure to which there is integration of management and an efficient national and regional policy of development (Aguilar 2006), that effectively generates greater social benefits, particularly in terms of diminishing social inequality through a promotion of competition and growth. Otherwise, neither the SPP nor the recommendations of the Work Group will have a major social impact.

SPP and Its Objectives for Development at the Northern Border[28]

SPP's general objective is to improve the competitiveness of the North American industry in global markets by increasing economic opportunities for all of its members and at the same time, to maintain elevated standards of health and security for the population.[29] The SPP mentions attending to the following particular objectives: increase productivity, promote sectoral collaboration in facilitating businesses, improve efficiency and security of the transportation system in North America, work toward the free flow of capital and an efficient supply of financial services in all of North America, invest in all of the countries, make movement of goods efficient, improve the quality of life, and protect the population against illness.

Following is an analysis of the principal objectives of the SPP in matters of border development. The analysis emphasizes the subjects of transport, quality of life, and public health.

One of the most important sources of bottlenecks in trans-border commercial relations between Mexico and the United States has been the system and infrastructure of transport. There is also a need to improve the security conditions of the transport and to hinder the traffic of migrants, drugs, and prohibited substances in general.

---

28   To identify the achievements of SPP see SPP 2005 and SPP 2006.
29   See http://www.usembassy-mexico.gov/sTrade_partnership.html

Nevertheless, structural deficiencies, such as Mexican centralism, lack of financing, and pressures generated by urban growth in the Mexican border cities have conditioned the development of the transport infrastructure, impeding advances toward increased planning. Increased efficiency in the processes of urban planning in the border cities is necessary, considering the expectations of population growth and commercial transport.[30]

Improving the Quality of Life

To improve the quality of life, the following has been proposed: co-responsibility for the natural environment; increased cooperation in improving air quality, including reduction of sulphur in fuels, mercury emissions and marine emissions; improvement in water quality through bilateral and trilateral cooperation, and through existing regional organisms, such as the International Commission for Waters and Limits and the International Mixed Commission; programs against the propagation of invasive species in both coastal and fresh waters; strengthening of alliances and incentives for conserving the habitat of migratory species to protect biodiversity; formulation of complementary strategies in co-responsibility for oceans; focus on the ecosystem; creation of a trustworthy and safe supply of food, facilitating at the same time commerce of agricultural products; searching for common foci regarding food safety; clarifying identification, handling, and recuperation in respect to risks of diseases related to food, animals, and plants; development of regulations related to agricultural biotechnology in Mexico, Canada, and the United States through the work of the Biotechnology Initiative of North America.[31]

This is one of the new and fundamental proposals in matters of development put forth by the SPP. Since 1994, greater attention has been given to the environmental problem with a vision toward sustainability.[32] However, bi-national agreements have been insufficient in substantially reducing environmental degradation derived from water and air pollution in the border cities of northern Mexico,[33] The SPP should be conceived of as an opportunity to advance toward the institutionalization of efficient mechanisms of environmental trans-border cooperation, with a focus on local environmental problems.

Different institutional efforts promoted in respect to environmental problems that have been analyzed from a perspective of Water Basins have permitted

---

30   See US Department of Transportation and Mexico Secretariat of Communications and Transportation 2004. *Binational Border Transportation Infrastructure: Needs Assessment Study*, July.

31   See http://www.usembassy-mexico.gov/sTrade_partnership.html

32   For a closer analysis of the importance of the environment from the perspective of development in Mexico see Gilbreath, J. 2003.

33   See the diagnosing of this system of problems in SEMARNAT and EPA 2003.

an identification of the system of problems and the generation of strategic information (Castro, et. al. 2006). However, one of the principal challenges of the focus on Water Basins is in the creation of a trans-border management scheme or, particularly, a Joint Consulting Committee for water and air management at the Mexico-US border.

Another structural problem is particularly associated with inefficient urban, environmental, and water management stemming from the Mexican side. Additionally, US authorities show little support for a joint approach to the problems. This issue has created trans-border environmental threats.[34] In spite of the fact that authorities in both countries acknowledge the issues, difficulties in establishing trans-border mechanisms in urban and environmental matters continue to exist.

If, in the coming years, advances have not been made in achieving greater control of air and water pollution at the Northern Mexico border, improvement in the quality of life will be affected in Mexican and US border communities.

The emphasis on security policy has not diminished the prioritization of the subject of the environment. This agenda has acquired importance for itself in local and state ambits, and in certain trans-border contexts.

The implementation of the Bi-national Environmental Program has permitted the border to acquire relevance for itself. However, the structural problem is rooted in the fact that for most local and state governments, developing an environmental agenda based on management and an efficient and sustainable policy has not been a priority.

Additionally, governments have lacked a focus on development (Aguilar 2006), without which environmental problems in matters of water and air have worsened over the years.[35] The SPP represents another opportunity for Mexican governments to build a proposal of environmental development in the context of security.

Protecting the Population against Illnesses

In order to protect the population against illnesses, the following has been proposed:strengthening trans-border coordination in public health matters regarding watchfulness, prevention and control of infectious diseases (for example, endemic flu); improving the health of the native population through specific bilateral and/or trilateral activities, for example, through promotion and education in matters of health; preventing illness and supporting research; and developing cooperation initiatives within the framework of the International Conference on Reconciling Technical Requisites for the Registry of

---

34   See the diagnosis of such a system of problems in SEMARNAT and EPA 2003.

35   For a diagnostics of the trans-border environmental situation see SEMARNAT and EPA 2006.

Pharmaceutical Products for Human Use to identify and adopt the best practices for the registration of medicinal products.[36]

The health problem is fundamental in Mexican and US border communities (Rangel, G., González, R. 2006), where unequal access to public services and environmental pollution create health problems.[37] These problems could increase as the population is expected to grow in the coming years. The situation also demands an improvement in living conditions through better access to funding options and through strategies emphasizing bi-national collaboration. A more efficient intergovernmental focus on health matters in Mexico, in general, and in northern border municipalities, in particular, is needed.

Cooperation and solidarity in the North American region was demonstrated in April 2009 when Mexico and the US faced the emergence of a new virus, H1N1, a cross-border threat. As the outbreak occurred in Mexico, steps were quickly taken there to control the disease by making it public, alerting the entire world, shutting down the country for up to three weeks, and closing schools and restaurants. Meanwhile the Obama Administration preferred not to take any extraordinary measures (such us closing the border) to halt travel or commerce between the countries. It was seen as efficient cooperation between the Department of Homeland Security in the United States and the Ministry of Public Health in Mexico (Kilroy, Rodríguez Sumano, Hataley 2010).

Working together, the highest expressions of responsibility, accountability and transparency were made clear. By alerting the other regions in the hemisphere in a timely manner, Mexico allowed them to implement preventive measures in order to abate the propagation of the virus.

The economic and social objectives proposed by SPP are important because they permit an advance toward an integral conception of security matters and development. Their possible success depends, among other aspects, on their not being predominated only by security and economics.

The governmental challenge for Mexico is in getting the US government to advance toward a balance in security, economic, and social policies. Otherwise, the social problems in Mexico will worsen, provoking more labor migration toward the United States, poverty, urban insecurity, environmental pollution, and a rise in the drug trade.

Strengthening the abilities of Mexican authorities associated with development is vital. Mexico must understand the problem of global insecurity and must establish social alternatives. Mexican authorities must conceive of a focus on strategic management in matters of development. Such strategic management should include a proper diagnosis of options for change, a design of efficient public policies, which implies the creation of social benefits, creation of responsible

---

36   See http://www.usembassy-mexico.gov/sTrade_partnership.html
37   See Mexico-United States Border Environmental Program 2012.

and efficient public management, and also the creation of political capacity for generating agreements.

The strategic management in matters of development should also be characterized by a participative process of reform, a correct identification of sector priorities, a periodic performance evaluation, a neutral platform to raise consensus, and nevertheless the integration of local, state, and international cooperation.

The implementation of these aspects is based on a focus and conceptual perspective of public management that permits attending to problems of development in a context of global insecurity.[38]

In summary, a greater impact of the SPP in Mexico will depend on the consideration of political, economic, social, and managerial factors.

This is a result of a lack of knowledge about the SPP, the financial limitations, a deficient national and transnational intergovernmental management, more emphasis on security, adding bureaucratic and political difficulties in joining security with development. The list of factors that are limiting the impact of the SPP is larger and also includes an inefficient development policy in Mexico, differing social perceptions of the process of integration, disarticulation of national, state, and local programs in matters of regional and local development, limited capacities for public management and of policy for establishing development programs, lack of vision and strategic capacity for establishing border development, inefficient management and intergovernmental cooperation in Mexico on border management matters, disequilibrium between economic growth and unresolved social issues.

These limitations also have to do with the different agendas that the three countries are facing, and only in a convergence scenario are improvements to be seen. A common agenda of these countries is the nature of the threat that Canada, Mexico, and the United States collectively face, and significance must be given to economic security and domestic policy considerations.

The security concerns for the United States and the threat of global terrorism increased in 2001, but with President Barack Obama, the United States has focused more on the threat of Mexico's war on its drug cartels and the related criminal violence.

Mexico is more concerned with the drug cartels and the nature of transnational organized crime. But also it fears that undocumented immigrants and terrorists will cross the border, especially considering the consequences of closing the borders and the catastrophic economic impact that would ensue. Three areas that have witnessed an increase in security cooperation among the three countries are natural disasters, pandemic influenza, and drug trafficking (Kilroy 2010). With a common agenda it seems less possible to deal with financial limitations for solving the problems. A good example is the Merida Initiative, where large funds were released for drug trafficking.

---

38   Such a proposal is developed by Ramos, J. 2004.

Conclusions

The principal purpose of this paper is to analyze the SPP in matters of promoting a development policy in the framework of global insecurity, particularly in the scope of the Northern Mexican border.

The SPP aims to integrate the issues of security and defense, incorporating economic and social elements. The alliance is posed because the North American region is considered vulnerable to various security threats, an increase in foreign competition, and unequal economic development within the region. It is important to encourage the security of the region in a parallel way and to try to obtain the wellbeing of citizens in the three countries that comprise it.

A focus on development in the framework of the SPP presents some limitations, because the US government has generally focused more on security. However, the implementation of the development agenda under the SPP from 2005 to 2006[39] indicates the Department of Commerce has promoted important actions. There are two agendas in security and prosperity matters that are not being managed jointly, due to bureaucratic difficulties. Border communities on both sides have been affected by delays in crossing, resulting in lower sales in US businesses on the border and less tourism in the Mexican border cities.

Critiques of US-Mexican cooperation, especially under the Merida Initiative, include the lack of efforts to assist at-risk youth and to curb unemployment and other social problems in communities plagued by drug trafficking. Also, heath aspects such as addiction treatment or prevention of violence are not included, and emphasis is mainly on training and equipping Mexican security forces.

The Obama's administration has given its full support to the drug war, but the US is responsible for reducing gunrunning and demand for drugs. There are signs of drug policy reform in domestic policy that could eventually affect the way foreign counternarcotics efforts are viewed.

To improve security, advanced detection technologies, intelligent risk management strategies, infrastructure upgrades, better personnel training and enhanced technology are needed. Programs like the Mérida Initiative are woven into a more holistic US drug policy focusing on reducing demand as well as supply, where US and Mexican counternarcotics programs have to be complementary, rather than duplicate each other's efforts. They should anticipate future funding requests for more institution building, including law enforcement training.

A greater impact of the SPP in Mexico in matters of border development depends on factors of a political, economic, social, and managerial nature, including: lack of knowledge about SPP, deficient national and transnational intergovernmental management, bureaucratic and political difficulties in the articulation of security with development, inefficient policies on matters of development in Mexico, disarticulation of national, state, and local programs in matters of regional and

---

39   SPP 2005. *Report to the Heads of State, op. cit* and SPP 2006. *Report to the Heads of State II*, op. cit.

local development, and an absence of vision and strategic capacity for establishing border development, among others.

A challenge to the policies of security and development in Mexico and the United States in the coming years is whether in fact both governments will have the political volition and institutional capacity to conceive an integral focus on security matters and development, in which both priorities form part of the national and bi-national governmental agenda, and whether an advance will be made in diminishing national social inequalities and in achieving greater agility at the border crossings. Without changes the SPP will be one more bi-national strategic project that does not generate social impact and does not allow a more equitable distribution of the benefits of free trade.

References

Agenda for Security. SPP 2005. Available at: http://usinfo.state.gov/esp/Archive/2005/Mar/23-657503.html

Aguilar, I., 2006. *The Agenda for the Regional Development of Mexico: Current Challenges and New Directions*, at *Seminar on Management of Local Development Local in Mexico*, COLEF, 17 November.

Alliance for the Security and Prosperity of North America (SPP) 2005. Available at: http://www.usembassy-mexico.gov/sTrade_partnership.html

Amartya Sen 2003. *Delivering the Monterrey Consensus*, Economic Paper No. 48., May, 129.

Arcos, C. 2006. *The challenges of a border security policy of the US with Mexico*, in Seminario *Binacional Seguridad Nacional y Fronteriza en la Relación Mexico-Estados Unidos*, El Colegio de la Frontera Norte (COLEF), Tijuana, B. C. 12 February.

Barajas I. 2006. *The regional development of Mexico: Current challenges and new directions,* paper presented at *Seminario La Gestión del Desarrollo Local en Mexico*, COLEF, 17 November.

Benítez-Manaut, R. 2004. *Mexico and new challenges in hemispheric security,* Washington, D.C. Woodrow Wilson International Center for Scholars, Latin American Program, 65.

Bonner, R. 2003. *Master's Lecture in "Safety and Security in North American Trade,* Center for Strategic and International Studies, Washington, DC, 16 July.

Bonner, R. 2005. Conference before the US Chamber of Commerce Washington, D.C., 18 November 2005, Available at: www.cbp.gov.

California Department of Transportation 2004. *Bottleneck Study: Transportation Infrastructure and Traffic Management Analysis of Cross Border Bottlenecks,* November.

Carlsen, L. 2007. *Extending NAFTA's Reach* [Online: Americas Program, Center for International Policy (CIP)]. Available at: http://americas.irc-online.org/am/4497

Carter, A. 2001. *The Architecture of Government in the Face of Terrorism.* International Security 26(3): 5-23.

Castro, J. et. al. 2006. Mas allá de la Generación de Información para la Gestión de Cuencas Hídricas: La experiencia del Consejo Consultivo de la Cuenca Hídrica Binacional del Río Tijuana, paper presented at the *VIII Border Institute for Cooperation in the Planning and Operation of Transborder Water Basins: Sharing Information at the Borders*, Río Rico, Arizona, May 22-24.

Comer, J.S. Assistant Special Agent in Charge, Phoenix Field Division DEA 2006. *Pushing the Border Back: the Role Intelligence Plays in Protecting the Border*, presentation before House Permanent Select Committee on Intelligence, Sierra Vista, Arizona.

Consejo Mexicano de Asuntos Internacionales (Mexican Council on International Issues) (CMAI), American Assembly, Columbia University, El Colegio de la Frontera Norte, ITAM 2003. *Assembly of North America*, Monterrey, N.L., September.

Consejo Mexicano de Asuntos Internacionales (Mexican Council on International Issues) (CMAI), 2006, *Memorandum for the President-Elect of Mexico: External policy in the first 100 days of the administration*, Mexico, November.

Council on Foreign Relations, Canadian Council of Business Leaders and CMAI 2005. *Construction of a Community in North America*, New York. Available at: www.cfr.org

CSIS and ITAM 2004. *US Mexico Border Security and the Evolving Security Relationship.* April.

Fernández de Castro, R. Ruiz Sandoval, E. (coords.) 2006. *The International Agenda of Mexico 2006-2012. Mexico in the World*, Editorial Arithe, April.

General Accounting Office (GAO) 2002. *Combating Terrorism: Intergovernmental Cooperation in the Development of a National Strategy to Enhance State and Local Preparedness*, 2 April.

GAO 2003. Richard M. Stana, Director Home and Security and Justice Issues, before the Subcommittee on Infrastructure and Border Security, State Committee on Homeland Security, House of Representatives, 16 June.

GAO 2006. *Homeland Security: Recommendations to Improve Management of Key Border Security Program Need to be Implemented*, Washington, D. C., 14 February.

GAO 2006. *Information Technology: Customs has made progress on Automated Commercial Environment System, but it faces long standing management challenges and new risks*, Washington, D.C., 31 May and Homeland Security: US-VISIT.

GAO 2006. *Border Security: US-VISIT Program Faces Strategic, Operational and Technological Challenges at Land Ports of Entry*. Washington, D.C., December.

GAO 2007. *Homeland Security: Management and Programmatic Challenges Facing the Department of Homeland Security.* GAO-07-398T, 6 February, Available at: http://www.gao.gov/cgi-bin/getrpt?GAO-07-398T

GAO 2007. *Secure Border Initiative: SBInet Expenditure Plan Needs to Better Support Oversight and Accountability.* GAO-07-309, 15 February, Available at: http://www.gao.gov/cgi-bin/getrpt?GAO-07-309

GAO 2007. Homeland *Security: US-VISIT Has Not Fully Met Expectations and Longstanding Program Management Challenges Need to Be Addressed.* GAO-07-499T, 16 February. Available at :http://www.gao.gov/cgi-bin/getrpt GAO-07-499T

Gilbreath, J. 2003. *Environment and Development in Mexico: Recommendations for Reconciliation*, CSIS, Washington, D.C.

Heyman, D., Wais, E. 2008. *Homeland Security in an Obama Administration* [Online: CSIS, Center for Strategic & International Studies] vol. 1, no.1. Available at: http://csis.org/files/media/csis/pubs/081203_hls_smart_brief.pdf

Homeland Security and Secretaría de Gobernación 2005. *Alliance for the Mexico-United States Border*, Report of Advances, 2002-2004, January.

Kilroy, R., Rodríguez Sumano, A., Hataley, T. 2010. Toward a New Trilateral Strategic

Security Relationship: United States, Canada, and Mexico, in *Journal of Strategic Security*, Vol 3, No.1, edited by J. Tamsett, M.A., Henley-Putnam University Press, 51-64.

Maira, L. 2002. *The United States Before the Change in International Scenery*, in *Revista Mexicana de Política Exterior*, IMRED, num. 65, 11-42.

Merrill, J. Director, Western Hemisphere Affairs, International Security Affairs, Department of Defence, Pentagon, Washington, DC. Program of International Visitors, State Department, *The Fight Against Terrorism and International Crime.* 30 January 2004.

Mexico-United States Border Environmental Program 2012 in http://www.epa.gov/usmexicoborder/index_esp.htm.

National Drug Intelligence Center 2003. *National Drug Threat Assessment 2003.* Executive Intelligence Policy Summary, Washington, DC, April.

The Office of Homeland Security, 2002. *National Strategy for Homeland Security*, July, Washington, DC.

Olson, E. 2009. *Police Reform and Modernization in Mexico* [Online: Woodrow Wilson International Center for Scholars Washington, DC]. Available at http://www.wilsoncenter.org/news/docs/Brief%20on%20Police%20Reform%20and%20Modernization.pdf

Partnership for Prosperity, 2002. *Creating Prosperity Through Partnership, Report to President Vicente Fox and President George W. Bush*, Monterrey, March 22.

Partnership for Prosperity, 2002. Partnerships Works, *Report to President Vicente Fox and President George W. Bush*, November 22.

Press conference by President Obama, President Calderón of Mexico, and Prime Minister Harper of Canada. 2009. Cabanas Cultural Center Guadalajara, Mexico, The White House: Office of the Press Secretary.

Ramos, J. 2004. *Transborder Management and Cooperation at the Mexico-United States Border in a Framework of Global Insecurity: Problems and Challenges.* Editorial Porrúa, CMAI and H. Cámara de Diputados.

Rangel, G., González, R. 2006. *Health situation at the Northern Mexican border"* in Gerardo Ordóñez and Marcos Reyes (coords.), *The Challenges of Social Policy at the Northern Border in Mexico*, COLEF and Plaza and Valdes, Mexico.

Rethinking the US-Mexico Border. 2009. [Online: Woodrow Wilson International Center for Scholars Event]. Available at: http://www.wilsoncenter.org/index.cfm?fuseaction=events.event&event_id=559683

Ribando Seelke, C. 2010. *Mérida Initiative for Mexico and Central America: Funding and Policy Issues* [Online: CSIS, Center for Strategic & International Studies] Available at:http://www.wilsoncenter.org/topics/pubs/M%C3%A9rida%20Initiative%20for%20Mexico%20and%20Central%20America%20Funding%20and%20Policy%20Issues.pdf

Sánchez, R. 2000. Bi-*national Cooperation on Environmental Regulation Enforcement*, paper presented at XIV National Congress, Mexican Association of International Studies-ITESM, 5-7 October, Monterrey, N.L.

Salinas, C. 2004. *Foreign Affairs* in Spanish, "Diez años de TLCAN y el fracaso de Cancún", January-March.

San Diego Association of Governments (SANDAG) and California Department of Transportation (CALTRANS) 2006, *Economic Impacts of Border Wait Times at the San Diego-Baja California Border Region*, Final Report, 19 January.

SEMARNAT and EPA 2003. *Mexico-The United States Environmental Program: Border 2012*, April. Available at: http://www.epa.gov/usmexicoborder/index_esp.htm

SEMARNAT and EPA 2006. *The Environmental Situation in the Border Region 2005*, US-Mexico Border Indicators.

South County Economic Development Council, San Diego Dialogue, Tijuana Trabaja, "Who Crosses the Border-2001", Project Overview. Preliminary Information. October.

SPP 2005. *Report to the Heads of State*. Annex. June.

SPP 2006. *Joint Declaration,* March 2005. *Report to the Heads of State*. Appendix. June.

SPP 2006. *Report to the Heads of State II*, August.

US Department of Transportation and Mexico Secretariat of Communications and Transportation 2004. *Binational Border Transportation Infrastructure: Needs Assessment Study*, July.

US Government. 2002. *Strategy of National Security of the United States,* Available at: http://usinfo.state.gov/espanol/.

Weintraub, S. 2004. *NAFTA's Impact on North America: The First Decade,* CSIS.

Wait times at the borders of Mexico and Canada Available at: http://apps.cbp.gov/bwt/

The White House. 2001. *Joint Statement between the United States of America and the United States of México.* March 22, Monterrey, Mexico.

Whitney, M. 2010. *Obama's Role in the Militarization of Mexico: An Interview with LauraCarlsen* [Online: Americas Program, Center for International Policy (CIP)]. Available at: http://www.globalresearch.ca/index.php?context=va&aid=16654

Who Crosses the Border-2001, Project Overview. Preliminary Information, October.

Wise, C. 2002. *Organizing for Homeland Security,* Public Administration Review; Washington; Mar/Apr, vol. 62, no. 2, 131-144.

WWICS, CMAI and ITAM 2005. *The United States and Mexico: Forging a Strategic Partnership,* Report of the Study Group on US Mexican Relations, Washington, D.C.

Chapter 7

Plan Colombia and the Mérida Initiative: Policy Twins or Distant Cousins?[1]

John Bailey

Introduction

In October 2007 US President George W. Bush and Mexican President Felipe Calderón announced the Mérida Initiative, a joint undertaking to confront growing challenges by organized crime, especially drug-trafficking organizations, to democratic governability in the region.[2] Named after the city where the presidents had met in March 2007 (along with Guatemalan President Oscar Berger-Perdomo), the "Mérida Initiative" (MI) quickly drew comparisons with "Plan Colombia" (PC), which also targeted trafficking-related crime and violence. Labeling it the "Plan Mérida" some critics pointed to flaws in PC, such as undermining of national sovereignty, insufficient attention to socioeconomic development, failure to reduce drug production and trafficking, and inadequate attention to human rights violations, especially by government forces. Proponents of the MI, on the other hand, were quick to emphasize a major difference between PC and the MI (especially that no US military personnel would be stationed on Mexican territory), and some also pointed to successful lessons from PC that might apply to the MI.

As is customary in controversial policy debates, symbolic politics takes center stage. Plan Colombia is reduced to a symbol of US imperialism and human rights oppression, or of international cooperation to resist narco-guerrilla terrorism, depending upon one's point of view. The purpose of this article is to compare and contrast the policies with respect to country contexts, problem profiles, and a series of programmatic features; and to consider "policy learning" and implications for security alliances.

Are PC and the MI policy twins or are they distant cousins? I argue that they are more like half-brothers. As the common partner, the United States emphasizes a supply-oriented, anti-drugs security policy, but Colombia and Mexico are quite

---

1   Revised version of a paper presented at the Institut des Amériques, VI Colloque International, "Politique étrangère dans les Amériques: Entre crises et alliances," Paris, 21-22 Novembre 2008. Daniel Ortega-Nieto lent research assistance; Marc Chernick and Margaret Daly Hayes provided helpful suggestions but bear no responsibility for the result.

2   See Selee 2008, CRS 2008a, and CRS 2009 for detailed descriptions of the Mérida Initiative program components and finance.

different partners. As the older brother, PC is a response to a problem context that differs from Mexico's in important respects. Also, the nations involved have experienced some policy learning since 2000, and US perceptions of its own responsibilities have evolved, at least at the level of discourse. Both PC and the MI are responses to perceived crises, and they produce ad hoc bilateral and sub-regional alliances. The interesting issue is whether the ad hoc responses may evolve into a more coherent regional or multilateral security architecture.

Country Contexts and Policy Characteristics

Some key points about country contexts and policy characteristics are set out in Table 7.1 and can only be summarized here. Mexico is a much bigger policy partner than Colombia. In comparative terms, Mexico is more than twice as populous as Colombia, has over forty percent more land area, more than five times the gross domestic product (GDP), and more than three times the central government budget outlays. Colombia is a unitary system (but with significant decentralization), while Mexico is federal. One of the implications is the much greater complexity of Mexico's police-justice system. Colombia has a national police, closely tied to the army. Mexico relies much more on state and local police forces, with a comparatively small national force. Due to acute, systemic problems of corruption and incompetence in the civilian police-justice system, the Mexican army has been assigned a leading role in anti-drug law enforcement, but the army's role is more improvised than institutionalized. There are two implications to note: First, the Mexican army is among the most closed of national institutions in terms of transparency and accountability; second, it has a long history of an anti-US institutional culture. The leading role of the Mexican army creates a further complication: It reinforces the US tendency to militarize anti-drug security policies. Above all, Mexico shares a 2,000-mile land border with the United States, which–among other things–puts its internal security situation higher on the US policy agenda.

The problem profiles of the two countries also differ in important respects. Violence associated with organized crime is a significant challenge in both countries, but in quite different contexts. If we take 1948 as a point of reference, Colombia entered (more accurately, re-entered) a phase of profound internal war, while Mexico began a long phase of consolidating internal peace based on the hegemonic rule of the Institutional Revolutionary party (PRI). Insurgency forces (especially the Revolutionary Armed Forces of Colombia, Fuerzas Armadas Revolucionarias de Colombia--FARC) have waged a forty-year armed struggle against the Colombian government, with varieties of rightist self-defense forces multiplying and complicating the violence. One estimate suggests that in 2006 the FARC controlled approximately 30 percent of national territory (CRS 2008b: 6). Colombia's primary challenge is to terminate the internal wars.

Table 7.1   Contexts and Characteristics of Plan Colombia and the Mérida
             Initiative

	Plan Colombia	Mérida Initiative
Country context	Population 45 M*; 1.14 M. sq. km.; GDP=US$250B* (2008); GDP/cap=US$5,174; budget expend=US$65B; unitary, with significant decentralization; 32 departments, 1,100 counties	Population 110 M; 1.97 M. sq. km.; GDP=US$1,142B (2008); GDP/cap=US$10,747; budget expend=US$227B; federal, with 32 states, 2,400 counties
Problem profile	Major guerrilla insurgencies; generalized violence; major producer & trafficker of illicit drugs; limited central government presence; corruption in police-justice system	Minor regional rebellion; producer & major trafficker of illicit drugs; rapid upsurge in trafficking violence; localized challenges to government presence; acute corruption in police-justice system
Policy origins	1999-2000; US proactive in policy design	2007-08; US reactive in policy design
Policy scope: goals & countries	Internal security & anti-trafficking; social justice; development. Primary= Colombia; secondary=Peru & Ecuador	Internal security; law enforcement & justice admin.; Primary=Mexico; secondary=Central America & Caribbean
Policy targets	Insurgency (FARC; ELN); self-defense organizations; drug crop eradication; criminal justice system; economic development (e.g., crop substitution)	Counter-drug; counter-terror; border security; public security & law enforcement; institution-building & rule of law
Time commitment	2000-06; succeeded by similar follow-on policies	Fiscal year 2008 through fiscal year 2010, with indications of extension
US financial commitment	US$4.5B; US currently seeks reduced commitment	US$1.3B appropriated for 2007-2010; considerable delays in disbursing funds
US commitments for internal policy	Reduce drug demand	"Genuine partnership"; Reduce drug demand; halt weapons trafficking, precursor chemicals, money laundering

Note: * M = million; B = Billion.

Sources: International Monetary Fund, World Economic Outlook Database, October 2008; CIA World Factbook <https://www.cia.gov>; CRS (2008); GAO (2008); CRS (2010).

In contrast, guerrilla insurgency is not an issue in Mexico. The Zapatistas are a minor regional rebellion, confined mostly to parts of the state of Chiapas on the far southern border with Guatemala. The Ejercito Popular Revolucionario (Popular Revolutionary Army) is a shadowy, largely marginalized group with bases in the State of Guerrero and the Federal District. Mexico's key challenge is a sharp upsurge in criminal violence beginning in about 2005 and escalating in subsequent years.[3] It is associated with drug trafficking in the sense of trans-national smuggling and retail distribution to the rapidly-growing internal drug markets. The confluence of rivers of drug money, trained manpower, and high-power weapons has produced well-organized, politically-effective, hyper-violent trafficking organizations that are capable of challenging the government's police-justice system and the army. While most of the violence is concentrated in perhaps five or six of the 32 states, the trafficking organizations can strike anywhere in the country and almost at will.[4] In comparison, the height of Colombia's drug gang violence was in the late 1980s and early 1990s. Since that time the trafficking organizations have adopted lower-profile, less violent methods. In summary, Colombia is a case of a complicated internal war in which drug production and trafficking play a significant role; Mexico is a case of hyper-violent criminal organizations that use terrorist-like methods to challenge the government and society.

The origins of PC and MI are different. As originally proposed by president Andrés Pastrana (1998-2002), Plan Colombia covered five areas: the peace process, economic growth, anti-drug production and trafficking, reform of justice and protection of human rights, and democracy-promotion and social development. Pastrana sought assistance from the European Union and a number of other countries. Following an internal debate, the US government emphasized the anti-narcotics theme to the point that other countries were reluctant to participate. Pastrana's original logic (shared by various other international actors) was that a negotiated peace could set the stage for economic development, institutional reform, and conditions to reduce drug trafficking. The US government, in contrast, insisted that solving the drug issue would starve the resources to FARC and other insurgency groups and hasten the end to the war. Other themes, such as human rights and the peace process, were secondary (Chernick 2008: 129-137).[5] In all this, the US government played an active–even intrusive–role.

---

3   A major Mexico City daily newspaper reports an escalation of deaths associated with organized crime violence: 2005, 1,537; 2006, 2,221; 2007, 2,673; 2008, 5,630. "'Narcoguerra' alcanzó a civiles," *El Universal* on line (January 1, 2009).

4   Drug gangs have employed numerous terrorist-like tactics such as beheadings and displays of threatening banners on streets and city squares. They have murdered top-level national and state police officials and scores of army personnel, including a retired army general who was about to assume police duties in a town in Quintana Roo. See "Ejecutan a general y escoltas en Cancún," *El Universal* on line (February 4, 2009).

5   A US-based human rights group has reported: "For Planners of US assistance to Colombia, non-military programs have always been an afterthought. Four out of five

With respect to MI, in contrast, the George W. Bush administration made a conspicuous effort not to take the initiative but to respond to Mexico (and subsequently to the Central American and Caribbean countries). This is because, given the long history of intervention (perceived or real), US government initiatives in sensitive areas of public security and law enforcement aroused Mexican nationalist responses that could be fatal to the Initiative. Also, President Calderón's government was more narrowly focused on repressing drug-related criminal violence, a focus that the US government shared.

The resulting policies thus differ in scope and targets. Even in its narrower version, PC included democracy-promotion and institutional development, with more ambitious components of economic development (e.g., crop substitution), and some attention to human rights. The policy targets reflect the US interpretation of the problem context. Originally, PC focused on anti-drug programs. Following September 11, 2001, the US policy shifted to include strong attention to anti-terrorism, with more active support for initiatives against the FARC and self-defense forces. Those targets put more attention on the Colombian army and police and themes of air mobility and operational intelligence. Primary attention in PC went to Colombia, with comparatively minor funding to Ecuador and Peru. Though subject to review by the Barak Obama administration, MI will likely remain more narrowly focused on internal security and institution building in law enforcement and justice administration. The language of anti-narcotics terror can be found in MI documents, and the main targets are trafficking organizations, security along the border, and institution building. Human rights was a sensitive issue because of Mexico's rejection of assistance conditioned on standards imposed by the US government. Although initially focused on Mexico and Central America, MI was subsequently broadened to include Haiti and the Dominican Republic.

With respect to time and money, PC ran from 2000 to 2006, and was followed by a similar set of policies in a PC, Phase II (2006-11). The US government spent about US$4.5 billion through 2006 and $6.1 billion through 2008 (CRS 2008b). The current debate in the US government concerns reducing US support and encouraging greater burden bearing by the Colombian government. As originally announced, US government commitment to the MI runs through 2010, although US officials intimate a longer-term commitment. Set originally in the US$1.5 billion range for 2008-10, US government financial commitment is presently uncertain and subject to debate in the current congress. Given Mexico's much larger economy and public sector budget, the dollar amounts of US assistance will likely be relatively small, which will reduce the leverage that the US government can exercise in Mexican internal policies.

Finally, US commitments for its own internal policy are much greater in the case of MI–at least at the declaratory level–than for PC. US rhetoric calls for a "genuine partnership" with the MI countries. This should be underlined as a significant shift

dollars in US aid goes to Colombia's armed forces, police, and fumigation program" (CIP 2006: 5).

in policy toward much greater engagement in the regional security challenge and a stronger commitment to make internal adjustments to ameliorate conditions that exacerbate insecurity. More specifically, the US government commits itself to reducing drug demand, halting the flows of precursor chemicals and weapons into the region, and addressing problems of bulk cash smuggling and money laundering.

Policy Learning and Alliance Possibilities

Plan Colombia evolved over the first half-decade of the 21st century, while the Mérida Initiative began in December 2008. I argue that important policy learning occurred in PC's implementation. Whether lessons learned will affect MI remains to be seen, but Mexican authorities have shown great interest in the Colombian experience.[6] Also, the priority given to public security in various sub-regions of the Americas is a factor influencing options for various types of alliances. The Inter-American Treaty of Reciprocal Assistance, the so-called Rio Treaty of 1947, is generally regarded as an "institutional zombie" left over from the Cold War, a relic largely irrelevant to 21st-century regional security challenges. MI may become one of several factors shaping new alliance possibilities.

One lesson that Colombians emphasize is the need for a strategic approach to addressing internal violence.[7] We can point to an important shift toward strategic thinking and policy development in PC in about 2003, with president Alvaro Uribe and "Plan Patriota." Gonzalo de Francisco (2006) identifies two distinct phases in drug trafficking in Colombia. In about 1980-93, trafficking was characterized by major cartels that operated with coca base imported mainly from Bolivia and Peru. In the second phase, roughly 1990-2003, coca crops were cultivated on a large scale within Colombia, with cocaine produced and trafficked by smaller, less-confrontational criminal groups. He underlines the lack of a coherent government strategy to confront the guerrillas. "Missing from the public-policy agenda was a comprehensive, ongoing strategy, supported by all institutions and Colombian society itself, which could have impeded the growth of guerrilla forces" (de Francisco 2006: 97). Rather than reacting to guerrilla initiatives in an ad hoc fashion, the Uribe government expanded the size and strengthened the

---

6   In the first days of the Calderón administration, Mexico's Attorney General Eduardo Medina Mora led a high-level delegation to Bogota to consult with President Alvaro Uribe and top Colombian security officials. Medina Mora stated that the purpose of the visit was to "exchange experiences, views, and learn reciprocally about common problems, security problems, about exchange of information about how to better combat organized crime." A high-level contact group begun in 2003 would be reactivated. "México usará experiencia de Colombia en lucha antinarco," *El Universal* on line (January 26, 2007).

7   See, for example, a statement by Colombia's defense minister: "'Recomendable, tener una política integral para combatir al narco': Manuel Santos," *El Universal* on line (November 29, 2006).

operational capacity of the army and police and adopted a harder, more proactive offensive against the insurgent forces.[8] His government also developed a more integrated political-military-development approach, one which carries overtones of US policy in Iraq (clear, hold, consolidate). Thus, the successor policy to Plan Patriota is called Plan Consolidación (GAO 2008: 11-14).

A second, tragic, lesson is that the human rights violations associated with PC were unacceptably high. A coalition of human rights organizations reports that during 2000-08, an estimated 20,000 were killed by paramilitary, guerrilla, and state forces, and more than 2 million persons were displaced. Most of the displaced took shelter in precarious camps around larger cities. Other reports put the number of internally displaced at more than 3 million, with another 500,000 Colombian refugees and asylum seekers outside the country (CRS 2008b: 26). In all, "Colombia continues to face the most serious human rights crisis in the Hemisphere, in a rapidly shifting panorama of violence" (Haugaard 2008: 4). Clearly, effective human rights safeguards are needed for the MI, a point to which I return below.

A third lesson comes from the operational levels in PC. Over time, significant improvements were made in uses of intelligence, air mobility, communications and coordination, and organizational capacity (e.g., police special units) (GAO 2008). Given the expanse and inaccessibility of much of Colombia's territory, air mobility is critical. US General (ret.) Barry R McCaffrey reported: "Make no mistake–the key difference that US financial and military support has made in the past eight years is funding, training, maintaining, and managing a substantial increase (total rotary wing assets 260 aircraft) in the helicopter force available to the Colombian Police, the Army, the Air Force, the counter-drug forces, and the economic development community" (McCaffrey 2007: 5-6). The improved mobility was supplemented by the creation of effective units such as the army's Aviation Brigade and the creation of an army Counternarcotics Brigade and new mobile units in both the army and national police (GAO 2008: 27-30). Early indications are that the MI will give priority to air mobility and to strengthening the capacity of the Center for Research and National Security (CISEN), Mexico's internal intelligence agency.

A fourth lesson concerns the long-standing US emphasis on supply-side strategies to reduce drug production and trafficking. For the US there is a growing awareness that such supply-side, anti-drug approaches are necessarily limited. Most of the rationale for PC from the US perspective was to curtail drug production and trafficking from Colombia. However, the US Congress's independent audit agency

---

8   "[Uribe] voted not to negotiate with any of the armed groups until they declared a cease-fire and disarmed. In addition, Uribe implemented new laws giving the security forces increased power, and instituted a one-time tax to be used to increase the troop strength and capabilities of the Colombian military. He increasingly equated the guerrillas with drug traffickers and terrorists, and initiated a military campaign, called *Plan Patriota*, to recapture guerrilla-controlled territory" (CRS 2006: 3).

reported bluntly: "Plan Colombia's goal of reducing the cultivation, processing, and distribution of illegal narcotics by targeting coca cultivation was not achieved" (GAO 2008: 17). The vast amounts of resources invested in crop eradication and interdiction have little lasting effect on the price and purity of illegal drugs in US markets. This finding should inform the internal political debate as a new administration takes office. The innovation with MI is an explicit commitment to invest more resources in the reduction of demand, but the commitment was not reflected in budget requests submitted by the outgoing Bush administration.

A fifth lesson for the United States is the growing awareness that military forces and approaches have uses and limitations with respect to anti-trafficking operations and that institution building with respect to police and justice administration is a lengthy, expensive challenge. Thus, the MI grants priority to reforming police and justice administration in the participating countries (CRS 2009: 16-19). My sense, however, is that US policy-makers do not grasp the enormity of the problems they confront. There are at least three priority issues. First, new approaches are needed that can combine military, police, intelligence, and socio-economic development capacities in a coherent strategy to deal with heavily armed, mobile, and politically astute trafficking organizations. Second, due largely to the incapacity and corruption of the civilian police, armies necessarily take the lead role in anti-trafficking operations in Mexico and several of the Central American and Caribbean countries. Third, operational intelligence is a key instrument against trafficking organizations, and this capacity is weak to nonexistent in the MI region.

Approaches that combine military, police, intelligence, and socio-economic development capacities might lead to institutional innovation of new types of national and transnational hybrid organizations (highly unlikely) or to much-improved inter-organizational coordination within and among the MI governments (also unlikely).[9] Organizations are profoundly resistant to change. Part of the resistance is cultural: Armies protect national sovereignty against other armies; they prefer not to be treated as internal police forces. Interagency coordination also implies uncertainty and struggles over credit-claiming; thus, part of the resistance is due to competition for scarce resources.

Beyond inter-agency and inter-governmental coordination is the question of forging a regional security strategy. A strategy implies setting priorities among goals over some time period, then translating the goals into tactical operations and linking these to agency tasks and resources. Even a national strategy, as the Colombian government claims, would be a signal accomplishment. Much more

---

9   The US Department of Homeland Security is a testament to the enormous difficulty of coordinating 22 agencies under one roof in one country. That said, the organizational experiment underway at the US Southern Command (Miami, Florida) and its operational task force based in Key West bears close scrutiny. The task force brings together US military, intelligence, and police agencies with those from several Caribbean and out-of-region countries. Southern Command authorities claim a number of successful joint operations against trafficking organizations. (Author interviews, December 2008).

common are official documents that list national goals, or regional operations that target a particular set of problems.

A second set of problems is over-reliance on armies, in good part due to police corruption and incompetence. One issue is that armies are usually not trained for internal policing (Bailey and Dammert 2005). This can lead to ineffectiveness against organized crime or ordinary problems of public security. It can also lead to serious human rights abuses as military methods and weaponry (e.g., highway checkpoints, routine searches, interrogation) are brought to bear against civilian populations. This is especially the case if the military are exempt from civilian justice. Another issue is that reliance on the military can shift from a stop-gap measure to business as usual. This retards innovation by taking pressure off governments to move more aggressively on police-justice reform. Army involvement also can imply the inculcation of military organization and culture in shaping reformed police forces. Prolonged involvement also exposes the military to trafficking-related corruption.

Operational intelligence is the key to acting against organized crime. "Operational" means various types of information that specific government agencies can use to act against criminal organizations or activities. The information can be financial, such as real estate transactions, purchase of luxury vehicles, tax administration, or money laundering. It can relate to the identification and location of a particular person or vehicle, which in turn requires accurate data bases. It often relies on communications intercepts and information provided by paid informants or government agents operating clandestinely. Whatever the type of information, operational intelligence requires organizations that can analyze useful information effectively, communicate the information to the appropriate law enforcement agency in a timely fashion, and protect themselves from penetration by criminal organizations through corruption or infiltration. Ideally, the organizations are accountable to democratic oversight, operating within a functioning legal framework. We lack extensive research on intelligence agencies, but my sense is that they are weak to nonexistent in the MI region. Dammert (FLACSO 2007:111-136) suggests that the Central American and Caribbean countries lag substantially behind Peru and the Southern Cone with respect to professionalism, inter-agency coordination, and democratic oversight. She ranks Guatemala and Costa Rica slightly above the neighboring countries (*Ibid.*: 124).

Mexico is *primus inter pares* in MI's "genuine partnership," and the issues sketched above will present enormous challenges in implementing joint strategies against organized crime. Two leading Mexican jurists sum up their country's institutional situation in especially bleak terms: "Any analysis of the Mexican criminal justice system must start from a certainty: It is so flawed we can say without fear of exaggeration that it is completely bankrupt" (Carbonell and Ochoa Reza 2007: 20).[10] Corruption in the police is comparatively widespread and

---

10   President Calderón has been harshly critical of Mexico's police-justice system as well. "Calderón señala fallas en sistema de seguridad," *El Universal* on line (October 2, 2008).

reaches from the municipal preventive (uniformed) police to the top of key federal forces.[11] Mexico's internal intelligence agency, the CISEN, suffered neglect during the Vicente Fox administration (2000-06) and only recently is getting substantial increases in resources.[12] The Mexican army is overextended and carries much of the battle against organized crime on its own.[13] The government claims to employ a comprehensive strategy against organized crime, but its real strategy appears simpler and more straightforward: use the military to pulverize the trafficking organizations into smaller, less potent gangs so that state and local authorities can reclaim effective control over territory.[14] In sum, the major interlocutor with the United States in the MI suffers severe institutional weaknesses that will require decades to remedy.

The Rio Treaty has become largely irrelevant to contemporary security threats. In what ways might the MI influence longer-term and more institutionalized security alliances in the region? Both PC and the MI reinforce close interaction at the bilateral and sub-regional levels. The interesting question is whether these programs might interact with initiatives already underway, such as the Central America Integration System (SICA), the Caribbean Community (CARICOM), and the Security and Prosperity Partnership of the North American Free Trade Agreement. Apart from these organizations, considerable consultation and interaction exists among countries.[15] Also, the OAS has put public security high on its agenda and is promoting regional consultations.[16] Brazil is taking leadership on security cooperation in South America, although Venezuela has its own agenda. While there is still no clear path toward a regional architecture, the various "bottom-up" activities may generate momentum toward broader regional security alliances.

---

11   See, for example, "Corrupción frena el plan para reestructuar la PFP," *El Universal* on line (January 21, 2009). The Corporación Latinobarómetro (2005), reports that the percentage of those surveyed who respond that they have a lot or some confidence in the police is a regional average of 37 percent. Chile is at the high end with 64 percent, and Mexico is near the low end with 22 percent.

12   See "Duplican el presupuesto para el Cisen," *El Universal* on line (November 14, 2008).

13   As an important symptom, 347,055 soldiers deserted during 1985-2006. For the most part, these were enlisted personnel with only basic training in weapons and tactics, but the numbers included 2,754 officers as well. See "Desertaron 100 mil militares con Fox," *Milenio* July 17, 2007.

14   The formal strategy can be gleaned from PGR (2008).

15   Mexico, Colombia, Guatemala, and Panama recently met to confer on regional anti-crime cooperation. See "Poyectan bloque regional anti-crimen," *El Universal* on line (January 15, 2009). Guatemala, El Salvador, and Honduras border police cooperate to the point of using common uniforms.

16   I was surprised to see the extent of consultations on security issues already underway in Central America and the Caribbean, as reflected in the comments of the participants from those regions in a workshop, "Realizing Mérida's Potential: Strategic Cooperation among Mexico, Central American and Caribbean States, and the United States," held at the Institute for National Strategic Studies, June 26-27, 2008.

Conclusion

The Mérida Initiative demonstrates that corruption and violence related to organized crime have reached a critical level in the Caribbean Basin countries, and that the United States is beginning to redefine the problem from one of law enforcement to that of a significant threat to democratic governability in the region. In using the language of "genuine partnership," pledging substantial resources, and committing itself to important domestic policy adjustments to help ameliorate insecurity in the region, the MI may represent a significant change. The obvious caveat is that the initiative appeared relatively late in the George W. Bush administration, the responses to date are largely at the rhetorical level, and the Barak Obama administration has yet to define its policies toward the region.

Though it might be misplaced optimism, my sense is that the past decade has brought about policy learning with respect to more effective ways to confront the violence and corruption associated with organized crime. The learning will be especially useful because the challenges presented especially by drug-trafficking organizations have grown more ominous at the same time that police-justice-social development institutional infrastructure has deteriorated in much of the region.

References

Bailey, J. and Dammert, L. 2005. Reforma policial y participación militar en el combate a la delincuencia. Análisis y desafíos para América Latina. *Revista Fuerzas Armadas y Sociedad*, 19:1 enero-junio, 2005, 133-152.

Carbonell, M. and Ochoa Reza, Enrique. 2007. The Direction of Criminal Justice Reform in Mexico. *Voices of Mexico*, (81), Sept.-Dec., 20-24.

CIP—Center for International Policy. 2006. "Plan Colombia-Six Year Later". Washington, D.C.: November.

Chernick, M. 2008. *Acuerdo possible: Solución negociada al conflicto armado colombiano*. Bogota: Ediciones Aurora.

CIA—Central Intelligence Agency, *World Factbook* https://www.cia.gov [accessed 15 November 2008.]

Corporación Latinobarómetro. 2005. *Informe latinobarómetro* available at: http://www.observatorioelectoral.org/documentos/data/info-latinba-2005.pdf.

CRS, 2006--Congressional Research Service, *Plan Colombia: A Progress Report*, CRS Report for Congress RL32774, 11 January.

CRS, 2008a–Congressional Research Service, *Merida Initiative: US Anticrime and Counterdrug Assistance for Mexico and Central America*, CRS Report for Congress RL32250, 7 July.

CRS, 2008b–Congressional Research Service, *Colombia: Issues for Congress*, CRS Report for Congress RL32250, 12 September.

CRS, 2009–Congressional Research Service, *Mérida Initiative for Mexico and Central America: Funding and Policy Issues* R40135, 13 January.

CRS, 2010—Congressional Research Service, *Mérida Initiative for Mexico and Central America: Funding and Policy Issues* R40135, 21 January.

Dammert, L. 2007. *Reporte del sector seguridad en América Latina y el Caribe* Santiago, Chile: FLACSO.

GAO, 2008—United States Government Accountability Office, *Plan Colombia: Drug Reduction Goals Were Not Fully Met, but Security has Improved; US Agencies Need More Detailed Plans for Reducing Assistance.* GAO-09-71; October.

de Francisco Z, G. 2006. "Armed Conflict and Public Security in Colombia," in *Public Security and Police Reform in the Americas,* edited by Bailey, J and Dammert, L. Pittsburgh, PA: University of Pittsburgh Press: 94-110.

Haugaard, L., et al. 2008. *A Compass for Colombia Policy* Washington, D.C., October.

McCaffrrey, B. R. 2007. "Memorandum for: Colonel Mike Meese, United States Military Academy," 3 October.

Selee, A. 2008. *Overview of the Merida Initiative* Washington, D.C.: Woodrow Wilson International Center for Scholars, May; available at: http://www.wilsoncenter.org/news/docs/Analysis.Merida%20Initiative%20May%208%202 02008.pdf [accessed 10 November 2008.]

Olson, E. 2008. *Six Key Issues in US-Mexico Security Cooperation* (unpublished paper, available at: http://www.wilsoncenter.org/news/docs/Olson%20Brief. pdf [accessed12 November 2008].

PGR—Procuraduría General de la República. 2008. "Lineaminetos del nuevo modelo de política mexicana contra la delincuencia organizada". (Febuary).

Chapter 8

Overcoming the Perceived Objections and Actual Obstacles to a North American Continental Common Transborder Security (NACTS)

D. Rick Van Schoik

"Typically human creation: It is physically invisible, geographically illogical, militarily indefensible, and emotionally inescapable. An interval of resonance... an interface... an irritation...charged with intensities." Marshall McLuhan in Borderline Case, 1977

"Air defense plan inspired by 9/11 gets 2nd look: Terror threat at issue. Costly program raises question of priorities during two wars." Thom Shanker and Eric Schmitt, Headline in New York Times, November 20, 2009

Introduction

As described by Canadian McLuhan above, Borders and their defense, have always complicated international relations. While the European Union was prompted by security and defense concerns to blur its borders in the half century following World War II, it is unclear exactly what direction North America is moving toward in the 21st century. Prior to September 11th, serious talks were underway to promote the idea of an external or common perimeter, a continental defense, a zone of tranquility or confidence, a common security within North America (herein called an external perimeter which promotes a North American Continental Common Transborder Security – NACTS). Movement by sectors of civil society and several government agencies tended to create the sense that a *de facto* external perimeter was being constructed. Headlines like the one from the *New York Times* serve to raise the question of what the relative costs and benefits are and what approach nations might take to pursue such a common security. These questions are explored in this paper.

The strategic concept of an external perimeter is founded in a knowledge-based society and a public good, in a desire by some to extend some forces of sovereignty outside borders in the notion of the advantage of a continental common enemy and shared security assets, and in the desire of both bordering countries of the United States to overcome being less secure due to their proximity to a target nation and a drug consuming nation. It is a strategic concept idealizing the exchange of intelligence, technology, and law enforcement to screen and inspect goods and people for mutual assured security. See Brunet-Jailly (2002 and 2007), Century Fund (2002), Council for Foreign Relations (2005), Herzog (1992), Jimenez (2004), Pastor (2008) and Rudolph (2005) for general discussion of North American security as a concept.

Transborder policy scholars have universally discovered disconnections between serious local security concerns and the centralized power decisions made elsewhere in national capitals. The two scales, perspectives, and orientations (a line in the sand versus a continent) intersect in interesting ways in the context of the external perimeter. This paper examines the concept of the continental external perimeter, looks at a handful of obstacles, and outlines a road map to a common security.

Historical Background

It is ironic that the common external threat of the Nazis in World War II that led to a special relationship between the United States and Canada for the purpose of joint wartime manufacturing, and that eventually spread to Mexico and concluded in a free trade agreement, also extended to a common defense and security stances, and then a new common threat early in the 21st century (global extremist terrorism) reversed that half century of cooperation.

In our lifetimes, the momentous events in the history for borders have been facilitating NAFTA, the thickening and tightening of the border in response to September 11th, and the latest chapters now, pending transborder and international responses to the financial meltdown, the recession, and the narcoinsurgency.

NAFTA did not so much change border dynamics as it confirmed the role of North American borders as enablers and facilitators of the trade trends that were occurring anyway. Border operations were attempting to respond to the need to move more people, raw product and produce, and finished assembled goods across the border. Transportation routes were envisioned to facilitate NAFTA trade within the continent, and to some extent other continents, to ensure North America remained the most productive and competitive trading bloc in and with the world by planning trucking, sea, air, and rail ports.

For the past fifteen years people have questioned the extent of positive change and prosperity NAFTA has brought versus the local borderland costs and impact to some industries. The borderlands, as the entry point, welcoming location, and "door mat" of NAFTA, suffered for whatever gains the three nations enjoyed.

The response to September 11th slowed and in some cases reversed much of the progress made in the first decade of NAFTA. At many academic conferences on borders as early as 2007 the terms "thicker", "stickier", and "denser" were often used to describe the reaction to September 11th.

In 2009 the above factors, confounded by the current mega-global recession and the latest threat to security - spillover of drug-associated violence - prompts nations to rethink the unnecessary tightening of the border operations, to rededicate funds and personnel away from fences back to the ports of entry, to reduce the transactional costs of borders, to make North America competitive worldwide again, to cooperate on transboundary environmental, energy, and ecological issues, and to enhance the regional collective security by moving the border operations even farther away from the geographic border and making them the last line of defense instead of the first.

Framework for Discussion

The organizing central frame of this paper is that "telescoping" up from borderlands at the local scale through the sovereign national concern through the North American regional/continental orientation to the global perspective with the lens on transborder risk assessment that enables not only more efficient border operations (i.e. less transborder transactional costs) but also enhanced regional and national security. The main argument of this article is that there is no understanding of the common threats and vulnerabilities that North America has or of the probability, exposed populations, and possible results and consequences of those risks.

Transborder security concerns range from mundane customs, vehicle safety, pathogen, agricultural, and endangered species checks and inspections to human labor and skill mobility, immigration and citizenship, and refugee sanctuary processing and to searches for illicit materials, drugs, and contraband, and finally to prevention of terrorism, weapons, bioterrorism, and other "1% solution" entry.

Risk: Perceived Versus Actual

Threat or perceived threat is not risk, but the reality is that perceived threats must be dealt with. Even though origins of risk perceptions stretch back centuries, they are as real today as in the past. To move forward we must accommodate or at least recognize the legacy perceptions and historic memory as a crucial context for negotiation.

Perceptions run deep and long. As an example, Mexico's doubts about the United States go back to the days of the Republic of Texas and war between the two nations. Those tensions result today in a refusal to allow law enforcement officers to carry arms in Mexico and a refusal to join the US in any military command (i.e. North or South Command). Things have thawed only recently. The most dynamic change was the overthrow of the PRI by the PAN almost a decade ago, with which many anti-US suspicions were thrown out as well.

This paper will identify, classify, and analyze perceived objections and actual obstacles in order to derive an objective vision of such a North American

Continental Common Transborder Security (NACTS) by examining historical and current movement towards NACTS by such diverse and important players as: North Command/North American Aerospace Defense Command (NORAD), the environmental community, NAFTA, Security and Prosperity Partnership (SPP) and its current form in 2009, the North American Leaders Summit (NALS), and others (such as the Mérida Initiative), in an attempt to lay out a roadmap to a more cooperative continental common security.

Past inquiry by the author has delved to some degree into the actual obstacles and objections to NACTS, but even more so into the perceived (and no less unreal) challenges. The actual or perceptual risks include a range of arguments primarily about three concerns: sovereignty, asymmetry in the three nations' readiness to assume a continental defense stance, and a range of regulatory factors related to customs, immigration, and refugees.

Concerns about sovereignty are more perceptual than actual but are not to be discounted. Those high in political life, who know they would risk the most if they were wrong, support this idea. Past Canadian Deputy Prime Minister John Manley saw the problems as one of "definitions", and more recently US Ambassador John Negroponte expressed the "pooling of laws" not as a problem but as a solution to the quagmire of regulations we have today. Sidney Weintraub cites the European Union retention of sovereignty even in their merging. "How attributes of sovereignty are defined" may end in a "sharing of sovereignty," he claims (2004). As recently as the last North American Forum in October 2009, ex-secretary of US Department of Homeland Security (DHS) Tom Ridge and past Canadian Deputy Prime Minister and the first Canadian Public Security Minister Anne Mclellan have seconded the notion of a common perimeter over any sovereign concerns.

Though many doubt the ability of the Mexican defense to grow into a continental role, the US Coast Guard (USCG) has recently complimented the Mexican navy for its ability to integrate with USCG and US Navy (at least in the relatively borderless maritime realm). Admiral Stavridis as South Command commander tried to integrate Mexico as part of a larger diplomatic relationship until the militarization of the border and the drug war raised tensions again.

Most of the concerns about the perils of integration are within the US federal government and Departments of Defense, where movement is slow. For example, misalignment among federal departments (i.e. the Department of State has a North America desk while the Department of Defense has a Northern Command and a Southern Command, neither of which integrates Mexico completely into its planning) threatens to stall movement.

The recommendation that Mexico, as the largest nation that does not send troops to the UN peacekeeping forces, do so, might have the beneficial side effect of thawing perceptions of Mexico and providing a "ball field" elsewhere for them to begin to relate to the US military power structure.

Though seemingly less important than sovereignty and security, harmonization of national regulations, customs rules, and even rules of origin standards are especially sticky wickets. Recent proposals by the Canadian Blueprint for US

Engagement called mutual recognition (for example in the case of pharmaceuticals) might move us to a common appreciation of how much we have to gain and how little is risked in such talks. Such mutual recognition agreements are necessary to move to discussions of a common external tariff or a customs union.

Rationale for a Common Perimeter Security

Arguments about the need for movement towards a common perimeter are derived from several arguments. Functionalism or utilitarianism theory would reduce the transactional border costs. Transactional costs are estimated as high as 3 to 5 percent just for rules of origin by Rolf Mirus and calculated similarly as high by private industry in the actual costs of compliance with CT-PAT. Alcatel in Nogales, Sonora, Mexico, which flies its product deliveries out of the Tucson airport, reported that the company loses an estimated 3 percent of gross revenue to their cost of compliance with border security operations as part of their investment in the trusted shipper system (Harris 2008). The company says that the benefit of assured border crossing times is worth the investment. Compliance with drug-free shipments accounts for a growing component of cost of compliance with increased border security operations.

Mary Brooks in her review (2008) cites a series of studies related to economic losses due to border thickening. First she recognizes that the closed border on 9/11 did idle some automobile plants that until then depended on just-in-time deliveries.

STUDY	FINDING
Small	Trucks experience a $144 to $192 cost per hour of delay
Trickey	The border presents a 6% increase in cost of a manufactured good
Belzer	Delays at Ambassador Bridge costs trucks between $135 and $180M
Belzer et.al.	Budgeting for delays nationally costs trucks between $37 and $47M
Taylor	Uncertainty accounted for 2.7% increase in costs
Taylor et. Al.	Delays cost between $2.52 and $5.27B or about 1% of total trade
OCC	Total cost to Canada from systemic delays was $13.6B
DAMF	Total impact from truck delays was between $170 and $406M

The counterproductive conundrum cites border tightening as having an illogical, unintended, and ironic opposite effect. For example, the increased price of human trafficking *coyotes* and the increased cost of interdicting them are cause and effect spirals. Neighbors call for the blunting of US bullying and Bush Doctrine solidarity behind "Fortress America" and even for heightened competition for resources and access to strategic assets. The new shipping routes through the Canadian Arctic present themselves under global climate change scenarios.

Basis for Moving Forward

The idea of a common perimeter and shared security is more palpable and sought after by the borderlands that bear the cost of borders (congestion, security infrastructure and activities, transactional costs, and bisected eco-, hydro- and other systems). The common external perimeter therefore will be conceptualized and motivated by those in the periphery who have bottom-up and stakeholder concerns versus the nationalistic top-down view inside the government beltways that is often overly sovereignty- and security-oriented. The borderlands also can conceive of harmonizing internal borders and national rules to get to a state where an external perimeter is possible.

The matrix below shows contexts and roles of borders, from the local to the continental, as a frame for addressing and eventually overcoming concerns. Each subsequent larger scale or level will need to address concerns a level below it. The matrix is intended as a frame for the discussions of the facets of the arguments necessary to move to a NACTS.

SCALE	CONCERNS	CONTEXT	BORDER ROLE
Local	Environment, commerce, family, geography	Parochial, borderlands, metroplexes,	Ports of entry, customs, and other inspections *
National	Sovereignty, homeland security	US-Mexico, US-Canada, and Canada-Mexico relations	Fences and walls often into the wilds
Continental	Defense against terrorism, narco-violence, organized crime, and regular threats	From 3 bilaterals to 1 trilateral and a couple of intercontinental	NACTS
Global	Ultimate human security	Multinational international relations	Not applicable

* Inspections for illicit material, undocumented migrants, weapons, drugs, pathogens, hazardous materials, rare species, etc.

Don Alper says "We're all local somewhere" and suggests a building blocks metaphor with split-level/scale stakeholders at local and regional scales who hold real interests highest and who can advocate for real collaboration and for moving the actual border operations more offshore. He cites local and regional informal or irregular mechanisms and institutions such as the enhanced drivers licenses used by 116,000 people who move between Washington state and the province of British Columbia, Integrated Border Enforcement Teams (IBETS), native nation ID cards and other local successes. He contends the federal governments by default must favor the formal national posturing and positioning politics of past. Thickened collaboration to offset the thickened security starts locally. He goes on to say, "Real security is built on a foundation of true secure operations as witnessed on the ground" that is at borderland and ports of entry not in national capitols. (Cite quote)

How to Move the Agenda from Local to National and Eventually to Continental

The items below outline policy initiatives intended to map the road, design the vehicle, or actually begin to drive down the avenue towards a NACTS. The policy options are in no particular order. Taken together, they portray the advantages of and means to achieve a broader, longer-lasting or sustainable security.

Joint Risk Assessment and Management

Threat assessments enable moving the focus of defense vigilance and security operations from the internal continental borders to the external perimeter by showing that the three nations are exposed to common external threats and have similar vulnerabilities. As they tune their entry screening to the demands of the other two nations they complement mutual security. Vulnerability assessments enable comprehensive looks at the range of exposures and weaknesses in resistances and resiliencies.

Comprehensive Migration Reform in the US

Progress anticipated in 2010 to reform US immigration policies, to make Canadian refugee policy more transparent, and to gain control of the narco-insurgency in Mexico will make joint risk assessment based on more actual and less perceived threats and vulnerabilities possible.

P2R2 Becomes P3R3

The current DHS motto of prevent, prepare, respond, and recover (P2R2) can be expanded to include planning (the third P) with neighbors and building a common resilience (the third R). The capacity to react, respond to, and recover from any one of myriad catastrophes (storms, bioterrorism, pandemics, and droughts) enhances interoperability of response to any and even all incidents. The electrical blackout that devastated the Great Lakes area could have prompted a range of positive responses on the southern border. DHS underfunding of hazardous materials inspections and training only increases the likelihood of an event and then an ineffective or inadequate response to it. Thankfully one of the strongest trilateral readiness responses to come out of the SPP is the three nations' cooperation in anticipation of an influenza pandemic.

Long-term Planning

Coordinated increments toward an envisioned goal is only possible with concerted, continual efforts, and those are made possible only by long-range planning on joint challenges. For example, the apparent inability of the three transportation secretaries ordepartments to articulate a North American transportation scheme has been disappointing and stands as symptomatic of a reluctance to bite off the big idea and benefit from it.

Joint Border Management Authority and Facilities

The election in the United States prompted a number of recommendations from scholars, advocates, NGOs, and think tanks. One of the recurring themes relative to the border has been the idea of a Joint Border Management Authority. What has been missing is the detail of how it derives its authority and how it operates. One option is subsuming it under the authority of, and therefore deriving its power from, the US DHS (which is likely to retain its *de facto* title of border czar). Joint booths with combined operations exist at Sweet Grass, Montana and Stewart, Alaska.

Move the Border from the Border

The new US administration seizes the opportunity of to suggest venues, mechanisms, and institutions for developing NACTS. One approach is to "widen" and "unglue" the myriad activities that can occur away from the borders through use of technology (CyberPorts) and intelligence (farm or factory certifications) to make them less thick, sticky, and dense.

Build upon Success of PJBD, US North and South Commands

"The Permanent Joint Board on Defense was established by Canada and the United States on August 17, 1940 by joint announcement of President Franklin D. Roosevelt and Prime Minister William Lyon Mackenzie King at Ogdensburg, New York as the senior advisory body on continental military defense of North America. The board consists of both Canadian and American military and civilian representatives. The main purpose of the group is to provide policy-level consultation on bilateral defense matters. Periodically the board conducts studies and reports to the governments of the United States and Canada. The board, which is co-chaired by a Canadian and an American, meets semi-annually, alternating between either country." (Wikipedia).

The US Coast Guard-enforced 1000-mile Long Range Identify and Track (LRIT) systems for ships at sea and the NORAD for air and space creates a three dimensional entry-alert system. The figure below illustrates the LRIT system distances from the United States as one conceptualization of what an external perimeter might look like.

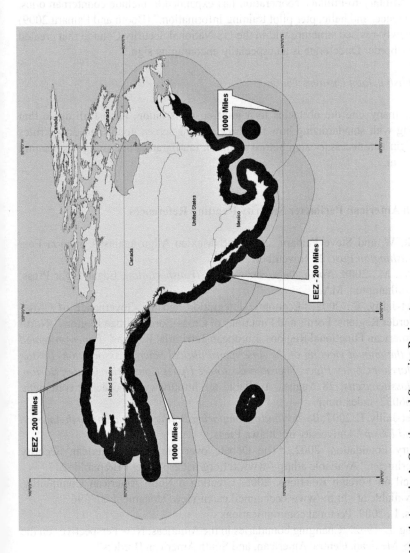

Figure 8.1   North America's Continental Security Perimeter

Share Intelligence and Technology

Mexico is more of a security user than producer. "But now, for the first time, the US and Mexico armed forces regularly exchange classified information in real time. Military-to-military cooperation has expanded to include counternarcotics, intelligence, and helicopter pilot training information." (Booth and Fainaru 2009) The newly-revised structure within the US National Security Council that created a Transborder Directorate is an especially encouraging sign.

Establish a Joint Customs Union

While many cite the obstacles to a joint customs union, almost all agree that starting with standardizing how the three nations screen goods and define rules of origin is a necessary step before common immigration and refugee screening can occur.

North American Perimeter Security Reading References

Booth, W. and Steve Fainaru. 2009. US Mexico Align against Common Foe. *Washington Post*, 22 November.

Brooks, M.. 2008. *North American Freight Transportation*. Edgar Elgar Press. Northampton, MA.

Brunet-Jailly, E.. 2002. "Economic Integration and the Governance of Cross-Border Regions: Forms and Functions of Cross-Border Urban Regions - North American Functional Regions, European Territorial Regions" *Paper presented at the annual meeting of the American Political Science Association, Boston Marriott Copley Place, Sheraton Boston & Hynes Convention Center, Boston, Massachusetts*, 28 August. Available at http://www.allacademic.com/meta/p66032_index.html

Brunet-Jailly, E. 2007. *Borderlands: Comparing Border Security in North America and Europe*. University of Ottawa Press.

Century Foundation. 2002. "The Debate over the North American Security Perimeter." Available athttp://www.tcf.org/list.asp?type=PB&pubid=277

Council on Foreign Relations. 2005. Creating a North American Community. Available at <http://www.ceocouncil.ca/en/view/?document_id=396

Harris, L. 2009. Personal communications.

Herzog, L. 1992. "Changing boundaries in the Americas: New Perspectives on the US-Mexican, Central American, and South American Borders"

Hristoulas, A. 2004. "Explaining Divergence in Foreign Policy: Canada, Mexico and North American Security" Paper presented at the annual meeting of the International Studies Association, Le Centre Sheraton Hotel, Montreal, Quebec, Canada, 17 March Available at http://www.allacademic.com/meta/p72784_index.html

Jimenez, J. 2004. "North American Security Perimeter and its Implications for North American Community". Paper presented at the annual meeting of the International Studies Association, Le Centre Sheraton Hotel, Montreal, Quebec, Canada. 17 March 17. Available at
http://www.allacademic.com//meta/p_mla_apa_research_citation/0/7/3/8/7/ pages73870/p73870-1.php
Negroponte, J. 2008. Remarks at the Fourth North American Forum. Available at <http://www.state.gov/s/d/2008/105999.htm>
Pastor, R.. 2008. *A North American Community Approach to Security.* Available at http://www.cfr.org/publication/8173/north_american_community_approach_ to_security.html
Rudolph, C. 2005. "International Migration and Homeland Security". Paper presented at the annual meeting of the International Studies Association, Hilton Hawaiian Village, Honolulu, Hawaii,. 5 March <http://www.allacademic.com/ meta/p69371_index.html>
Weintraub, S.. 2004. North American Integration: Migration, Trade, and Security: Big Issues Come in Combinations". Availabe at http://209.85.173.104/ search?q=cache:N9062wNXi0sJ:www.irpp.org/events/archive/apr04/ weintraub.pdf+north+american+perimeter+security&hl=en&ct=clnk&cd=4& gl=us&client=firefox-a

Jimenez, L. 2001. "North American Security Perimeter and its Implications for North American Community." Paper presented at the annual meeting of the International Studies Association, Le Centre Sheraton Hotel Montreal, Quebec, Canada, 17 March 17. Available at http://www.allacademic.com/meta/p_mla_apa_research_citation/0/7/8/7/pages75470p75470-1.php

Newcombe, T. 2008. Remarks at the North American Forum. Available at http://www.state.gov/s/d/2008/05999.htm

Pastor, R. 2008. A North American Community Approach to Security. Available at http://www.cfr.org/publication/8175/north_american_community_approach_to_security.html

Rudolph, C. 2005. International Migration and Homeland Security. Paper presented at the annual meeting of the International Studies Association, Hilton Hawaiian Village, Honolulu, Hawaii, 5 March. http://www.allacademic.com/meta/p69271_index.html

Weintraub, S. 2004. North American Integration, Migration, Trade, and Security. Big Issues "core Implications". Available at http://209.85.173.104/search?q=cache:Nj0AZ6MXj05J:www.frbsf.org/events/maili.../weintraub_north+american+perimeter+security&hl=en&ct=clnk&cd=1&gl=us&client=firefox-a

Chapter 9

Globalization and Regionalization in North America: Security and Prosperity. Is There a Place for Latin America in the US Geopolitical Picture?

José Luis Valdés Ugalde with Bernadette Vega

Introduction

The current US security strategy contains several relevant elements, and some of them are new. At the inter-American level, the most important issue is whether security will override indefinitely other important issues of US-Latin American relations. The end of the Cold War radically changed the global panorama and gave rise to the emergence of new actors and issues on the international agenda that are currently challenging the scenario of the world order. Terrorism, drug trafficking, and the fight against organized crime are some of the big problems to be tackled. September 11 produced a rigorous review of US security doctrine, giving rise to preemptive action and homeland security, which demonstrate how the United States concentrated on implementing unilateral policies by adopting a strategy towards guaranteeing security *"vis-à-vis* everyone and despite everyone." (Curzio 2007) The future of Latin America in US national security plans, at least in the short term, was relegated to a back burner, just as multilateralism became the mechanism *par excellence* for solving conflicts in the international arena. In the eight years of the George W. Bush presidency, the United States returned to a vertical unilateralism, with extraordinary implications for international security. The US also relatively abandoned some of the regions allegedly of importance, such as Latin America.

Latin America: A National Security Priority?

The relationship between the United States and Latin America plummeted to its lowest point during the administration of George W. Bush. US reaction to the terrorist attacks in New York and Washington was exclusionary, a fact that deepened the distance from a region that did not share its anti-terrorist obsession. The distance between the two Americas was determined by the fact that the US set foreign policy priorities based on immediate considerations and the return to "hard power": military solutions as the way to reposition the United States at a time when it was going through a crisis of hegemony, intensified by the president's obsessive and dogmatic foreign and national security policies. That particular moment favored the plans of the neo-conservative elite which, in the opinion of George Soros, used the terrorist threat as a cover for laying out a foreign policy already designed by the George W. Bush White House (Curzio 2007) .

In the National Security Strategy designed in 2002 as the official response to the September 11 attacks, Latin America would theoretically fit into each of the lines of action (The White House 2002). However, its strategic importance is only mentioned in two sections: the chapter dealing with defusing regional conflicts and the chapter that talks about the new era of global economic growth. The former proposes the formation of "flexible coalitions" with countries such as Mexico, Brazil, Chile, and Colombia, with which the United States identifies shared risks particularly in the priorities involving the fight against activities related to or derived from drug trafficking and extremist groups in Colombia. In the second chapter, the framers attempted to dredge up and make a priority of the dubious proposal to create the Free Trade Area of the Americas (FTAA) planned for 2005 and discussed at the Mar del Plata summit. Part of this proposal is the importance of signing free trade agreements with Chile and Central America and the need to resolve trade disputes with Mexico and the European Union. The hemisphere as a whole is also included in the energy issue, and a very specific proposal is made about implementing a program equivalent to The African Growth and Opportunity Act for the Caribbean basin.[1]

The Bush administration's heightened disinterest in the region has its most immediate precedent in the conservative philosophy that dominated all White House policies at that time. This philosophy is very well expressed in the Project for the New American Century, a think tank founded in 1997 by Robert Kagan and William Kristol.[2] The central question around which this initiative developed was whether the United States had the capability to mold the new century in favor of Washington's principles and interests; it also openly recognized that the country would be in danger if it did not meet the challenge of exercising global leadership.

---

1   The African Growth and Opportunity Act was signed May 18, 2000, and offers tangible initiatives to facilitate the continued efforts of African countries to open their economies and build free markets.

2   The Project for the New American Century was an initiative of the US neoconservatives who were disgusted by the politics of the administration of President Bill Clinton. Among its main proponents are Donald Rumsfeld, Paul Wolfowitz, Dick Cheney, and I. Lewis Lobby, key figures in the Bush administration. Project for the New American Century, Statement of Principles, on line at http://www.newamericancentury.org/statementofprinciples.htm.

This document, both a faithful and an enthusiastic reflection of neoconservative discourse, openly proposed the recovering of the principles that made the Reagan administration successful: a strong military, ready to face any challenge, a foreign policy that boldly promotes US principles, and a national leadership that would accept the US global responsibilities. George W. Bush's policies reflected the needs manifested in this initiative: an increased defense budget, stronger ties with the allies and the condemnation of regimes hostile to US interests and values, the promotion of the cause of political and economic freedom abroad, and the acceptance of the unique role of the United States and responsibility for preserving and spreading an international order friendly to US security, prosperity, and principles.

All this leads to the conclusion that Latin America was simply not included as one of the highest priority regions for several reasons, because it was not a fertile breeding ground for terrorist cells that threaten US national security, because it continues to be thought of as "the back yard of the United States" and does not represent a major serious national security crisis, because specific issues of interest can be more easily handled piecemeal, or because the supremacy of hard power relegates to the back burner issues that can be dealt with by non-military means. The fact is that, despite the discourse, Latin America was pushed down to second or third place on Bush's strategic long-term foreign policy agenda.

Indifference or Self-Interest

The distancing between the Colossus of the North and the rest of the southern region was not only the result of the 9/11 terrorist attacks; it had already insinuated itself into President Bush's plans when he occupied the White House. Nevertheless, his administration began a war against terrorism and at the same time underestimated the importance of its neighboring prime zone towards securing and ensuring territorial security in such a geopolitically essential spot. By putting such a high priority on terrorism, the United States neglected other issues that were also very important in the sphere of hemispheric security.

The return of the Republicans to the presidency in 2001 and the domination of right-wing extremism fixed the presidential sights on recovering military strength in other strategic regions. Once the Cold War was over, Latin America was no longer a region in dispute ideologically, and the nature of its political systems did not seem to be at high risk. The relationship was based on US bail-outs when localized crises broke out, such as the financial bail-outs in the 1980s and 1990s, but not on seeking greater proximity or a profound commitment. While the abandonment was already evident, the 9/11 terrorist attacks were the catalyst for distancing Latin America far from the foreign policy priorities of the White House. This was partially brought on by Latin America's tardy show of support after the attacks and the energetic rejection of the Iraq invasion by some important countries in the region such as Argentina, Brazil, Cuba, Venezuela, Chile, Mexico, and Peru.

The relationship between the two Americas at the time can best be described as a string of missed opportunities, in the sense that the United States forgot its promise of making its relationship with Latin America a priority, and issues that are *de facto* related to each other, such as migration, drug trafficking, and security have been fragmented. This is why in the very design of a monothematic foreign policy agenda–terrorism–a project of regional integration that included common prosperity as its most important boon was irrationally postponed, conditioning it to advances in democracy and security.

Because the two Americas share values, interests, and common goals, since the idea of "Western Hemisphere" was conceived different perspectives have been proposed for interpreting relations between the United States and Latin America (Russell 2006). Nevertheless, more than representing the web of relationships between the two Americas, this concept reflects the geopolitical worldview of the United States in its area of influence.

> [...] the term *Western Hemisphere* is linked to the archetypal geopolitical notion
> prevalent in the United States whereby the Western tradition (and/or the "*American*"
> version of it) had to have conditions for settling itself within a geographical piece
> of the American map. I argue that this term is a *territorial extension* (and an
> ontological representation) of the US conviction that the "American creed" and
> thereafter, the "American way," were the philosophical pillars of its conception
> of civilisation (i.e., the Monroe Doctrine's motto: "America for the Americans,"
> and the subsequent irrational imposition of the rules of containment and retaliation
> upon Latin Americans) (Valdés-Ugalde 2004: 200).

The concepts of "inter-American community" and "pan-Americanism" used during the Kennedy and Nixon administrations to support their respective foreign policies flow from this vision. However, their relevance in the twenty-first century is questionable, particularly since the end of the Cold War, when US and global foreign policies have changed their battlefronts and fundamental priorities, and the democracies in Latin America have taken alternate paths. In addition to the "Idea of the Western Hemisphere," Roberto Russell (2006) recognizes three other visions: that of the "growing irrelevance of Latin America," that of the "imperialist will and practice," and that of the "decline of US hegemony" in Latin America, particularly in South America. There are specific cases that could validate each of these focuses but at the same time reveal that they are materialized in a subtler rather than categorical way.

For example, the distancing suggested here is not an argument in favor of the focus on the region's irrelevance, given that there is a substantial difference between being not very important and being a secondary priority among the issues on the US security agenda. In this regard, Russell says: "The fact that other countries or regions of the world are at the center of Washington's radar does not make Latin America unimportant (Russell 2006)." Latin American migration to the north is undoubtedly relevant as an issue of *intermestic*[3] policy, particularly in the scheme of border security, just as the need to ensure regional trade flows is. But its exclusion or inclusion in an overall security strategy only shows the clumsiness, convenient omission, or best choice of decision-makers in Washington.

With a reductionist reading, energy alliances could shore up the theory of the *imperialist will and practice*. It is true that the region has been the stage for imperialist clashes and unbridled pragmatism, but it would be risky to suggest that every US move toward the south has been absolutely perverse. It is true that economic pressure, interventions, and a deepening of asymmetries have existed. But this kind of uni-directionality on Washington's part and generalized sustained Latin American docility do not jibe with the complexity of national and regional dynamics. Oil trade with Venezuela, on the one hand, and the differences with the Chávez regime, on the other, may be cynically convenient, but they respond to a legitimate national security need, guaranteeing energy supply. Juan Carlos Mendoza Sánchez says it very well: the Americans' perception of the world as seen through the eyes of a great power necessarily passes through the prism of *real politik* (Mendoza Sánchez 2003).

Finally, there is a *crisis of hegemony*, but in an international system just as convulsed: While 9/11 served as a catalyst for the crisis and the superpower's foreign policy turn, it deepened into growing anti-US sentiment, the strengthening of both state and non-state spheres of power, and the diversification of foreign policy issues very often overlapping with domestic ones. The decline in hegemony may well be happening, but it is also probable that it is really a dip in US hegemony as a result of the evolution of the international system, exacerbated by a series of specific, unfortunate presidential decisions like those previously mentioned.

US National Security vs. Hemispheric Security

The discussion of how Latin America fits into the national security and hemispheric security paradigm needs to be dealt with. Why has there not been a significant effort to integrate the hemisphere with regard to security? Is the United States really interested in getting involved in a hemisphere-wide security effort? Regardless of the focus used to analyze relations and of the conflict between security paradigms–national or hemispheric–the underlying factor derived from the traditionally paradigmatic US hegemony has been Washington's reticence to accept reciprocity in its foreign relations. The disinterest and lack of thoughtfulness in Bush's Latin American policy were part of the big puzzle whose central pieces are the absence of understanding, sensitivity, and mutual knowledge. It is a proximity unresolved on both sides for many reasons. For the US, security agendas are non-negotiable; for that same reason agendas of common risks cannot be agreed upon mutually.

---

3   Issues that are both of the international and domestic interest for both countries.

When US security is in question, it is the United States that establishes the canons and, in the name of defending its own security, it commits excesses: human rights violations against its nationals and foreigners, demands for harmonization of security policies, etc., which, in the name of hemispheric security either subordinate or mishandle issues that are priorities for the Latin American countries.

To date, no hemispheric project has had sufficient weight to be viable and doable. The Security and Prosperity Partnership of North America (SPP) seems to be the only regional security mechanism, and there the United States imposed its will. In it, security strategies subordinate the Mexican regional prosperity priorities. Without going further into an analysis of the SPP, it is worth noting that in the gamut of regional or hemispheric frames of action, migration continues to be ignored. This is the case despite its implications as a risk to border security for sending, receiving, and transit countries. In addition, the partnership was forged in the framework of increasingly unilateral measures by Washington, like the militarization of the border and the proliferation of anti-immigrant civilian actions.

Securitization and Bilateralization in Latin America

The trend toward bilateral relations dominates US relations with the hemisphere in all of the sub-topics of integration, whether in matters of trade or security, and it is around the security issue that Washington has fostered its greatest bilateral commitments, especially with Mexico and Canada. The negative interpretation of the phenomenon arising out of US hegemony is that it would not necessarily need to commit itself in a multilateral game in which it does not obtain the benefits it obtains from the bilateralization of its relations. In policies to fight drug trafficking and to defend energy security, it has clearly expressed the idea of bilateralization because these are issues that represent a latent threat for US domestic and economic stability. For this reason strategic alliances have been created for the defense against threats, even sometimes producing divisive strategies contrasting with the characteristic, sometimes naked pragmatism to which Washington has accustomed us. From a different point of view, regionalism based on bilateral relations with the dominant actor (the US) can be justified by: a) the enormous and deep differences dominating relations among the Latin American countries (according to the nature and degree of economic independence, the commitment to international competition, the patterns of activity in the world economy, or the strength of their democratic institutions); 2) the asymmetries with the United States; and c) the degree of importance that the issue of risk has when the US weighs its priorities. There are cases to exemplify the bilateralization of regional security issues: Colombia and Mexico, with regard to militarization due to drug trafficking; and Brazil and Venezuela, in the negotiations around the issue of energy security. US fragmentation of security strategy has led to the implementation of bilateral models such as the Plan Colombia and the Mérida Initiative, and to different aid packages to fight against drug trafficking in Colombia, Mexico, Central America, and the

Caribbean. There is a different level of cooperation than that of the certification processes that from 1986 to 2002 were the central tool for cooperation regarding the fight against drugs.

Since 2000 Colombia has received an investment of about US$5 billion to fight drug trafficking and the guerrillas (80 percent earmarked for military spending, particularly on special equipment like helicopters to transport combat troops and airplanes to fumigate and destroy illicit crops) (Salazar 2007). The rest of the funds have been destined to programs to strengthen the justicial system and civil society, and also to experiment with alternative crops; almost US$20 million a year were invested in Colombia's judiciary, a minimal part of the total (less than 3 percent). Nevertheless, it is worth noting that, at least until 2007, Colombia was the only survivor of the continual budget cuts for the region; in fact, it is the program that benefits from the largest US aid package outside of the Middle East and Afghanistan. There are contradictory perceptions of the results of the Colombia program. According to one US Justice Department official, it may be the most important investment today in terms of results dollar per dollar. On the other hand, Ricardo Vargas, of the Andean Initiative, says that since the plan has been in place there has been no drop in the drug supply in the United States. The prices to the consumer have tended to drop, the quality of the drugs tends to rise, and, in general, the availability has not been affected. He even says that the drug cartels and their links to the guerillas have been strengthened (Sanchez 2007).

In Mexico the situation is even more delicate, not only because of the risks that seem implicit in the acting of organized crime, drug trafficking, and the massive flow of migrants, but also because of the type of relationship with its northern neighbor. There is deeply rooted confusion about the definition of relations between Mexico and the United States, which are not as formal as they could be due to an imperfect (and unnecessary) friendship and a not-very-prosperous (and urgently needy) society. Basing the relationship on friendship and not on a partnership has been a historical mistake; it tends to compromise the national interests of the less powerful actor given the absence of reciprocity and recognition of mutual priorities. In addition, little importance is placed on the risky complexity of the geographical proximity and dual identity–being both part of Anglo and Latin America–and the lack of agreement on bilateral and multilateral policy issues. It would seem that the geographic realities act to the detriment of Mexico, since its proximity to the United States limits and reduces instead of broadening Mexican international policy opportunities, although this is sometimes more a result of Mexico's confusion about knowing what it wants. However, because of its proximity and interdependence with the US, Mexico–even more than Canada–is an actor of the highest importance for preserving US security, as the SPP initiative and the existence of NORAD prove.

As a result of the unfortunate link that has been drawn between migration and terrorism since 9/11 (Rosas 2003), and, given the risk of undesired crossings, the militarization of the entire security strategy became a reality along the border. Curzio points appropriately to the fact that not even in the design of smart borders did the US thought about adopting a multilateral focus involving Mexico, Canada, and the United States to reinforce the idea of a shared North America. It simply preferred to negotiate bilaterally, and Mexico accepted stricter border controls and (explicitly and implicitly) a more rigid migratory regime as its own (Curzio 2007).

The Mérida Initiative (MI), passed by the US Senate on May 22, 2008, initially also budgeted US$1.4 billion for fighting drug trafficking and organized crime. The law stipulated that Mexico would receive US$400 million the first year, US$85 million less than what President George W. Bush had proposed (BBC 2008). Seven Central American countries and two Caribbean countries (the Dominican Republic and Haiti) are included in the initiative, with US$65 million earmarked for them. It should be mentioned that this bill was not approved without frictions, since the US legislature wanted to establish conditions regarding police transparency and the prosecution of members of the security forces accused of human rights violations for paying out the aid, which amounted to suggesting intervention in Mexico's internal affairs.

Pragmatism and bilateralism are also regular practice in energy matters. In this sphere, the United States shows rather crudely its strategic interests precisely with the actors that are exercising sub-regional leadership. Regarding the fundamental issues like oil and international finance, pragmatism characterizes the relationship between the United States and Venezuela. Jorge I. Domínguez underlines this fact when discussing the US bi-polar personality *vis-à-vis* Latin America, exemplifying it with the fact that Venezuela has continued fulfilling its oil export commitments to the United States and the that US has not imposed an embargo on oil imports from Venezuela (Domínguez 2007). To what extent do public bilateral differences project the most precise image of the state of relations? We can say that the US condemnation of the Hugo Chávez government has not been due to US support for democracy as a political mechanism for staying in power, but more because of the political risk that the illegitimacy of those mechanisms would pose, for example, for international investments in Venezuelan bonds.

To exemplify this pragmatism in US-Venezuela relations, see figure 1. The United States imports 63 percent of the oil it consumes domestically (13.468 million barrels a day in 2007, or 25 percent of world oil consumption).[4] The main US suppliers are Canada, Saudi Arabia, Mexico, and Venezuela, in order of volume. On the other hand, the growth rate in imports from Brazil makes it the country with the third-fastest growing rate among crude oil suppliers; Canada is in eighth place, and Venezuela, tenth, placing Brazil and Venezuela as the only Latin American countries at the top of the list. Meanwhile, despite the fact that Mexico has increased its exports 211.4 percent since 2003, indicators for 2006 to 2007 show a 0.1-percent reduction in exports.

---

4   Energy Information Administration, "US Imports by Country of Origin 2002-2007", available on line at http://tonto.eia.doe.gov/dnav/pet/pet_move_impcus_a2_nus_ep00_im0_mbblpd_a.htm.

Table 9.1   US Imports by Country (2002-2007)

Country	2002	2003	2004	2005	2006	2007
All	11,530	12,264	13,145	13,714	13,707	13,468
Persian Gulf	2,269	2,501	2,493	2,334	2,211	2,163
OPEP	4,605	5,162	5,701	5,587	5,517	5,980
Saudi Arabia	1,552	1,774	1,558	1,537	1,463	1,485
Venezuela	1,398	1,376	1,554	1,529	1,419	1,361
Nigeria	621	867	1,140	1,166	1,114	1,134
Algeria	264	382	452	478	657	670
Angola	332	371	316	473	534	508
Iraq	459	481	656	531	553	484
Ecuador	110	145	245	283	278	203
Kuwait	228	220	250	243	185	181
Non-OPEP Countries	6,925	7,103	7,444	8,127	8,190	7,489
Canada	1,971	2,072	2,138	2,181	2,353	2,455
Mexico	1,547	1,623	1,665	1,662	1,705	1,532
Russia	210	254	298	410	369	414
United Kingdom	478	440	380	396	272	277
Brazil	116	108	104	156	193	200

Source: Energy Information Administration, *US Imports by Country of Origin 2002-20*

Table 9.2   Countries With Highest Growth of Exports to the US

Country	Growth (2003 to 2007)	Growth (2006-2007)
Kazakhstan	275.3%	275.3%
United Arab Emirates	244.5%	147.8%
Brazil	505.3%	133.9%
Libya	No exports	131.3%
Nigeria	317.5%	120.6%
Algeria	841.8%	120.2%
Indonesia	122.9%	117.5%
Canada	269.3%	116.2%
Saudi Arabia	200.4%	112.1%
Venezuela	237.1%	111.2%
Angola	295.3%	107.4%
Russia	163.3%	102.7%
Kuwait	189.9%	100.5%
Iraq	237.8%	-2.5%
Mexico	211.4%	0.1%

Source: Workman 2008.

The growing US dependency on oil and oil derivative imports, despite being the world's third crude oil producer after Russia and Saudi Arabia, has created an important concern that oil may be a risk to national security.[5] This is why the Energy Security for the 21st Century plan (The White House 2008) emphasizes the need to strengthen domestic oil production (also as a mechanism to counter pressure on oil prices), to increase standards of efficiency and the use of alternative fuels (by passing the 2007 Energy Independence and Security Act that urges fuel producers to use at least 36 billion gallons of bio-fuels, and encourages the "Twenty in Ten" initiative to achieve a 20-percent reduction in the use of oil by 2010), and recognizes the need to invest in alternative energy sources, as President Barack Obama has already done. In the second week of his administration, Obama issued executive orders to encourage auto manufacturers to produce more fuel-efficient vehicles as of 2011, and later he instructed the Environmental Protection Agency (EPA) to review decisions against state initiatives to impose stricter measures.[6]

The US strategic alliance with Brazil was necessary as part of a search for allies in the region with which relations are not as conflictive as with Mexico. The big difference between relations with Mexico and relations with Brazil is that the United States recognized Brazil as an ally, and Brazil, in turn, demanded to be treated as a partner. In addition to embodying an inclusive multilateral leadership, a partnership with Brazil would represent a decisive strengthening of ties with the MERCOSUR bloc and an immediate link to the rest of South America. Simply put, the MERCOSUR nations all together represent 45 percent of the population of Latin America and the Caribbean, almost 60 percent of regional gross domestic product, and more than 40 percent of US investment in the region, but less than 15 percent of US trade (Lowenthal 2007). For practical reasons, the US and Brazil seem to recognize that their agreements are more important than the disagreements they have over relations with others, specifically the discord between the United States and Venezuela and Luiz Inácio Lula da Silva's relatively cordial relationship with Chávez. Brazil is a global player, member of the BRICS; it has opened most of its economy to international competition; it plays an important role in world trade and in trade negotiations, shown by its leadership role in the Doha Round negotiations. As Olga Pellicer states, together with India and South Africa, Brazil's activism and influence in the global South is dominant, as it is among the medium-sized powers, including Mexico, despite the reticence with which our country deals with its responsibilities and prerogatives (Pellicer 2006).

With regard to alternative energy sources, the United States has sought to establish an energy alliance with Brazil in order to increase ethanol use to reduce

---

5   Energy Information Administration, "Producción Mundial de Petróleo Crudo 1960-2007," available on line at http://www.eia.doe.gov/aer/txt/ptb1105.html.

6   The first of these orders would ensure that by or before 2020, all US vehicles would get a minimum of 35 miles to the gallon, which would represent a savings of more than 2 million barrels a day. The second order would allow state governments to impose stricter limits on carbon dioxide emissions.

fossil fuel consumption and possibly to reduce Venezuela's influence. Brazil is the largest exporter of ethanol and a leader in bio-fuel technology, particularly for fuels produced from sugar cane, which is more efficient than US-produced corn-based fuel. Brazil's replacement of 40 percent of national gasoline consumption and the fact that 70 percent of vehicles for sale are hybrids are the result of government investment since 1970 in the ethanol industry (Reel 2007). Despite the fact that the United States (with subsidies) produced more ethanol than Brazil (without subsidies) (4.855 billion gallons and 4.491 billion gallons respectively), the US still had to import 1.7 million gallons, mostly from Brazil, to satisfy its demand.[7]

A Renewed Insertion of Latin America in the Future Security Strategy

Situations change, and, in line with the hegemonic theory, US supremacy has an irregular course as long as it continues to want to maintain its position as dominant power, as it seems to be achieving despite the aforementioned crises. The "hegemonic presumption," a term coined by Abraham Lowenthal to describe regional relations with the United States, existed and was effective in a context of bi-polar competition characteristic of the Cold War (Lowenthal 2007). However, in today's international order, the idea of a Western Hemisphere as an inclusive, generalizing concept is no longer valid. The image of a "consolidated back yard" no longer fits in with the diverse nature of twenty-first-century Latin American countries either. This old notion of US hegemony over Latin America seems to have definitively lost its validity.

At the end of the Bush administration, relations with Latin America were not completely healthy, possibly because of limited communication and prevailing mistrust in inter-American relations. The current fronts will continue to exist; security will keep its place as the number one priority. But, Latin America will also continue growing and projecting itself as a region of dynamic, influential, diversified actors. These are all weighty reasons for the United States to revisit the relationship with renewed vigor, not with timid approaches, but with fresh focuses that do not solely encompass the interests of the Colossus of the North. Perhaps this has started to happen given the renewed interest the Obama administration has shown in the region. Washington is seeking and perhaps proposing a new strategy beyond the issue of security at the expense of a healthy and credible relationship with the continent.

---

7   "Market Research Analyst: World's Ethanol Production Forecast 2008-2012," March 5, 2008, on line at http://www.prlog.org/10054934-market-research-analyst-world-ethanol-production-forecast-2008-2012.html.

References

BBC. 2008. Claves: Iniciativa Mérida. *BBC Mundo*, 27 June. [Online] Available at: http://news.bbc.co.uk/hi/spanish/latin_america/newsid_7473000/7473437. stm [Accessed: 7 April 2010]

Curzio, L. 2007. *La seguridad nacional en México y la Relación con Estados Unidos*. Mexico City: CISAN-UNAM.

Domínguez, J. I. 2007. Las relaciones contemporáneas Estados Unidos-América Latina. Entre la ideología y el pragmatismo, in *Foreign Affairs en Español*, 7 (4), 3-10.

Energy Information Administration. *Producción Mundial de Petróleo Crudo, 1960-2007*. [Online] Available at: http://www.eia.doe.gov/aer/txt/ptb1105. html [Accessed: 7 April 2010]

— *US Imports by Country of Origin 2002-2007*. [Online] Available at: http://tonto. eia.doe.gov/dnav/pet/pet_move_impcus_a2_nus_ep00_im0_mbblpd_a.htm [Accessed: 7 April 2010]

Free Press Release Distribution Service. 2008. Market Research Analyst: World's Ethanol Production Forecast 2008 - 2012. [Online] Available at: http://www. prlog.org/10054934-market-research-analyst-world-etTEL. CASA (614) 430-35–45hanol-production-forecast-2008–2012.html [Accessed: 7 April 2010]

Lowenthal, A.F. 2007.Estados Unidos y América Latina a inicios del siglo XXI, in *Foreign Affairs en Español*, 7 (1), 156-173.

Mendoza Sánchez, J.C. 2003. La seguridad hemisférica en las relaciones Estados Unidos-América Latina: Hacia una nueva era en la cooperación internacional, in *Cooperación y conflicto en las Américas. Seguridad Hemisférica: un largo y sinuoso camino*, edited by M.C. Rosas. Mexico City: UNAM-Centro de Estudios de Defensa Hemisférica-Universidad Nacional de la Defensa.

Pellicer, O. 2006. *Mexico – a Reluctant Middle Power?* [Online] Available at: http://library.fes.de/pdf-files/iez/global/50417.pdf [Accessed: 7 April 2010]

Project for the New American Century. 1997. *Statement of Principles*. [Online] Available at: http://www.newamericancentury.org/statementofprinciples.htm [Accessed: 7 April 2010]

Reel, M. 2007. US Seeks Partnership with Brazil on Ethanol, *The Washington Post*, 8 February. [Online] Available at: http://www.washingtonpost.com/wp-dyn/content/article/2007/02/07/AR2007020702316.html [Accessed: 7 April 2010]

Rosas, M.C. 2003. ¿Existe la seguridad hemisférica?, in *Cooperación y conflicto en las Américas. Seguridad Hemisférica: un largo y sinuoso camino*, edited by M.C. Rosas. Mexico City: UNAM-Centro de Estudios de Defensa Hemisférica-Universidad Nacional de la Defensa.

Russell, R. 2006. América Latina para Estados Unidos: ¿Especial desdeñable, codiciada o perdida?. *Nueva Sociedad,* 206 (November-December), pp. 48-62.

Salazar, H. 2007. Plan Colombia: diferentes balances. *BBC Mundo,* 22 August. [Online] available at: http://news.bbc.co.uk/hi/spanish/latin_america/newsid_ 6959000/6959605.stm [Accessed: 7 April 2010]

Sanchez, M. 2007. Un nuevo énfasis para Plan Colombia, *The Washington Post.* [Online] Available at: http://www.washingtonpost.com/wp-dyn/content/ article/2007/03/15/AR2007031501496.html [Accessed: 7 April 2010]

The White House. 2008. *Energy Security for the 21st Century, Reliable, Affordable, Environmentally-Sound Energy.* [Online] Available at: http://www.whitehouse. gov/infocus/energy/ [Accessed: 7 April 2010]

— 2002. *The National Security Strategy of the United States of America.* [Online] Available at: http://georgewbush-whitehouse.archives.gov/nsc/nss/2002/nss. pdf [Accessed: 7 April 2010]

Valdés Ugalde, J.L. 2004. *Estados Unidos: Intervención y poder mesiánico. La guerra fría en Guatemala, 1954.* Mexico City: CISAN-Instituto de Investigaciones Jurídicas-UNAM

Weintraub, S. 2007. La situación energética en el hemisferio occidental, *Foreign Affairs en Español,* 7(3), 47-60

Workman, D. 2008. *USA Oil Imports by Country 2007.* [Online] Available at: http://import-export.suite101.com/article.cfm/usa_oil_imports_by_country_ 2007. [Accessed: 7 April 2010]

PART 3
The Governance of Territorial Borders and Bilateral Relations

Chapter 10
Borderlands: Risky Spaces or Safe Places? 'Real and Imaginary' Borders – (Re)Framing Identity and Privilege

Elaine Correa

Introduction

What does it mean to be identified as a member of a nation – a citizen? Does citizenship, regardless of diversity in representation, imply membership with privileges and rights conferred to the individual? The relationship and interconnection of identity formation, citizenship and the exercising of rights within the shifting and often unsettled borderland terrain may reflect the complexity and contradictions inherent in framing or reframing borders within North America. For many people these contested borderlands may simultaneously represent safe and risky spaces based on the construction of real and imaginary border divisions, status or position, documentation, and location of residency. With the intention of securing safety and guaranteeing the entitlement of rights and associated privileges of citizens, the border then becomes either a gateway of access or a wall of resistance. Within the framework of contemporary North American debates, the border serves as the great divide between "us" and "them", protecting citizens while maintaining social order and control.

With constantly changing demographics in North America, and the increase in attention to smart and secure borders in the name of national security, the notion of identity formation as interconnected with citizenship and the exercising of rights that an individual may assert as part of his or her citizenship status raises many controversial questions. For example, who is defined as comprising "us", and subsequently who is categorized as "them" when issues of citizenship beyond passports and documentation are challenged? Is there a space between "us" and "them" where identity formation and citizenship exist as part of a broader national identity? What does identity as related to citizenship mean today within the context of a global response to the threat of terrorism to national security, and the creation of smart and secure borders?

Under the current global concerns for security that relate to international collaboration for anti-terrorism initiatives, the complexity and understanding of citizenship for those nations comprised of people from diverse racial, ethnic, and religious groupings has become increasingly more difficult. Within Canada, the cherished Canadian Charter of Rights and Freedoms, along with the enshrinement of Multicultural Policy into official legislation, has fostered not only the expectation of rights, but encouraged the exercising of rights by diverse groups of people. In the United States, the Constitution and the Declaration of Independence are considered the framework of US ideals and values recognizing the vision of US identity and distinction. Although ongoing challenges to the established practices of North American societies lend credibility to the high value that these nations offer as diverse societies, the impact of exercising these rights may also illuminate differences that are categorized to distinguish the "us" from the "them". Particularly these categories may be employed in terms of determining citizenship as related to identity both nationally and internationally. The prevention of movement and the blocking of access, or entrapment and containment of individuals based on identity as interconnected with citizenship and rights contributes to the "paradigm of suspicion" (Shamir 2005), that is utilized to determine and direct who is deemed acceptable (non- threatening as opposed to subversive) to earn or be granted the "license to move" (qualified as low-risk through social screening) both across and within the "real and imaginary" borders. Therefore, it is imperative to recognize the relationship between identity formation, citizenship and the exercising of rights in a re-bordered North America, not only in terms of visible constructions of difference aligned with color and physical appearance, but also in terms of ascribed or demarcated status of "authorized" and "unauthorized" aliens. New technologies for defining and framing those individuals considered as "undesirable" for perceived threats of criminality, terrorism, and subversive behavior are interconnected with the direction in which rights and privileges are accorded people moving within the borderlands of both "real and imaginary borders" in which the association of identity with privilege may represent either a risky space or a safe place.

Real and Imaginary Borders

In Canada, the complexity of identity formation in relation to rights for Canadians from within and outside the nation offers a unique perspective to reframing identity and privilege. As Len Kuffert (2003) has stated, "for many Canadians, the idea of what defines Canada is linked with real or imagined cultural differences between Canadians and other national groups, or even differences among Canadians themselves" (107). These perceived differences that define and contribute to the categorizing of "us" versus "them" also have been framed within political discourses. For many Canadians, such identity formation in relation to citizenship and rights may require juggling in between these spaces that are delineated within socially constructed categories of "us" versus "them". While people may suffer from unwritten exclusionary practices embedded within institutional parameters, the language of difference can also be equally problematic (Taylor 1994).

The border between the United States and Mexico provides an obvious example of institutional parameters where the language of difference demarcates visually the distinction between "us" and "them". The US Department of Homeland Security had aligned and demonstrated its concerns for protection, with the initial failure of the SBINet project, "a new border protection program based largely on high-tech surveillance systems to create a virtual fence" (Ackleson 2009: 346). It is quite puzzling and rather disturbing that as people in other parts of the world celebrate the 20th Anniversary of the decline of the Berlin Wall, the United States of America fortifies her border with Mexico with the erection of a physical border wall, and seeks proposed "virtual border" alternatives to enhance protection initiatives along its shared border with Mexico. The use of real border divisions (as in the case of Mexico) versus the somewhat imaginary border lines drawn between Canada and the United States, reflect the differences in border policy, which appear to fluctuate and lack consistency, as perceived threats to US society. Although border control has been an "interest driven process firmly rooted in politics" (Ackleson 2009: 347), seeking new ways to advance border policies with a long-term vision rather than short-term, crisis-oriented mode of operation, may in fact reframe real and imaginary borders more effectively. The value of intended mechanisms of the joint accord "Our Shared Border", which focuses on facilitating trade and coordinating policy to efficiently manage the frontier, may serve to shift fear-based initiatives which foster false dichotomies of people towards challenging prevalent conceptions of identity and privilege used to decipher those categorized as "us" versus "them".

The discrepancies in approaches to deal with border politics and concerns are magnified further when reflecting on the advances that have occurred with the destruction of the Berlin Wall. As Germany continues with the "Abbau" of real and imaginary borders, which literally means the "un-building" (deconstruction), painting a picture by reversing the process of something tangible or intangible that was put in place, the United States moves in completely the opposite direction with the visible symbol of historical protectionist aggression. Additionally, as the real borders are framed for the purpose of protection and hindering the enemy from penetrating precious territory, such as in the case to the North, where the United States has simultaneously increased the level of security with Canada in efforts to "serve and protect" its people, the intersection of physical barriers and prolonged border crossing delays serves as another reminder that these differences matter.

The concentration on differences may also help to support binary divisions of "us" versus "them", which can contribute to greater separation between groups (Taylor 1994). Additionally, these distinctions can be used to subvert attention away from common shared identities that are cultivated through social and cultural exchanges by magnifying those aspects of physical visible identity within an aura of suspicion associated with group members who share specific visible distinctions or differences. It is therefore not accidental that the lack of knowledge about visible minorities of color has culminated in the association and representation of their differences by dominant group members as non-differentiable. Hence, if the relationship of terrorism is linked to identity in the form of skin color, or visible traits for males (turban, beard and mustache) and equally identifiable visual markers for females through dress codes and religious symbols or traditional cultural clothing (veil, *hijab*, chador, and *burqa*), then it would not be unexpected or surprising that divisions between "us" and "them" would be more acute and reflective of the way identity is framed with privilege.

In addition to the visible traits of identity that serve to differentiate "us" from "them", the adherence to a "club membership" mentality is pervasive in the treatment and assessment of those defined as "authorized" or labeled as "unauthorized" aliens. Here the association with this type of membership status that is aligned with specific privileges or rights serves to justify and legitimate a form of temporary acceptance that may be issued to those providing a desired service or benefit to the US labor force. Take for example the process of border inspection and the cases of "authorized" versus "unauthorized" aliens entering the United States to serve the economic marketplace. Although a greater emphasis on rhetoric reflects heavy media coverage and negative campaigns centering on "illegal aliens" taking jobs away from legitimate, hardworking, God-fearing US citizens, little attention and focus is actually directed to the benefits of this labor force and the significance of its contribution to the US economy. Eduardo Porter (2005) stated in the *New York Times* that the estimated 7 million "illegal immigrants" in the United States provided the fractured US Social Security System as much as 7 billion dollars a year of surplus through taxes withheld from their wages. Additionally, he contended that the projected taxable earnings and revenue allocated from the labor of "illegal immigrants" were anticipated to cover social security benefits for US residents. While "unauthorized" immigrants are not accorded the membership status that deems them as legitimate citizens within the Unites States, with rights and associated privileges, their economic contributions ironically support the very structure that denies them recognition for the value of their labor.

According to the Office of Homeland Security, there were an estimated 6,650,000 "unauthorized" Mexican immigrants in the United States in 2009. As a group, Mexicans comprise the largest number of "unauthorized" immigrants to the United States. While "unauthorized" immigrants under the Immigration and Nationality Act (INA) Section 245(1) are "unauthorized" to work till they have been granted Legal Permanent Resident Status (LPR) and are accorded beneficiaries of Temporary Protected Status, (TPS), it is quite revealing how flexible regulations are when H-2A nonimmigrant visas are temporarily issued to the same class of agricultural workers who are otherwise typically barred entry to the United States (Hoeffer, Rytina and Baker, 2010). According to Shamir (2005), there have been 48 different categories of nonimmigrant visas to the United States as of 2004. The visa system allows for the careful sorting of people whose individual identities are deemed necessary to enhance the quality of the labor force from those who are considered redundant, or worse, a burden (209). Yet it appears that, at least for a conditional period of time, when the agricultural sector dictates a demand for workers in the unskilled category, the sorting or selection process of prospective immigrants may be compromised, with the end justifying the means.

Within these spaces of "us" versus "them", the discussion of citizenship and the exercising of rights as aligned with identity formation become increasingly more complex and contradictory. From the perspective and location of the US border inspector, those individuals who were once assessed under a negative collective identity may individually receive partial benefits if their contributions to the US economy are needed. Undocumented Mexicans may fit this classification and be temporarily tolerated as a disposable labor force. However, within the binary classification of "them", these individuals are denied the exercising of rights associated with legal status, and are further devalued as people based on their identity formation as "other", where their individual and collective differences matter.

Defining the "Other" – Differences that Matter

Because the "other" is created within the borderlands relating to how knowledge and power are understood, and where identity and citizenship beyond official documentation are considered, it is necessary to discuss the value assigned to the "other". Knowledge of what constitutes a collective identity and associated rights operates like a border, defining "outsiders" and "insiders" while actively legitimatizing insiders (Mohanty 1997). Challenging what constitutes the border invokes questions of how these borderlines are drawn; who has access, and what is needed to enter? Redefining the border involves reformulating what counts as the inside.

The struggle between insiders and outsiders over who should be positioned on the inside, as well as what knowledge should be represented and why, remains a contested space. These borderlines define what type of knowledge counts and who has or should have access to it. For those defined as "other", the struggle over representation is a struggle over knowledge (Mohanty 1991), where the knowledge and voice of the "other" from the inside has remained non-existent. "Authorized" and "unauthorized" aliens do not invoke tremendous compassion in the assessment of their status as residents in the United States. These individuals are not viewed as real members of society, but rather considered outsiders within. Their contributions to the US economy are often negatively conflated with stereotypical representations about them that construct their identity as inferior, undesirable individuals, unworthy to claim the legitimate rights and privileges aligned to US citizenship. Despite the differences among "unauthorized" immigrants, from a variety of geographical locations around the world, these individuals are lumped together as possessing a shared identity from their experiences of "illegal" entry, which is used to make them appear the same. Particularly interesting, however, is how the representation and greater focus and subsequent emphasis is placed on people of color as "unauthorized" immigrants, despite the diversity of racial groups of people from around the world who fall into this category in the United States. The homogenizing effect of differences, aligned with the status of illegal entry effectively operates to deny people of color (as the representative image associated with "unauthorized" status), any legal recognition or legitimate voice to assert their rights.

In 2009, the Canadian Minister of Citizenship, Immigration and Multiculturalism, Jason Kenney, announced that new restrictions would apply to Mexicans wishing to enter Canada as visas would now be required. This change in status means that nationals from Mexico who travel to Canada will first need to apply for a Temporary Resident Visa. The imposition of a visa was justified as a means to address the increase of refugee claims from Mexico, which have tripled since 2005. According to Kenney's July 19, 2009, news release, "In 2008, more than 9,400 claims filed in Canada came from Mexican nationals, representing 25 per cent of all claims received. Of the Mexican claims reviewed and finalized in 2008 by the Immigration and Refugee Board, an independent administrative tribunal, only 11 percent were accepted." Kenney stated that the purpose for imposing visas was to "manage the flow of people into Canada and verify bona fides...and to process the genuine refugee claims faster. The visa process will allow us to assess who is coming to Canada as a legitimate visitor and who might be trying to use the refugee system to jump the immigration queue". Kenney contends that, "It is not fair for those who have been waiting patiently to come to Canada, sometimes for years, when others succeed in bypassing our immigration system." Thus it appears that Canada, similar to the United States, is willing to provide temporary adjustments to official policies when unskilled labor is needed for economic gains. However, this shift in thinking appears to operate as a matter of convenience with little regard to consistency and benefits to those exploited by marketplace demands. Additionally, the focus of addressing illegal immigration concerns by visa restrictions seems to be specifically directed towards Mexico. If "unauthorized" immigrants comprise a vast array of people from numerous countries and racial and ethnic backgrounds, it is indeed troubling that the focus of Kenney's initiative is directed solely on geographical proximity rather than addressing the underlying components that contribute to this concern.

Evidently, the "other" then is defined by those differences that matter, but those same differences can be conveniently restructured as less problematic when the services of the "other" are needed. The power to name the "other" systematically serves as the power to control and determine, if not dictate, what rights and privileges are accorded this group. Therefore, how the "other" is identified will impact how citizenship, identity formation, and rights will be framed or reframed in terms of their collective space and subsequent privileges.

Identifying the "Other"

The role of identity is significant to the description of the "other". As Patricia Hill Collins (1991: 39) has indicated, the "status of being 'other' implies being 'other than' or different from the assumed norm of white male behavior". Thus the concept of identity is partly shaped by recognition of identity or its absence (Taylor 1994). Trinh T. Minh-ha (1990) has provided a theoretical definition of identity in which she explored the complexity of defining identity for the "other". Minh-ha (1990: 371) uses a binary framework to capture the existing tensions of difference within society when she states that:

> Identity in the context of a certain ideology of dominance has long been a notion
> that relies on the concept of an essential, authentic core that remains hidden to
> one's consciousness and that requires the elimination of all that is considered
> foreign or not true to the self, that is to say, not- I, other. In such a concept the
> other is almost unavoidably either opposed to the self or submitted to the self's
> dominance. It is always condemned to remain in its shadow while attempting at
> being its equal. Identity, thus understood, supposes that a clear dividing line can
> be made between I and not – I, he and she; between depth and surface, or vertical
> and horizontal identity; between us here and them over there...The search for
> an identity is, therefore, usually a search for that lost, pure, true, real, genuine,
> original, authentic self, often situated within a process of elimination of all that
> is considered other, superfluous, fake, corrupted or Westernized.

Identities are often claimed in opposition to the norm, as Stuart Hall (1990: 225) suggests, whereby "identities are different names we give to the different ways we are positioned by, and position ourselves within, the narrative of the past." Thus the formation of identity is in relation to multiple constructions, such as race, gender, class, nationality, sexual orientation, and ability. Within the discussion of smart and secure borders, the notion of identity formation is integral and interconnected with citizenship and the exercising of rights.

In the constructions of a re-bordered North America, while color and physical appearance are utilized to frame identity and assertions of citizenship, the actualizing of rights is further subjugated to scrutiny in terms of the privileges ascribed to the status of "authorized" and "unauthorized" aliens. It is quite striking that in the case of "unauthorized" workers, greater emphasis seems to be placed on geographical proximity to the United States, and visible identity, as in the case of Mexicans. These individuals form a type of poster board representation in defining who might constitute this group of "unauthorized" workers based on their appearance.

Most recently, Arizona Governor Jan Brewer signed a bill into law making the failure to carry proof of citizenship or legal status a crime. As of April 2010, any immigrant who cannot produce the documentation attesting to his or her legal right of residence can be arrested, fined $2,500 and jailed for up to six months

(Samuels 2010). This law justifies the right of local police authorities to interrogate any individual they may suspect as "unauthorized". The police can demand that individuals provide documentation to justify their right to be living and working in the state. Support for this law was based on the premise that by providing local authorities the power to interrogate individuals deemed suspicious they could help address the problem of "unauthorized" workers in the state. The fact that the state of Arizona is home to many "authorized" Mexican-Americans who may now be subject to scrutiny and search raises questions to how their Constitutional Rights will be protected under these investigative, ethnic profiling procedures of the "other".

The creation of boundaries between people based on history, culture, or both form a type of dominance and resistance which is defined through the word identity and experienced differently at border stations North and South of the United States. According to Friedman (1996: 3), the new geography of identity is poly-vocal and often contradictory. She has stated that "those whose daily survival most depends on understanding identity as the product of complex intersections and locations have provided the most leadership as they reflect upon their often double or triple marginalization within the institutions of higher education and knowledge." Thus the voice of the "other" is based on a multiplicity of intersecting social constructions and power differentials that shape the discourses of identity. Those whose identity reside in locations whereby difference, or "being other" is framed in opposition to the dominant discourse may experience hegemonic practices of power and control at border crossings that are contradictory and conflict driven at times. Perhaps those locations of identity where privileges are extended to the "other" (as in the case of clergy, or those identified with the dominant religious affiliations) represent the exceptional positive experiences of border exchanges within a climate of exacerbated fear and heightened tension within North America. The reframing of identity and associated privilege may elucidate the necessary shift that post-colonial theorists have argued must occur in order to ensure that the participation of marginalized and oppressed peoples voices are acknowledged within contemporary constructions of knowledge and the struggles aligned with the dilemmas of difference (Anzaldua, 1990, Spivak 1990, West 1993).

Re (Framing) Identity and Privilege

Undeniably, the impact of the media as a means of representation for diverse people is a major contributor to the types of images that are available in society as well as how identity is defined, accepted and reproduced. The institutional structure of our consumer society has oriented our culture (and its attitudes, values and rituals) more towards the world of commodities (Jhally 2003). Since advertising presents consumption as a way of life, it is imperative that consumers are able to think for themselves in order to learn how to analyze not just the meaning of advertising, but also the place of the advertising industry in our society and our lives.

Sut Jhally, in *Image-Based Culture –Advertising and Popular Culture* (2003) indicates that advertising is a communication system "through" and "about objects" since it does not merely tell us about things but rather relates to us how things are connected to important domains of our lives. In our multicultural society, people not only see images of what constitutes being different through various media forms (such as television programs and magazines), but images of difference are also reinforced in opposition to ideas of normalcy viewed through daily practices and reinforced through security practices. Often the common shared experiences that all people encounter regardless of their race, ethnicity, social class, physical ability, or sexuality are represented from the dominant groups' perspective. These representations are problematic since one group defines what is of value and how it should be framed for everyone. As Hussein, (2003: 40) has stated:

> Negative representations in popular culture reinforce, and are reinforced by, biased and at times hostile journalism in the mainstream news media, academic polemics that urge a confrontational and aggressive policies that are informed by anti-Arab bias and at times even involve the acting out of stereotypes received from popular culture. The result is a self-perpetuating vicious cycle of negativity about Arabs, Arab Americans, and Muslims, who have been all-too-successfully represented and accepted as 'the enemy' in contemporary American culture. Thus even as these stereotypes are increasingly critiqued and demystified by cultural observers, they retain their ubiquity and resulting negative impact on American relations with the Arab peoples and the circumstances for Arab Americans and Arabs living in the United States.

It is essential to recognize that many people of diverse backgrounds have assimilated and acculturated into a shared common Western culture in which they navigate rather successfully between two distinctly different worlds. Despite the lack of understanding and acceptance of their differences by members of the dominant group, many visible minorities as well as "unauthorized" aliens have aligned with North American values without the extended benefits and rights accorded by citizenship. These individuals continue to contribute and function as productive individuals without legal entitlements. Although they have lived and functioned as productive individuals within the US context, they still cannot escape their differences, regardless of the number of years they have served and labored in the country. Documented or undocumented they will always be "other" by virtue of their physical and visible differences, accompanied by either their lack of status or birthright.

It appears then that rights automatically conferred to the individual by virtue of citizenship no longer retain the same value when individuals enter border inspection stations. Citizenship rights conflated with identity hold questionable validity in the fight against terror. New technologies supporting the profiling of individuals in the name of protection have emerged, as have discourses that focus on a shared understanding of global protection over human rights. In the United States, racial profiling continues to be used by police for selecting whom to stop and arrest. Thus, stereotypical representations of non-dominant groups are dangerous, not only for those who do not conform to them, but also for those who are part of the dominant culture and view these images as reflections of what life should be for other people. It is essential then that appropriate spaces are provided wherein collective identities can be affirmed without distortion or oppressive images. For example, only when the experiences of white males as a universal standard are challenged can the social practices of race, ethnicity, or both, in which everyone participates, be fully explored and critically examined. As Howard (2006: 67) has argued:

> The luxury of ignorance, the assumption of rightness, and the legacy of privilege have for centuries functioned together to support and legitimize White dominance. The interaction of these three dynamics has formed the 'dominance paradigm', a pervasive and persistent worldview wherein White assumptions are held to be true and right, White ignorance of other groups is the norm, and White privilege flourishes essentially unchallenged and unacknowledged. The dominance paradigm has allowed Whites to continue to benefit from past and present dominance, with or without our conscious intent and awareness.

As McLaren (1988: 173) has further contended, these attitudes have created a "cultural encasement of meanings, a prison house of language and ideas" that has proven highly resistant to change. It is therefore imperative that the dominance paradigm be recognized and acknowledged in contributing to how identity and privilege operate within the framing of people and their experiences at border inspection stations within North America. Furthermore, the interchange and impact of identity and privilege at these locations of inspection and interrogation must be considered specifically in terms of how "whiteness" becomes invisible, while constructions of difference based on color are formulated as interconnected to terrorism.

In the United States, people of color have experienced some progress to renegotiate their identities and shift borders somewhat symbolically. Take for example the changes experienced by African-Americans from their struggle for civil rights in the early sixties to the current Obama Presidency. It appears that African-Americans have recreated their own identities in the United States within spaces that still remain highly contested. While some African-Americans have managed to redefine their identities within these reformulated spaces, for many others these shifts still remain symbolic since they continue to experience systemic and overt forms of discrimination based on stereotypical representations of them as a group. Lee (2005: 3) has argued that "Whiteness is both invisible and ubiquitous in defining 'American-ness'. Specifically whiteness is associated with all that is ostensibly good about the United States and being from the United States. Blackness, by contrast, is associated with all that is ostensibly bad about the United States and being from the United States. Feagin (2000) has argued that "the racist continuum runs from white to black from 'civilized' whites to 'uncivilized' blacks, from high intelligence to low intelligence, from privilege and desirability to lack of privilege and undesirability" (210). It appears that within North American societies race remains connected to the unresolved national discourse on identity (Feagin and Feagin 2008), which defines notions of "us" versus "them" relating to identity, privilege, and citizenship.

Similar to the experiences of other people from visible minority groups who are situated on the periphery based on constructions of difference in identity, Asian-Americans also experience negative interactions when international relations with Asian countries are tense (Lee 2005), as they are quickly viewed suspiciously as "un-American" people who may be potential threats to National Security. As indicated by Wu (2002), attitudes and behaviors by security officials towards Asians are highly influenced by international relations between the United States and Asian countries. Hence, despite the status and significance to be labeled as "honorary whites", Asian's carry the "stain of the perpetual foreigner" which means that Asian-Americans will not experience actual privileges that are conferred with "real" whiteness (Tuan 1998 as cited by Lee 2005).

The perception versus the presence of any real threat to US culture and society is apparent with discourses that presume dangerous natural tendencies aligned with immigrant cultures, or people who are viewed as different. The Patriot Act is a transparent example of anti-immigrant thinking, with rhetoric that can be used as a form of cultural racism or racism without race (Lee 2005). Similar to the notion of a color-blind perspective that denies the significance of race, cultural racism can be used to lock individuals and groups into a fixed and static representation of identity in which cultural differences are used to debase and control people (Spivak 1996) or reinforce representations of divergent identities from the dominant group with terrorism. Thus, by drawing attention to identity and privilege that rests within the traditional dominant discourses of white, middle class, male, Western, Judeo-Christian, or Eurocentric norms and values, a reframing of identity and subsequent privilege are challenged through conceptions of how differences in identity matter and are used to establish borders between "us" and "them".

Difference Matters – "Us" versus "Them"

"The border does not run between above and below but between you and me!"
– Graffiti in Kreuzberg, Germany

This articulation of the internalization of border concepts reflects the level and impact of framing and reframing distinctions between people where difference matters. Kreuzberg, Germany is one of the poorest neighborhoods in Berlin, with the highest percentage of people with a migration background. The concept of "difference" extends beyond normative differences in relation to the dominant group, whereby the challenge to difference as McCarthy (1993) has advocated requires a non-synchronous approach to difference, one that accounts for the intersection and relationship between race, class, gender, sexuality and disability (4). According to Young, (1990) how people think about difference must be interrogated if justice is to be served. (8).

Young (1990: 2) has argued that thinking about difference challenges our basic ideas about justice. Rather than building theories and justice based on abstract universal principles, we must pay attention to justice claims in particular local contexts, for it is only in these specifics that justice can be conceptualized and pursued. As Abu el-haj (2006:16) has cited, "differences are deeply embedded in relationships and mark the axes along which power is organized in society (Hare-Mustin and Maracek 1990, McCarthy 1990, McCarthy and Crichlow 1993, Minow 1990, Scott 1988, Young 1990). These differences are viewed as the property of particular individuals or groups (Rhode 1990, Unger 1990 as cited by Abu el-haj 2006) that reflect the position of how the dominant group assigns the label of difference in relation to its own normative standards. Martha Minow (1990: 20-21) aptly raises the dilemma of difference by questioning:

> when does treating people differently emphasize their differences and stigmatize or hinder them on that basis? And when does treating people the same become insensitive to their differences and likely to stigmatize or hinder them?...The problems of inequality can be exacerbated both by treating members of minority groups the same as members of the majority and by treating the two groups differently. The dilemma of difference may be posed as a choice between integration and separation, as a choice between similar treatment and special treatment, or as a choice between neutrality and accommodation.

As Minow (1990) contends, the "dilemma of difference" results from the broader, inequitable social arrangements that make differences matter in the way that they do in society. Additionally, by focusing on differences between groups, security initiatives may obscure variability within groups. Thus the principle of formal equality may assist in adhering to a principle of equal treatment whereby individuals who are alike should be treated alike, according to their actual characteristics rather than stereotypical assumptions made about them. This principle also can be applied either to a single individual, whose right to be treated on his or her own merits can be viewed as a right of individual autonomy, or to a group, whose members seek the same treatment as members of other similarly situated groups. What makes an issue one of formal equality is that the claim is limited to treatment in relation to another similarly situated individual or group that do not extend beyond same-treatment claims to any demand for particular substantive treatment.

It is unfortunate, however, that highly contentious claims for equal standards often culminate in simple-minded policies and practices that are undertaken in the name of equality and often produce highly inequitable outcomes. The re-examining of the reigning norms, assumptions, and values embedded in the contexts in which differences and inequalities are produced may enable security issues to be illuminated and handled through practices whereby the difficulties embedded in acknowledging fundamental equality for an individual, without denying differences or viewing certain differences as specific individual deficits, can be challenged more effectively.

Although the politics of recognition (Taylor 1994) may create opportunities for social action, this level of recognition may be limited by assumptions about differences. Here border policies may tend to focus too narrowly on visible aspects of culture that overlook the deeper issues of power, privilege, and domination embedded within the dominant groups' narratives and institutional structures. As Taylor (1992) has asserted, justice is served not by ignoring difference but by recognizing and focusing on it. Although individual identity includes specific characteristics, it must also be equally stressed that a collective identity can cross gender, race, sexuality, class, and disability lines. Here difference must be understood as relational. According to Taylor (1994) the examination of how discourse about recognition unfolds makes visible the exciting possibilities, as well as the limitations, of organizing ideas about justice around group differences. The space then between "us" and "them", where identity formation and border practices for assessing citizenship rights exist as part of a broader national identity may reflect a shared understanding of global protection, human rights, and value for the individual, regardless of constructions and locations of difference.

Borderlands: Risky Spaces or Safe Places?

What is your citizenship? What is the purpose of your trip? What are you bringing into the country? On the surface, these questions may be identified as standard protocol for inspection purposes; however, the implication of these questions and the consequences of the next series of questions that follow reflect a shift from protocol to interrogation. According to Lyon (as cited by Ackleson (2009: 338),

> contemporary border policies around the world result in both regulation and openness, sometimes simultaneously, leading to an evolving but uneven and tenuous border and mobility management regime. That regime tends to prioritize certain economic classes and trade interests but marginalizes "exceptions," such as economic migrants, refugees, and certain identity-based groups. Such a reading is consistent with an appreciation of new forms of state surveillance, at borders as well as at other sites both without and within the nation state. These represent a kind of 'social sorting" that has reached new heights in the wake of 9/11.

As a consequence, "security inspection procedures inject additional delays, paperwork and procedures, all of which have concomitant compliance costs"

(Ackleson 2009: 339) which result in a very different border-crossing experience for many people. While the extended period of time held at border crossings for dominant group members implies overly lengthy delays since 9/11, along with the heightened levels of security and questioning, these acts of inspection and or interrogation have been the norm or regular experience for people of color prior 9/11. It appears that very little has actually changed in the way that people of non-white color are viewed, treated, or interacted with at border crossings North and South of the United States. A more integrated global approach and practice whereby overt identification and alignment to categories of difference are recognized as components that influence the hierarchy of human worth or value may force a space for the diverse identities to exist without re-inscribing and exerting inequitable hegemonic practices of power and control.

As in the case of the practices historically embedded by the division created with the Berlin border wall, people now speak of the Wall as an image in their heads between the former East and West. It is possible to interpret such a message to mean that there is much more work to do to bring people together beyond taking down actual walls that separate people geographically. Thus, it is not sufficient to merely provide the appropriate politically correct rhetoric of equity that culminates in tokenized slogans about tolerance and respect, but rather to challenge how diversity in practice will promote equity for those individuals such policies were designed to serve and protect. Although cosmetic modifications to an environment may initially appear as a commitment to taking diversity to new heights, the lack of substantive change directed at practices that support inequity signal neither a paradigm shift in thinking nor an alteration in attitude. Therefore, in order to move between the real and imaginary borders in which identity and privilege may frame ease of access, security initiatives must be revised to ensure that borderlands are not risky spaces for marginalized groups, but safe places where individual rights are recognized, multiple identities are respected, and national citizenship is valued.

References

Abu el-haj, T. 2006. *Elusive Justice: Wrestling with Difference and Educational Equity in Everyday Practice*. New York: Routledge.

Ackelson, J. 2009. From "Thin" to "Thick" (and Back Again?): The Politics and Policies of the Contemporary US-Canada Border. *American Review of Canadian Studies*, 39(4), 336-351.

Anzaldua, G. 1990. *Making Face, Making Soul - Haciendo Caras, Creative and Critical Perspectives by Feminist of Color*. San Francisco: Aunt Lute Books.

Citizenship and Immigration, Canada (2009). News Release: Canada imposes a visa onMexico.http://www.cic.gc.ca/english/department/media/releases/2009/2009-07-13.asp

Collins, P. H. 1991. *Black feminist throught: Knowledge consciousness and the politics of empowerment*. New York: Routledge.

Feagin, J., and Feagin, C. 2008. *Racial and Ethnic Relations*. Upper Saddle River: Prentice Hall.

Feagin, J. 2000. *Racist America: Roots, Current Realities and Future Reparations*. New York: Routledge.

Freidman, S. 1996. Beyond gynocriticism and gynesis: The geographics of identity and the future of feminist criticism. *Tulsa Studies in Women's Literature*, 15:1, 13-40.

Hall, S. 1990. Cultural identity and diaspora. In J. Rutherford (Ed.), *Identity, community, culture and difference*. London: Lawrence Wishart.

Hoeffer.M., Rytina, N and Baker, B. 2010. Estimates of the Unauthorized Immigrant Population Residing in the United States: January 2009. Department of Homeland Security: Office of Immigration Statistics, Policy Directorate.

Howard, Gary. 2006. *We Can't Teach What we Don't Know*. New York: Teacher's College Press.

Hare-Mustin, R. T. & Maracek, J. 1990. Gender and the meaning of difference: Postmodernism and Psychology. In R. T. Hare-Mustin, & J. Maracek (Eds.) *Making a difference: Psychology and the construction of gender* (pp. 22-64). New Haven: Yale University Press.

Hussein, I. 2003. "They are absolutely obsessed with us" Anti-Arab Bias in American Discourse and Policy. In Tracy Ore (Ed.) *The Social Construction of Difference and Inequality: Race, Class Gender and Sexuality* (pp. 40-54) New York: McGraw- Hill.

Jhally, S. 2003. Image-Based Culture –Advertising and Popular Culture" In G. Dines and J. Humez (Eds.). *Gender, Race and Class in Media* (pp. 249-257) Thousand Oaks, California: Sage Publishing.

Kuffert, L. 2003. "A Commentary on Some Aspects of Canadian Culture". In K. Pryke and W. Soderlund (Eds.) *Profiles of Canada*, (pp. 97-116) Toronto: Canadian Scholars Press.

Lee, S. 2005. *Up Against Whiteness: Race, School and Immigrant Youth*. New York: Teachers College Columbia University Press.

McCarthy, C. 1990. *Race and curriculum: Social inequality and the theories and politics of difference in contemporary research on schooling*. London: Falmer Press.

McCarthy, C. and Crichlow, W. (Eds.) 1993. *Race, identity and representation in education*. New York: Routledge.

McLaren, P. 1988. "Critical pedagogy and the politics of education ". Social Text, (19-20), 153-185.

Minh-ha, T. 1990. "Not You/Like You: Post-Colonial women and the Interlocking Questions of Identity and Difference. In G. Anzaldua (Ed.), *Making face, making soul – Haciendo Caras: Creative and critical perspectives by feminists of color* (pp. 371-375). San Francisco: Aunt Lute Books.

Minow, M. 1990. *Making all the difference: Inclusion, exclusion, and American law*. Ithaca, NY: Cornell University Press.

Mohanty, C. T. 1991. "Under Western Eyes": Feminist scholarship and colonial discourses. In C. T. Mohanty, A. Russo and L. Torres (Eds.), *Third world women and the politics of feminism* (pp. 57-80). Bloomington: University of Indiana Press.

Mohanty, C.T. (1997). Dangerous territories: Territorial power and education. In L. Roman and L. Eyre (Eds.), *Dangerous territories: Struggles for difference and equality in education* (pp viii-xvii). New York: Routledge.

Porter, E. 2005, April 5. Illegal Immigrants Are Bolstering Social Security With Billions. *The New York Times,* retrieved April 25, 2010, from http://www.nytimes.com/2005/04/05/business/05immigration.html?_r=1

Rhode, D. L. 1990. Theoretical perspectives on sexual difference. In D. L. Rhode (Ed.), *Theoretical perspectives on sexual difference* (pp. 1-12), New Haven, CT: Yale University Press.

Samuels, T. 2010, April 24. New York politicians rip into Arizona immigration law, call it 'un-American. New York Daily News, retrieved April 26, 2010 from   http://www.nydailynews.com/news/national/2010/04/25/2010-04-25_pols_rip_ariz_immig_law.html#ixzz0mGFgpYBC

Scott, J. 1988. Deconstructing equality-versus-difference: Or, the uses of poststructuralist theory for feminism, *Feminist Studies*, 14(1), 33-50.

Shamir, R. 2005. Without Border? Notes on Globalization as a Mobility Regime. Sociological Theory, 23(2), (pp. 192-217), American Sociological Association: http://www.jstor.org/stable/4148882.

Spivak, G. 1990. "Can the subaltern speak?" In S. Harasym (Ed.) *The post-colonial critic: Issues, strategies, dialogues* (pp. 271-313). New York: Routledge.

Spivak, G. 1996. "Explanation and culture marginalia." In D. Landry and G. MacLean (Eds.).

The Spivak reader: Selected works of Gayatri Chakrovorty Spivak (pp. 29-52) New York: Routledge.

Taylor, C. 1994. The Politics of recognition. In D. T. Goldberg (ed.). Multiculturalism: A Critical Reader (pp. 75-106). Massachusetts: Basil Blackwell Limited.

Taylor, C. 1992. *Multiculturalism and the "politics of recognition."* Princeton, NJ: Princeton University Press.

Tuan, M. 1998. *Forever foreigners or honorary whites?: The Asian ethnic experience today.* New Brunswick, NJ: Rutgers University Press.

Unger, R. 1990. Imperfect reflections of reality: Psychology constructs gender. In R. T. Hare-Mustin & J. Maracek (Eds.), *Making a difference: Psychology and the construction of gender* (pp. 102-149), New Haven,CT: Yale University Press.

West, C. 1993. The New Cultural Politics of Difference. In C. McCarthy and W. Crichlow (Eds.), *Race, identity and representation in education* (pp. 11-23). New York: Routledge.

Wu, F. H. 2002. *Yellow: Race in America beyond black and white.* New York: Basic Books.

Young, I. M. 1990. *Justice and the politics of difference.* Princeton, NJ: Princeton University Press.

Chapter 11

Nationalist Policies, Immigration, and Policy Boomerangs: "Three Strikes and You Could Be In"

Imtiaz Hussain

Introduction

The fact that the North American Free Trade Agreement (NAFTA) was not renewed when its originally stipulated 15 years expired in December 2008 exposed two conditions holding North American integration hostage: the first is the relationship between regional economic integration, immigration, and the state of the economy; and the second is the inherently nationalistic preferences over collective action in each of the three countries. Both can be squeezed for more theoretical light. Economic demand-supply explanations of one kind or another have influenced the literature on Mexican emigration, emphasizing how hopes of better living standards drive many from below the margin northwards (a per capita income of $33,900 in the United States versus $5,780 in Mexico at the start of the 21st Century),[1] and the availabilities of low-wage Mexican workers entice US producers (in both farms and factories) to recruit immigrants over their possible US counterparts. Yet, how US immigration policies also contribute to this flow has not attracted as much attention, motivating my argument: In implementing their immigration policies, US decision-makers unwittingly opened the door to more Mexican immigrants, both legal and illegal. Extant paradigms cannot, and immigration-related rhetoric will not, satisfactorily explain this. To understand the theoretical argument, attention must first rivet on empirical dynamics–first how the problem has festered, then on the big policy-making picture at the national (federal) level, and finally on how this differs from the smaller, but noisier local-level imprints. The article subsequently draws conclusions and projects implications.

The Escalating Empirical Problem

Breaking NAFTA's fifteen years into three unequal phases illustrates part of the first special relationship. Whereas the first phase incorporates both the negotiations

---

1   Figures from D. Campbell (2001).

of 1992-93 and the initial implementation from 1994, the second can utilize 9/11 as a turning point, not necessarily because of the dawning of the age of terrorism, but due to a philosophical shift accompanying the change of US and Mexican administrations from 2000; in the third, NAFTA acquires a past tense, that is, after 2008.

In the first phase, the 107 consecutive months of US economic expansion became the longest phase of continued economic growth (overtaking the 106 months during the 1960s), though not the strongest (1961-9: gross domestic product growth of 52.6%; 1982-90: 37%, 1991-2000: 36.8%), in the entire twentieth century (Passel and Suro 2005, Polzin 2000, Wortley 2000), and served as a North American locomotive. This was an occasion auspicious enough to (a) fuel the demand for low-wage workers–and with them, illegal immigrants;[2] (b) search for foreign markets; and, as a result (c) boost trade-investment to make them conducive to regional economic integration. The pattern was clear: Regional economic integrative efforts moved behind the North American steering wheel, while immigration concerns were relegated to the back seat. Trade-offs between NAFTA members promised a mutually positive outcome if (and only if) the economic upswing continued.

By the turn of the century, a cool-off was underway, but whose consequences were too far off to be immediately visible. Just the economic build-up of the 1990s was enough to prod Mexican President Vicente Fox Quesada to make what his first foreign secretary, Jorge Castañeda, would call *the whole enchilada* proposal on September 4, 2001:[3] to marry migrant flows with the trade and investment flows across North American boundaries, much like the European Community had permitted almost from the outset. That 9/11-related events captured headlines for a long time should not obscure the impact of 9/4: The US Congress immediately rejected the visiting Fox's *enchilada* proposal, prompting Fox to delay his sympathy phone call to his US counterpart, George W. Bush, after the 9/11 attacks. The relationship between immigration problems and regional economic integration showed its true color: a possible zero-sum trade-off. A flailing US economy could support neither regional economic integration nor immigration. Not only did it have to look beyond North America to be viable, making Doha Development Agenda (DDA) goals priorities at the 2003 Cancún WTO ministerial meeting, and resuscitating the Free Trade Area of the Americas spirit, at least until the January 12, 2005 Monterrey summit (Hussain 2004: 1-16 on DDA, Carlsen 2005, Starr 2004 on FTAA), but border restrictions also had to be accommodated.

In the final analysis, the third phase, coinciding as it did with the mortgage-driven 2007-08 recession, was aptly characterized by the North American September 2009

---

2   J. Passel (2002) believes 5 million undocumented migrants arrived in the United States during the 1990s, increasing by 500,000 each year rather than the expected 2-300,000 annually.

3   One can find the details from any concurrent newspaper, and the one used here is by D. Campbell (2001). For a *chilaquiles* (slightly less upbeat) view, see M. Cooper (2004).

Guadalajara Summit outcomes: Regional economic integration would be kept at bay until the United States had sorted out the Mexican immigration problem to suit a domestic audience. Economic collapse rather than 9/11-related aftershocks pulled the trigger since some of the highest annual increases in Mexican legal and illegal emigration followed 9/11, not to mention the peaking of the remittances earned. Yet when the economy crashed, more Mexicans returned from the United States than ever before.

Concealed by these dynamics was the policy-based special relationship: Nationalistic policies became second best at a time of immense technological growth, expanding production, and evaporating boundaries. They also compounded the problems. Here the United States can be singled out to dramatize the second North American special relationship being held hostage even though it did not monopolize the nationalistic outlook. By investigating every nook and cranny to explain why Mexicans migrate to the United States (supply factors), how Mexican workers are sought in the United States (demand factors), and what the ripples of consequences entail (from US bilingual apprehension to record-breaking Mexican remittance earnings), legions of scholars may be unwittingly ringing false alarms. Even if all economic demand-supply factors have been exhausted, North America's immigration problem is unlikely to be fully explained, let alone resolved, because of the equally unwitting boomerang effects of policies made in Washington, D.C., and state capitals.

The puzzle of North American immigration governance may be less in the demand-supply dynamics than in not sufficiently recognizing how nationalistic policies widen the immigration door structurally–to the point of compelling collective governance when it is being eschewed the most.

Washington Policy-making: The Big Federal-level Picture

Pointing US fingers at Mexico for not arresting the immigration problem has become so institutionalized that we don't always notice that rationalist policy-making worsens the immigration problem. Though George W. Bush's presidency will be associated with the building of a border-wall between Mexico and the United States, in turn linking it with 9/11-triggered security concerns, walls were being built around the San Diego-Tijuana border area from as early as 1994. Dubbed Operation Gatekeeper, this wall at the busiest North American port-of-entry would not have been built if unwitting errors had not been made in prior US legislations.

At stake was illegal Mexican immigration. During Jimmy Carter's presidency, the Special Commission on Immigration and Refugee Policy (SCIRP), established by Congress in 1978, became the first to address illegal US immigration. By then about 1 million were estimated to enter the United States annually (LeMay 2004: 6, but see ch. 1), and of the 3-6 million already in the United States, two-thirds were Mexicans–the largest US immigrant group–prompting the need to build safeguards (Batalova 2008). The most important collection of safeguards emerged in the Immigration Reform and Control Act (IRCA), passed in the House of Representatives by a 238-173 margin on October 15, 1986, in the Senate by a 63-24 margin two days later, and signed by Ronald Reagan into law on November 6 that same year–showing the urgency behind developing a legislative constraint.

Borrowing from the failed Simpson-Mazzoli bills of the early 1980s, IRCA asked for employer sanctions and gave teeth to the SCIRP proposal to adopt guest worker programs for Mexicans. Even though two such programs were opened for Mexicans (Legalizing Authorized Workers, or LAWs, and Seasonal Agricultural Workers, or SAWs), one cannot help but be struck by how similar they were to the 1942 *bracero* program (Tiedeman 1999). Adopted as a war measure to substitute male farmers drafted into the military, the annual *bracero* program recruited Mexican farmers who simply did not return to Mexico, so much so that in 1964 the *bracero* program was terminated.[4] Here was the first instance of an immigration policy not working, even beginning to boomerang, but more important, here was the innocuous seed it sowed that would grow into crisis proportions thirty years later and was beyond human imagination: Not only was there a Cold War-driven soft-spot for immigrants and refugees in countries being victimized by or becoming vulnerable to communism (Cuba and Mexico, respectively), but also the relative strength of the US economy during the 1960s diluted scattered grassroots concerns of immigrants shaking US society.

Exogenous factors also contributed to making IRCA some sort of an immigration Rubicon. Two deserve attention, one within the United States, the other within Mexico, and both at least indirectly related. The US development was the 1965 Immigration and Naturalization Act (INA). It was a noteworthy gesture to displace the country-specific quota system in existence at the time, but the preference system it created also would snowball into nightmares of sorts. The third preference, for example, opened the door to professionals and scientists, thus expanding Indian immigrants by 3,000 percent, Vietnamese by 1,900, Thai by 1,700, Pakistani by 1,000, Korean by 1,328, and Filipino by 1,200: these immigrants could then utilize the second preference whereby spouses and unmarried children of permanent residents could also be brought in. Within ten or 20 years, as Michael C. LeMay notes, "there were more Filipino physicians in the United States than native-born black doctors" (2004: 6). By the twenty-first century, even native-born white professionals would face the job-market heat for reasons created innocuously by a past policy and which current policy could not control. Mexicans increasingly faced their wrath for no reason except to follow the "huddled masses" before them–to the land of liberty and opportunity.

For Mexico, the most important preference was the sixth, designed to cater to skilled and unskilled workers in short US supply–in other words, *bracero* under a glossy name, made glossier still by IRCA's adoption of what came to be called guest-worker programs. The point not to be missed is how a vibrant

4 *Bracero* program was officially called the Labor Importation Program, 1942-64.

economy lubricates the transition from a guest worker to US permanent resident status–and then to exploiting the second INA preference (Waldinger and Reichl 2006). An economic downturn, on the other hand, sparks local reactions, scattered though they were in the economically healthy 1960s, feeds into nativism and anti-immigrant sentiments, and becomes the residual wild-card capable of holding politicians at bay in elections, pushing would-be emigrants from legal routes to illegal, and expanding the desirable immigrant base even as INA's third preference expanded the desirable base.

A different development within Mexico also made IRCA a negative landmark: the 1965 Border Industrialization Program whereby *maquiladoras* were expected to absorb low-wage workers and would-be migrants in conjunction with US manufacturers shifting production to Mexico to reduce costs. That they were largely located along the Mexico-US border, thus generating twin-city partnerships of sorts, profited from proximity to all types of high-skill infrastructures on the US side while reaping the most of low-skilled Mexican resources, hoping for long-term admixtures to ease the vast developed-underdeveloped gaps along those borders.

Those policy-making hopes were blown asunder for very secular reasons. While the *maquiladoras* emptied the Mexican countryside, making the border the gravitational center, across the country's heartland at first but eventually embracing the southern-most Mexican provinces (and ultimately connecting with the northern hopes of Central Americans), what welcomed the internal migrants were not the green pastures of a Mexican city with factories but the greener pastures and a job on the US side of the border. Their hopes of eventually crossing over were facilitated by *maquila* manufacturers' preferring women workers over men, thus liberating the males to (a) explore US transitions, (b) establish a US homestead, and (c) sponsor near and dear ones from Mexico.

Between INA and IRCA, from 1965 to 1986, enough figurative water had flown under the US immigration bridge to irretrievably alter US society and politics, regardless of any policy measures; and as it transpired, policies themselves became stop-gap measures against the rising tides–simply incapable of making wholesale changes at the local level from Washington when the socio-economic, socio-political, and socio-cultural dynamics had transformed irreversibly.

Against this background came the ace IRCA provision: amnesty for illegal immigrants residing in the United States. IRCA legalized three million illegal immigrants, two-thirds of whom were not only Mexicans but also suspicious of the gesture (Papademetriou 2004). As the pool of suspicious newly-minted US citizens expanded, the most significant message was the long-term legacy the provision left for would-be migrants: Get to the United States by however means, lie low for a while, and eventually an amnesty would come. Just as an immigration-friendly policy-approach between 1965 and 1986 whetted the hopes of so many Mexicans, among others, the illegal immigrant-friendly message of IRCA deepened and diffused those hopes within and outside Mexico.

The gap between the formulators and subjects of immigration policy-making deserves at least as much attention as the demand-supply economic factors in the immigration equation. Others may test a number of hypotheses: (a) Whereas immigration policy-makers must compete with multiple policy proposals for attention and resources at any given moment while the citizens they represent show more issue-specific motivations, the gap is more likely to favor national over local interests—be those interests in business, social programs, or politics. If this proves to be valid, democracy may be shaken at the roots. (b) Whereas immigration policy-makers must address dominant domestic concerns to get votes in the first place, formulating feasible solutions may not be possible without involving foreign countries with which more interests than votes serve as the trigger. If this one also tests positively, then local politics will be globalizing faster through the policy-making networks, for good or for bad, than personal values and preferences—again creating a gap questioning the virtues of democracy and liberalism as their vices abound. (c) Whereas immigration policy-makers utilize all the constitutional powers and resources at the federal level, local politics reserve sufficient constitutional powers and resources directly and indirectly impacting immigration—creating yet another gap in interpreting laws for policy-making at the different levels. Not only is democracy at stake here, but also how immigration policy-making survives in such a hostile environment. As the next section reveals in exploring the third hypothesis, US immigration policy-making may be pushing (a) the tension between federal and state immigration policy-making to a breaking point; and (b) security over welfare considerations increasingly, reflecting a growing incompatibility with regional economic integration, dramatized by a cumulatively worsening economic cycle (for instance, a growing budget deficit souring moods and mental frameworks of the typical citizen precisely when illegal immigration seems to be peaking).

State-level Nitty-gritties: Tightening the Screws Unconstitutionally

Whereas the cream state-level legislation to unwittingly fuel southern immigration was California's 1994 three-strikes-and-you-are-out, it is noteworthy to examine two other state-level legislations which explicitly slammed the door on southern immigration—only either to fail completely or to kick up so much dust as to obfuscate the purposes behind US immigration policy. These are Proposition 187 ("Save our State" initiative), proposed by California's Governor Pete Wilson, on November 8, 1994; and Arizona's April 23, 2010 Senate Bill (SB) 1070. The first sought to deny education, healthcare, and welfare benefits to illegal immigrants, but it was deemed unconstitutional at the federal level by Judge Mariana R. Pfaelzer in November 1997. Two years later Governor Gray Davis halted appeals against that ruling. The second, Arizona's SB 1070 ("Support our Law Enforcement and Safe Neighborhoods Act"), makes it unlawful to be in Arizona without proper immigration papers, and thus accents racial profiling in a state with a 30% Hispanic population component by empowering the police to crack down on illegal individuals and their abettors, institutionalizing racism in the process.

California's Proposition 187

Introduced by Republican Dick Mountjoy, Proposition 187 propelled the underdog, Governor Pete Wilson, to victory in the November 1994 elections, even though it was dismissed by President Bill Clinton and dubbed "xenophobic" by Carlos Salinas de Gortari, the Mexican president. Although it got almost 59% of the votes cast on November 8, it was immediately challenged at the federal level. Federal Judge Matthew Byrne issued a restraining order, while in December 1994 Judge Pfaelzer issued a permanent injunction. The key issue was its unconstitutionality: infringing the federal government's powers (immigration belongs to the federal domain). This was repeated by Pfaelzer in November 1997, and, in spite of an appeal filed by Governor Wilson, his successor, Gray Davis, essentially killed the bill in 1999.

Proposition 187 sought to screen illegal immigrants at all levels of education, work, healthcare, and public benefits (Martin 1995: 255-61), given the high number of illegal immigrants already utilizing those services and welfare (Philip Martin, for example, notes up to 400,000 students with illegal immigration status boycotted schools due to the threatening nature of the legislation). It found support from such Republican presidential hopefuls as Patrick Buchanan, but opposition from William Bennett and Jack Kemp, both former secretaries in Republican administrations. In addition, while the mayor of Denver called for boycotting California, many local groups opposed the legislation entirely: the California Teachers Association, California Medical Association, California Association of Hospitals and Health Systems, the League of Women Voters, the Congress of California Seniors, California Civil Rights Initiative, the American Civil Liberties Union, Center for Human Rights and Constitutional Law, among others (Martis 1994, McDonnell 1997). Though the legislation was eventually scrapped, the social and political divisions only sharpened.

A similar attempt to create a similar legislation in Arizona capitalized on this souring mood, but never reached its launching pad. In April 2010, Arizona stunned the entire United States, not to mention Mexico, with a legislation reaching deeper and releasing more venom.

Arizona's SB 1070 Legislation

By requiring all immigrants to have their papers with them while in Arizona, SB 1070, which was introduced by Republican Russell Pearce in the Arizona Senate, opened up the gates to (a) racial profiling, (b) institutionalizing racism, and (c) favorable comparisons with apartheid South Africa's Pass Laws (Castañeda 2010:

20, Sigal 2010). Though signed into law on April 23 after a 35-21 vote largely along party lines, it was expected to go into effect on July 28, 2010. In spite of mounting opposition, the legislation is obviously popular in both Arizona, with almost 70% popular approval, and the rest of the United States, where an April poll found 51% of the people supporting the legislation (Sacks 2010). However, no other state in the United States has the power (perhaps the will) to ask any member of the public for their immigration status the way Arizona now can. An arrest can be made on the spot if there is "reasonable suspicion" for the police to believe the person is illegally in the United States (or if the person cannot supply one of the four types of acceptable identification cards: a valid Arizona driver's license; a valid but non-operating Arizona driver's license; any other valid federal, state, municipal government identification license; or a valid tribal identification license). Even with 460,000 illegal immigrants, Arizona's "mean spirited" measure against its two million Hispanics (accounting for 30% of the population), has invited immense rebuke (McArdle 2010).

Mexico reacted immediately. The legislation, President Calderón observed during his Washington meeting with US President Barack Obama in mid-May, "opens the door to intolerance, hate, discrimination and abuse in law enforcement" (Booth 2010: 5). In return, he slapped a "travel advisory" on Mexicans planning to visit Arizona. Mexico's six border states have planned to boycott Arizona, a gesture with enormous consequences given the bilateral Arizona-Mexico pattern of relationships: In 2009, 27.9 million people crossed to Arizona from Mexico, 12.8 million of them through Nogales; in 2008 there was about US$20.8 billion worth of two-way trade; Mexican visitors to Arizona spent US$2.7 billion during 2007-8, directly creating 23,000 jobs; Mexico is Arizona's largest trading partner; 65,000 Mexicans cross into Arizona to work each day (Gaynor 2010: 4); and 30% of Arizona's trade is with Mexico (Castañeda 2010: 20).

On top of these were the immediate endogenous losses in Arizona, at a time when it is carrying a hefty US$4.5 billion budget deficit during 2010 (American Immigration Council 2010). Estimates made at the University of Arizona's Udall Center for Studies of Public Policy suggest the US$44 billion generated by the state's immigrant workers in 2004 would be threatened, as would the 400,000 full-time jobs this sustains, while 35,000 Latin-owned businesses, with sales of US$4.3 billion and employment of 39,363 people in 2002, would also be exposed. According to the Perryman Group, removing illegal immigrants, as SB 1070 seeks to do, would cost Arizona US$26.4 billion in economic activity, US$11.7 billion in gross state product, and about 140,324 jobs (American Immigration Council 2010).

Opposition spread quickly. President Barack Obama chastised the law for being "misguided" (Mexico and the United States 2010:12), and undermining "basic notions of fairness that we cherish as Americans, as well as the trust between police and our communities that is so crucial to keeping us safe" (Archibold 2010). Several leading US cities adopted actual or potential counter-measures. Mayors in San Francisco (Gavin Newsom) and St. Paul, Minnesota (Chris

Coleman), for example, imposed travel bans on Arizona, as did Denver's public school superintendent (Tom Boasberger), while city councils in Austin, New York, San Diego, and Washington, among others, contemplate similar measures (Sacks 2010). Even local groups protested loudly, as did the Associated Students of the University of Arizona (Donovan 2010). While the Cardinal of Los Angeles likened the legislation to "Nazism" (Archibold 2010), Arizona's business community was hostile. In a meeting Governor Jan Brewer had been invited to on April 26, slogans conveyed nasty messages: "Brewer's AmeriKKKa"; "Brewer, am I dark enough to pull over?" and "No to Jan Crow". Inside, businessmen were "pissed" (McArdle 2010). While one journalist dubs SB 1070 a "Mexican Exclusion Act" (Dosaj 2010), referring to the shameful effects the 1882 Chinese Exclusion Act, the 1904 Japanese Exclusion Order, and the 1924 Japanese Exclusion Act had, others worry about how "it will generate unprecedented racial profiling," as well as "impact legal foreign workers, legal residents, tourists, and even American citizens" (Fierros 2010, "Racial profiling... ," 2010).

On the other hand, Steven A. Camarota of the Center for Immigration Studies reminds us that Arizona's illegal immigrant population expanded faster than anywhere else (335,000 in 2000 to 560,000 in 2008), 12% of its workers are illegal, 20% of those living in poverty are illegal immigrants, as are 33% of those without health insurance and 16% of students in state schools (Camarota 2010). The rationale behind Arizona's legislation appealed to some other states. Oklahoma, for example, is considering a similar legislation with a more punitive punch, for example, seizing assets and imposing harsher penalties (Sacks 2010). That grassroots discrimination against Hispanics is growing alarmingly is also brought out by an April 29, 2010 report of the Pew Research Center in Washington: Not only were Hispanics subjected to the most discrimination in 2009 (23% of those polled, as against 18% for blacks, 10% for whites, and 8% for Asians), but they also were facing more discrimination in 2009 than in 2001 (19% in 2001, as opposed to 25% for blacks, 9% for whites, and 8% for Asians, in 2001); Hispanics constituted 76% of the 11.9 million undocumented immigrants in 2008 and, of the 359,000 illegal immigrants deported by the United States in 2008, Hispanics constituted a whopping proportion (Pew Research Center 2010). That Arizona is not the lone wolf is evident in the record-breaking immigration-related laws (222) and resolutions (131) during 2009 across the United States, suggesting a polemic national debate in the US Congress is not far away (Archibold 2010).

Discussions of how immigration is tearing US society today increasingly drive electoral calculations, get driven by the recession, or both. Among the consequences: increasing questions about how democracy will work given the mammoth immigration levels, whether state-federal relations are sturdy enough for the growing problems in society and about governance, or if the assumptions behind foreign policy (for instance, consolidating the regional economic integration already underway) streamline with domestic imperatives. A viable immigration policy is simply impossible to construct in the United States today given those considerations. Yet, that is only half the picture—the better half. The other half, showing how legislation actually boosts immigration in a way that encourages illegal entry as part and parcel of legal admission, is well illustrated by another Californian legislation, this time harmonizing with federal provisions.

California's Three-strikes-and-you-are-out Legislation

Although "three strikes and you are out" carries California's name, it originated in the state of Washington in December 1993. Nevertheless, as home of the largest concentration of Mexicans (and Hispanics), California's experience with the legislation captures the entire story relevant to this research, even though many other states have since embraced similar legislations.

Adopted in March 1994, the legislation essentially means repeat offenders are to be placed out of free circulation–arrest, by another name–for life. While the offenses vary, the common crimes include murder (homicide), rape (sexual assault), and carjacking (other crimes against persons), to which California added lewd acts, other types of sexual offenses (lewd act on child, continued sexual abuse of child, penetration by foreign object, sexual penetration by force, sodomy by force, and oral copulation by force); robbery; felony (attempted murder, assault with a deadly weapon on a peace officer or an inmate, and assault with intent to rape or rob); committing other crimes against persons (any felony resulting in bodily harm, arson causing bodily harm, exploding device with the intent to injure/murder, kidnapping, and mayhem); property crimes (arson, burglary, and grand theft with firearm); drug offenses (drug sales to minors); weapons offense (any felony with deadly weapons or where firearm is used); and so forth (Clark, Austin, and Henry 1997: 1-2).

Lengthening the list was deliberate: As I discuss below, it incorporates almost all routine activities of gangsters, especially from Central America. Although in some states the offender can be "out" after two years (Arkansas, Connecticut, Georgia, Kansas, Tennessee, and even California), or even four (felony in Georgia and Louisiana), the legislation permits law-enforcement officials to deport immigrants. California led all other states in deporting immigrants under this legislation after 1994, and the obvious candidates were Central America's infamous gangs in Los Angeles: *Mara Salvatrucha* (MS-13) and Eighteenth Street (Mara 18 or MS-18), formed mainly by the children of war migrants from El Salvador, but also from Guatemala, Honduras, and Nicaragua, during the 1980s, who could not fit into US society, yet were seen as profiting the most during the 1992 Los Angeles riot, looting and inflicting violence. This is not to say there were no Mexican gangs. The Mexican Mafia (*La Eme* or EME) was, in fact, the grand-daddy of them all. As Max G. Manwaring reminds us, every gang "operating south of Bakersfield, California, and into northern Mexico[,] had to pay homage [to] and take orders from the EME " (2007). Both MS-13 and MS-18 formally broke from EME in 2005, even though the loyalties were never too deep from the very start.

Meanwhile, the United States government also got tough. The 1996 Illegal Immigration and Reform Responsibility Act (IIRRA) also adopted mandatory deportation by widening the offenses, essentially including lesser theft and forgery as aggravated crimes (Valentin 2006). The net result was not only to expand gangsters and prison populations in under-prepared Central American countries, but also, since these youths did not know anything about the country where their parents had been born (Ariana 2005), to increase isolation–and thereby more gang activities and a desire to return to the land they were deported from.

That Mexico lay in between Central America and California thickened the plot, as it were (Saltsman and Welch 2008). Gangster violence crept north and, since they serve as perfect vehicles of drug cartels, ongoing narco-trafficking assumed new colors, facilitating the passage of a different breed of *loaded* migrants through corrupt law-and-order officials in Central America and Mexico (Sullivan and Elkus 2009), and imposing a southern migration problem upon Mexico (Brands 2009). According to a 1997 Washington Office of Latin America (WOLA) report, at least 54 Central American cliques have US connections, with El Salvador boasting 10,000 *core* gang members, Honduras 40,000 (Elton 2003, Thompson 2004), and Guatemala 125,000. The US Immigration and Customs Enforcement (ICE), through its 2005 Operation Community Shield, netted over 1,415 members of transnational gangs (Valentin 2006), and, since 2003, deported 52,684 criminal aliens and 40,802 non-criminal aliens (Hispanics and Arizona's new immigration law 2009). Chris Kraul, Robert López, and Rich Connel argue, in the first 10 years of the "three strikes" legislation, over 40,000 youth criminals were returned to a Central America they did not know (Kraul, Lopez, and Connell 2005).

Manwaring detects a pyramid structure with four layers in these transnational gangs. At the top remain the international bosses, increasingly in league with cartels; then come the transnational leaders who "operationalize" trafficking, human smuggling (Francis 2008, Pelisek 2009), and other illegal shipments (France n.d.); but it is at the third and fourth levels within each country where all members execute these plans, either nationally (third) or in the specific neighborhoods (fourth). It is at this fourth level (*clickas*) where foot-soldiers are recruited, and where a strict hierarchy also exists, with *sympathizers* at the top, *aspirants* coming next, and *nobodies* falling at the bottom (Manwaring 2007:1 7-8).

The literature on gangs generally refers to the new transnational gangs as belonging to the third generation of gangsterism (Sullivan 1997), who "participate in the drug trade and myriad other illicit economies, and use violence and corruption to undermine the state" (Brands 2009). According to Hal Brands, while the first generation involved "street gangs," typically driven to "protecting their turf... from equally parochial rivals," second-generation gangs happen to be larger, "organized around illicit economies like drug-trafficking... . [with] links to transnational criminal organizations (TCOs) like drug cartels." Whereas the former "are horizontal rather than hierarchical," the latter "feature a more centralized leadership and a more hierarchic structure." By comparison, third-generation gangs "are sophisticated TCOs in their own right... . operate according to a division of labor," usually in multiple countries, standing "astride the line separating crime and insurgency" (Brands 2009: 2). These third-generation gangs "are the rarest of the lot, occupying the highest part of a pyramidal gang hierarchy," indulging in "drug-smuggling, arms-dealing, money laundering, kidnapping, human trafficking, and others."

While it would be naïve to say Los Angeles gangs would not have transnationalized had there been no "three strikes" legislation or a "get tough" US policy approach, how they have penetrated Mexican and Central American emigration is obvious. Heather Berkman and others, while not tracing the emergence of Central American gangs to California, insist the "three strikes" legislation "also fostered the creation and spread of gangs in Central America" (Berkman n.d., Reisman 2007).

What began on the one hand as economic demand-supply explanations of Mexican emigration has transformed into a transnationalized and illegal multi-product enterprise (Pastor and Alva 2004: 92-112); and on the other as a policy targeting migrants by invoking penal and criminal laws, deploying military methods, and retreating behind walls–all without curbing the illegal residents of the United States whose check and control becomes more difficult as they launder their status through marriage and other means.

Conclusions

At least five observations demand attention. First, though economic demand-supply explanations of Mexico-US migration are popular in literature, they can no longer cover the increasing complications of their subject–opening the scope to examine, for example, the cumulative effects of immigration, whether national and local policy-making streamline each other, the extent to which the state of the economy cuts into demand-supply dynamics, and what all of the above mean for regional economic integration between countries.

Second, the unintended consequences of immigration policy impose an independent line of inquiry. While federal-level US policies sought to legalize illegal Mexican immigrants over the long haul, local laws in California and Arizona, at least, sought to close the lid immediately, but pursued unconstitutional or unpopular routes. The dynamic between the two levels may just be starting, necessitating further exploration, comparison, and scrutiny.

Third, while stemming Mexican immigrants only opened the door for Central American counterparts, the question arises if immigration can in fact be stopped, especially at the illegal level, under democracy. Contradictory sentiments toward openness and closure either become the stuff of electoral politics (converting other viable issues into second-best pursuits) or a democratic constraint (limiting rights and freedoms). Where to draw the line along this slippery slope may become the litmus test in future electoral politics.

Fourth, in an age of terrorism, though US immigration policy-making is correctly demonstrating fewer economic than security considerations, the consequences may be detrimental to both: economically-driven would-be migrants will have to learn the language of security anew; and the crusade against *hard* threats, such as jihadists, might be weakened by shifting resources against *soft* threats. With the mushrooming of the illegal immigration-drug trafficking-money laundering nexus, it becomes increasingly difficult to (a) concentrate on any one specific threat, (b) avoid an escalation in policy responses, and (c) prevent the insulation of the larger society at both ends. With the inclusion of gang threats along the trails, the United States could easily be pushed from its pursuit (or defense) of democracy into a garrison state.

Finally, the new form of southern US immigration is uniquely transformative. Not only has the United States confronted fears of bilingualism, whether that is good or bad notwithstanding, but it also seems to be on the threshold of returning to a manichean epoch (characterized simply by a dual view of the world in which everyone and everything belonged only in a *good* or an *evil* category). An earlier manichean era was the Cold War, dominated by sentiments which can be best summarized by "better dead than red." The present also seems to be dominated by color: white or non-white. For one of the most ethnically and racially assimilated countries in the world this would represent a marked departure from some of its cherished principles and the constitution the Founding Fathers wrote.

What do these observations imply?

First, with the US immigration policy becoming some sort of a collective good (one country pays, other countries benefit), it is amazing why the unilateral approach that has not worked since World War I has not been replaced by a domestic collective approach. Federal and local levels of policy-making, for example, can quash or over-ride immigration problems better if they collaborate rather than work against each other. In turn, this would push citizens and social groups to show greater unity than they presently do, with factions of all kinds dotting the policy-making picture, stopping at the edge of what Aristotle called the perverted form of democracy: mobocracy. The absence of domestic collective action is also mirrored abroad.

Second, with Mexico facing a similar southern immigration problem as the United States–and cracking down on illegal immigrants as hard as the United States does in its own backyard–not only does Mexico become a critical country for the United States to partner on an equal basis, but also suggests, with Mexico's emigration patterns reaching a peak, why a joint crusade has not even been considered. Mexico becomes critical because, if it is lax in closing its own border, the United States faces the brunt of the impacts; and if it is tight in so doing, there is a distinct possibility Mexico might, for once, become an immigration "team player" with the United States. If Mexico collaborates, the momentum can be pushed south to Central America. The absence of a collective good otherwise produces a collective bad: one country's actions hurting other countries, such as Salvadoran gangsterism, Guatemalan drug-trafficking, Mexican cartel corruption, or US security walls in an area historically free of terrorism.

Third, challenging democracy so severely under an immigration policy-making context raises the question, what alternative is there? Immigration studies inform us of the inverse relationship between immigration on the one hand, and democracy and dictatorship on the other: Democracy encourages immigration, while dictatorships constrain immigration. Predicting the future may be presumptuous based on just that observation, but could we be unwittingly headed in an unpalatable direction—away from democratic traditions because of an immigration "not in my back yard" attitude?

Finally, with 10% of Mexicans living in the United States, as President Felipe Calderón Hinojosa keeps reiterating in the wake of Arizona's SB 1070 legislation (Booth 2010: 5), and with 25% of Mexico's working-age population in the United States, not extending NAFTA in one way or another was a mistake. The sheer weight of the transactions of this group (remittances, visits and gifts, merchandise spread of the cultural artifacts, and so forth), is enough to merit regional integration, even without considering trade, investment, and other formal indicators. Those transactions are not new, but formally converting them into collective goods (to eliminate the emergence of collective bads first, then to promote the common welfare) is an idea North America needs to put into practice, and the sooner the better!

References

American Immigration Council. 2010. The legal challenges and economic realities of Arizona's SB 1070. http://www.immigrationpolicy.org/just-facts/legal-challenges-and-economc-realities-ariz... Accessed May 24, 2010.

——. 2010. How much will Arizona's immigration bill (SB1070) cost? http://www.immigrationpolicy.org/newsroom/release/how-much-will-arizonas-immigrati... Accessed May 24, 2010.

Ariana, A. 2005. How the street gangs took Central America. *Foreign Affairs* (May–June).

Archibold, C. 2010. Arizona enacts stringent law on immigration. *The New York Times* [online], April 23. http://www.nytimes.com/2010/04/24/us/politics/24immig.html. Accessed May 24, 2010.

Batalova, J. 2008. Mexican immigrants in the United States. *Migration Information Source* [online], April. http://www.migrationinformation.org/USFocus/display.cfm?id=679. Accessed May 24, 2010.

Berkman, H. n.d. The politicization of the judicial system of Honduras and the proliferation of Las Maras. *Journal of International Policy Studies*.

Booth, W. 2010. For Calderón one state visit had dual agenda: cooperation on drug war and the SB1070 law, the main subjects. *The Daily News*, May 18, 5.

Brands, H. 2009. Third-generation gangs and criminal insurgency in Latin America. *Small Wars Journal* [online], July 4. www.smallwarsjournal.com/blog/2009/07/thirdgeneration-gangs-and-crim/. Accessed May 24, 2010.

Camarota, S.A. 2010. Center for Immigration Studies on the new Arizona immigration law, SB1070. Center for Immigration Studies [online], Memorandum, April 2010. http://www.cis.org/announcement/AZ-immigration-SB1070. Accessed May 24, 2010.

Campbell, D. 2001. Mexico goes for the whole enchilada: The president meets George Bush this week in a bid to secure a better deal for the millions of his compatriots living illegally in the US. *Guardian* [Online], September 5. http://www.guardian.co.uk/world/2001/sep/05/immigration.usa. Accessed: May 24, 2010.

Carlsen, L. 2005. Timely demise for Free Trade Area of the Americas. *Americas Program* [online], November 23. http://americas.irc-online.org/am/2954. Accessed May 24, 2010.

Castañeda, Jorge. 2010. Gratitude for Arizona: its aggressive law could spur action. *Newsweek*, May 24 and 31, 20.

Clark, J., J. Austin, and D. A. Henry. 1997. 'Three strikes and you are out': a review of state legislation. *National Institute of Justice: Research in Brief*, US Department of Justice, Office of Justice Program (September): 1-2.

Cooper, M. 2004. Immigration reform: a first step, but not the 'whole enchilada'. *Los Angeles Times*. January 4.

Donovan, L. E. ASUA approves anti-SB 1070 resolution. *Arizona Wildcat* [online], May 12. http://wildcat.arizona.edu/news/asua-approves-anti-sb1070-resolution-1.1479212. Accessed May 24, 2010.

Dosaj, T. 2010. Arizona law SB 1070 repeats history: SB 1070, like its anti-immigration predecessors, wrongly points at a single ethnic group. *The Daily Bruin*, May 11. http://wwwdailybruin.com/articles/2010/5/11arizona-law-sb-1070-repeats-history/. Accessed May 24, 2010.

Elton, C. 2003. Honduran police crack down on gangs: controversial law makes it illegal for youths to join. *Houston Chronicle*, September 7, A23.

Fierros, A. 2010. SB1070, divisive from praise to hate. *Examiner* [online], April 21. http://www.examiner.com/x-9270-LA-Border-and_Immigration-Examiner~y2010m4d21-... Accessed May 24, 2010.

France, C. N.d. The MS--13 and 18th Street gangs: emerging transnational gang threats. *CRS Report*, #RL34233, 8-13.

Francis, D. 2008. Mexican drug cartels move into human smuggling. *SF Gate* [online], March 31. http://www.sfgate.com/cgi-bin/article.cgi?f=/c/a/2008/03/31/MN8MV94C7.DTL. Accessed May 24, 2010.

Gaynor, T. 2010. Border businesses lose key Mexican clients: visitors boycott Arizona shops; $1 billion-a-day trade holds steady. *The Daily News*, May 24, 4.

Hispanics and Arizona's new immigration law. Pew Research Center, fact sheet. 2009.

Hussain, I. 2004. After Cancún: G21, WTO, and multilateralism. *Journal of International and Area Studies* 11, no. 2 (December): 1-16.

Kraul, C., R. Lopez, and R. Connell. 2005. 4 presidents seek help in gang battle: Central American Readers say the groups pose a treat, augmented by US deportation of criminals. *Los Angeles Times*, April 2.

LeMay, M. C. 2004. *US Immigration: A Reference Handbook*. Contemporary World Issues Series. Santa Barbara, CA: ABC-CLIO.

McDonnell, P.J. 1997. Prop. 187 found unconstitutional by federal judge. *Los Angeles Times* [online], November 15. http://www.humnet.ucla.edu/humnet/linguistics/people/grads/macswan/LAT23.htm. Accessed May 24, 2010.

Manwaring, M. G. 2007. A contemporary challenger to state sovereignty: Gangs and other illicit transnational criminal organizations in Central America, El Salvador, México, Jamaica, and Brazil. US Government, Strategic Studies Institute [online], December. http://www.StrategicStudiesInstitute.army.mil/pubs/display/.cfm?PubID=837. Accessed May 24, 2010.

Martin, P. 1995. Proposition 187 in California. *International Migration Review* 29, no. 1 (Special issue): 255-63.

Martis, N.H. 1994. #187 illegal aliens: ineligibility for public services: verification and reporting. *California Journal* [online]. http://www.calvoter.org/archive/94general/props/187.html. Accessed May 24, 2010.

McArdle, P. 2010. Business community angry about SB1070, Arizona Governor 'going down in flames'. *Examiner* [online], April 27. http://www.examiner.

com/x-31778-Tucson-Life-in-Photos-Examiner~y2010m4d27-Busi...
Accessed May 24, 2010.

Mexico and the United States: an unappetizing menu. *The Economist*, May 22, 2010, 42.

Papademetriou, D. G. 2004. The Mexico factor in US immigration reform. *Migration Information Source* [online], March. http://www.migrationinformation.org/ Feature/display.cfm?ID=210. Accessed May 24, 2010.

Passel, J. 2002. New estimates of the undocumented population in the United States. *Migration Information Source* [Online], May. http://www.migrationinformation. org/Feature/display.cfm?D=19. Accessed May 24, 2010.

Passel, L., and R. Suro. 2005. Rise, peak, and decline: Trends in US immigration, 1992-2004. Pew Hispanic Center Report, September 27. Washington, D.C.

Pastor, M., and S. Alva. 2004. Guest workers and the new transnationalism: possibilities and realities in an age of repression. *Social Justice* 31, nos. 1-2: 92-112.

Pelisek, C. 2009. Human smuggling ring busted by ICE; Avenues gangsters linked. *LA Daily* [online], October 14. http://blogs.laweekly.com/ladaily/crme/human-smuggline-ring-in-Los-an-1. Accessed May 24, 2010.

Polzin, P.E. 2000. US economy expansion longest on record: can the 'new economy' take the credit? *Montana Business Quarterly* [Online], March 22. http://www. allbusiness.com/government/573737-1.html. Accessed May 24, 2010.

Racial profiling, SB 1070 will go hand in hand. *Arizona Star* [online], April 16, 2010, editorial. http://azstarnet.com/news/opinion/editorial/article_al10573e6-03dd-5c13-b345-a84a74fb4. Accessed May 24, 2010.

Reisman, Lainie. 2007. Violence in Central America. Testimony to US Congress, House Foreign Affairs Committee, Subcommittee on the Western Hemisphere [online], June 26. http://www.globalsecurity.org/military/library/ congress/2007_hr/070626-reisman.htm. Accessed May 24, 2010.

Sacks, E. 2010. Battle over Arizona's SB 1070: Oklahoma eyes similar immigration law; city councils eye boycotts. *New York Daily News* [online], April 30. http:// www.dailynews.com/news/national/2010/04/30/2010-04-30_battle   _over_ arizona... Accessed May 24, 2010.

Saltsman, T. W., and B. J. Welch, III. 2008. Maras in Central America: national security implications of gang activity south of the border. *Small Wars Journal* [online], May 3. www.smallwarsjournal.com/blog/2008/08/maras-in-central-america/. Accessed May 24, 2010].

Sigal, B. 2010. Minnesota protest against SB-1070, Arizona's racist anti-immigrant law. *Fight Back News* [online], April 27. http://www.fightbacknews. org/2010/4/27/minnesota-protest-against-sb-1070-arizonas-rac...   Accessed May 24, 2010.

Starr, P. 2004. US-Mexico relations. *Hemispheric Focus* 12, no. 2 (January 9): 8pp.

Sullivan, J.P. 1997. Third generation street gangs: turf, cartels, and netwarriors. *Transnational Organized Crime* 3, no. 1: 95-108.

Sullivan, J. P., and A. Elkus. 2009. Plazas for profit: Mexico's criminal insurgency [online], April 26. *Small Wars Journal*, from: www.smallwarsjournal.com/bolg/2009//04/plazas-for-profit-mexicos-crim/. Accessed May 24, 2010.

Thompson, G. 2004. Gunmen kill 28 on bus in Honduras: Street gangs blamed, *The New York Times*, December 24.

Tiedeman, M. D. 1999. Los Braceros, 1942-1964 [online], April 7. http://www1.american.edu/TED/bracero.htm. Accessed May 24, 2010.

Valentin, C. S. 2006. Big kids falling through international cracks: Transnational youth gangs on the global stage. *Brown Policy Review* (Fall).

Waldinger, R., and R. Reichl. 2006. Second-generation Mexicans: getting ahead or falling behind? *Migration Information Source* [online], March. http://www.immigrationinformation.org/Feature/display.cfm?ID=382. Accessed May 24, 2010.

Wortley, J. 2000. A record-breaking economic expansion. *Senate Fiscal Agency: Topic of Legislative Interest.* Washington, D.C.

Chapter 12

What's in a Visa? Considerations of the Canada-Mexico Relationship within North America's Security Discussions

Olga Abizaid[1]

Introduction

The Canadian government's decision in the summer of 2009 to impose a visa requirement on Mexican citizens–and the impact it had on ties between Canada and Mexico–attracted for the first time the attention of analysts, students of North American integration, and the general public to the least explored side of North America: the Canada-Mexico relationship.

The prevailing tendency to look almost exclusively at developments in the Canada-United States and Mexico-United States relationships to explain North American dynamics does not provide us with many points of reference to understand the Canada-Mexico relationship in North America or to appreciate how the visa decision may also have a regional dimension. To better understand, it is perhaps useful to bear in mind that the bilateral relationship between Canada and Mexico has been determined and affected by the trilateral relationship–even if it is incipient–and by the relationship that each nation has with the United States. In turn, the bilateral relationship could serve to strengthen or weaken trilateral ties.

Most explanations in Canada about the newly imposed visa argue that it was an unfortunate casualty of domestic politics, the response of a continuous series of problems caused by a flawed refugee system that was in need of reform (Mayeda 2009).[2] In Mexico this decision was perceived as evidence of the preference of Conservative Prime Minister Stephen Harper to deal bilaterally with the United

---

1   Olga Abizaid is Director of the Research Forum on North America at the Canadian Foundation for the Americas (FOCAL), a think tank based in Ottawa. The views expressed in this chapter are hers only and do not necessarily represent the views of FOCAL.

2   On July 14, 2009 Canada removed the exemption of visa requirements on Mexico and the Czech Republic arguing that these two countries accounted for more than half of a staggering number of refugee claims. It has been argued too that many of these claims were made by people under the advice of so-called "immigration consultants" that profited from existing loopholes in the Canadian refugee system. Before this something similar happened with Chile and Costa Rica.

States and as an illustration of the consequent loss of importance of the strategic value of the Canada-Mexico relationship (Studer 2009).

The disconnection between these two appreciations is not easily explained, unless we place the discussion within the broader North American security agenda and draw a line between Canada's decision to impose a visa on Mexican citizens and other initiatives undertaken unilaterally by the United States and Mexico. To do so would allow us not only to see a continuum at the regional level between national immigration measures undertaken by the three countries, but also to perceive that the decision to impose visa requirements on Mexicans is not a policy preference exclusive to the Conservative Party, but part of a process that began after the September 11, 2001 (9/11) attacks on United States, when the Liberal Party was in power. Despite partisan statements regarding the visas, there is a high degree of consensus between the two major parties in Canada's Parliament on immigration policy. Another missing piece in these perceptions is the fact that one of the areas where the Canada-Mexico relationship has thrived since 2006 is precisely security cooperation, even though other areas seem to have reached a plateau.

This chapter will argue that the relationship between Canada and Mexico presents a good example of the contradictions that emanate from the driving forces of integration in North America. On one hand, just like what happened in terms of trade after the passage of the North American Free Trade Agreement (NAFTA), where an incipient relationship grew exponentially, cooperation on security between Canada and Mexico has been on the rise and is likely to continue thus in coming years. On the other, it illustrates how in the absence of a stronger North American governance infrastructure, national policy decisions crafted in Canada and Mexico—while coherent in the context of their own bilateral relationship with the United States—may negatively impact the Canada-Mexico relationship, and by doing so, weaken the effectiveness of the three countries in dealing with existing North American security challenges. This is particularly clear in the realm of border management and the attempts of each of country to create national immigration policies that are compatible with measures implemented in the United States.

Security: An Emerging Bilateral Agenda in the Aftermath of 9/11

Increased bilateral cooperation in the realm of security may be surprising given that traditionally this was not an area where Canada and Mexico shared many common interests (Woods and MacLean 2000, Abizaid 2004). However, the predominance of security within the North American agenda since 9/11 opened a window to gradually incorporate this issue into the bilateral agenda.

Canada and Mexico were both affected by the defensive reaction of the US government post-9/11, which in practice implied a major distortion at the borders with its two neighbors. More important, it changed the premises of interaction in North America; security now trumps trade, and NAFTA is no longer in itself a guarantee of preferential access to the US market. With very high degrees of interdependence with that market, the economic security of Canada and Mexico depended on being able to move legitimate goods and people across the border with the United States.

It was clear that to retain that access Canada and Mexico were bound to cooperate with the United States to repel security threats in the region and to shift them away as much as possible from the US borders. This process has entailed a progressive reinforcement of border controls in all ports of entry to the United States and a gradual move toward the creation of a security perimeter surrounding the three countries. In both of these spaces Canada and Mexico bear part of the responsibility.

The creation of a regional security area–or "zone of confidence" as it is often called in Canada–that identified potential threats to North America has facilitated a rapprochement between Canada and Mexico. While terrorism was the most important security threat as defined by the United States, other threats including organized crime and irregular migration were also considered dangerous activities to security in the region.

The need to eliminate potential security threats at the border places Mexico's fight against organized crime and drug trafficking as a priority for US security. However, this is not an area of interest exclusive to the United States. Public security in Mexico is also an important issue for Canada in light of the significant flows of Canadians traveling to this country every year, which in 2009 amounted to over 1.1 million, and the presence of over 2,300 Canadian firms on Mexican soil (FOCAL 2010a: 4).

Cooperation in this area also has a domestic dimension. It can be explained by the fact that both administrations–Stephen Harper's and President Felipe Calderón's–have made the rule of law one of their domestic priorities, something that creates new incentives for them to expand existing governance and institution-building collaborative work, incorporating issues such as reform of the security system (including the judiciary), as well as other much broader security issues. The inclusion of security in the bilateral agenda also found fertile soil given the lack of historical baggage regarding armed confrontations between the two countries, and as such was perceived to be more natural than cooperation between Mexico and the United States (FOCAL 2010a: 4-5).

The combination of regional and domestic shared concerns provides common ground to work together on North American security that did not exist before. It also creates enough ground for Canada to provide assistance–upon request by Mexico–to the strengthening of its institutional capacity to cope with security threats, in the understanding that bilateral efforts will strengthen trilateral ones.

Security cooperation is still in the early stages. As of now it has centered on fostering dialogue, exchanging information, and building trust, but it is likely to expand in the future (FOCAL 2010a). This was evident with the creation of a multi-track process within the Canada-Mexico Joint Action Plan for 2007-08[3] aimed at promoting dialogue on security, defense, and public safety in order to address issues like organized crime or irregular migration (DFAIT 2007). This process encompasses all bilateral initiatives related to security, including:

1. The annual government-wide security policy consultation coordinated by Canada's Department of Foreign Affairs and International Trade (DFAIT) and Mexico's Foreign Relations Secretariat (SRE).
2. The bilateral working group on security led by the Canadian Ministry of Public Safety and the Mexican Center for Investigation and National Security (CISEN), whose purpose is to strengthen cooperation under the Security and Prosperity Partnership (SPP),[4] and deal with law enforcement and security system reform (e.g. crime prevention, anti-corruption, judiciary, correctional system, and reinsertion programs), border administration, migration, emergency management, and critical infrastructure protection. It is also in charge of coordinating dialogue on issues of public safety, including management of health pandemics and disaster prevention and relief.
3. The political-military talks, originally launched in 2006, where Canada and Mexico discuss civilian-military relations and peace-support operations.

Canada and Mexico also created a working group on consular affairs to foster information exchanges between the authorities of the two countries on cases related to their citizens and broader migration issues.

Under this umbrella of initiatives exchanges have been fostered and cooperation on institution strengthening has evolved. In recent years a number of visits and inter-departmental exchanges between Mexican and Canadian personnel from the Ministries of Public Safety, Justice, National Defence, and the Royal Canadian Mounted Police (RCMP) have increased.

For example, throughout 2009 Canada participated in training programs to strengthen the capabilities of Mexico's Federal Police Force, alongside other countries including the United States, France, and Colombia. Spanish-speaking officers from the RCMP went to Mexico to train federal police recruits in forensic interview techniques, and more than 250 Mexican medium-level officers and 42 commanding officers traveled to Canada to attend a seminar on managerial, investigation, and intelligence skills at the Canadian Police College (Office of the

---

3   The Canada-Mexico relationship lacks major institutions driving it. Hence, bilateral declarations and plans of action are important indicators of the vision of the two countries on the bilateral relationship.

4   The Security and Prosperity Partnership (SPP) is a trilateral intra-bureaucratic ad hoc mechanism to enhance security, economic prosperity, and the well being of citizens. Launched in 2005 in Waco, Texas, the SPP was a conglomerate of multiple initiatives mainly concentrated at the regulatory level.

Prime Minister 2010). This was the last portion of a training program that began in Mexico and included modules in Colombia and the United States (Embassy of Mexico in Canada 2009).

The Influenza A (H1N1) pandemic outbreak in 2009 offers another example of the emergence of the security agenda between Canada and Mexico. Particularly it illustrates how the North American Plan for Avian and Pandemic Influenza, agreed to by Canada, Mexico, and the United States in 2006, served as the basis for crucial bilateral cooperation in 2009 to manage the rapid spread of the disease in North America.[5] Canada's epidemiologic experience, developed in the aftermath of the outbreak of Severe Acute Respiratory Syndrome (SARS) in 2002-03, was decisive in the identification of the virus. Moreover, bilateral cooperation served to develop protocols to control the crisis (FOCAL 2010b: 7, Peschard-Sverdrup 2010: 6).

Exchanges also have increased between the Justice departments from both countries, particularly in light of Mexico's switch to adversarial trials, enshrined in constitutional reforms that entered into force in 2008. In 2010 a delegation of Mexican judges from the states of Chihuahua, Morelos, and Zacatecas visited Canada to learn about the Canadian justice system and to learn about the adversarial court system. The Mexico office of the United States Agency of International Development financed the visit. (Embassy of Mexico in Canada 2010). As in the case of police training, Canada's contribution is done in tandem with initiatives undertaken with the United States.

Canadian-Mexican efforts to strengthen Mexico's institutional capacity in security procurement through a reform of the judiciary system and the modernization of law enforcement agencies coincide with the priorities set in this area between Mexico and the United States in March, 2010, as complements to the Mérida Initiative. In particular, Mexico and the United States will join efforts to strengthen democratic institutions in Mexico, especially the police and justice sectors, and to institutionalize reforms to ensure the rule of law and respect for human rights.

Continued interest in work on security was reiterated during Felipe Calderón's visit to Canada in May 2010. During this visit a new Canada-Mexico Joint Plan of Action was signed, laying out the priority areas identified by both countries until 2012. Included in these priorities is the recognition of the threat that organized crime and pandemics pose to regional security and a commitment to strengthen cooperation in order to ensure their citizens' security (Office of the Prime Minister 2010, DFAIT 2010).

---

5   In the meeting of the Security and Prosperity Partnership (SPP) in 2006, Canada, Mexico, and the United States pledged to protect their citizens in the event of a regional pandemic outbreak. To prevent and control the spread of avian or influenza pandemics the three countries established principles of cooperation, including: information sharing mechanisms among governments, coordination within and among the three countries to manage the outbreaks effectively, and protocols to manage responses and to communicate with the general public (Security and Prosperity Partnership 2007: 2).

In addition to the plan of action, three initiatives were launched[6], one of them including a pledge of almost C$4 million worth of programs going through 2011 out of the C$15 million allotted annually for the Anti-Crime Capacity Building Program for the Americas.[7] The programs announced in the context of Felipe Calderón's visit are aimed at strengthening judicial reform in Mexico and enhancing its anti-corruption capacity. They include training and education programs in adversarial trials for Mexican judges, the development at the national and state levels of coherent licensing standards and codes of ethics for lawyers that would be in line with this new court system, and the harmonization of criminal legislation within Mexico and the strengthening of prosecution service (Office of the Prime Minister 2010, Dade and Abizaid 2010).

Anti-crime cooperation is another area where Canada and Mexico see potential joint action in Central America and the Caribbean. During a State visit to Mexico in December 2009, Governor General Michaëlle Jean identified this area of shared interest in her address to Mexican senators (Governor General of Canada 2009). In light of the importance given to the Americas by both countries' foreign policy, and the stated commitment of the three North American countries to work in tandem in the hemisphere and to strengthen inter-American organizations (*Joint statement by North American Leaders*, 2009), cooperation in this area was expected.

The governor general's statement, however, was the first concrete mention of collaboration in the Americas, despite reiterated statements by Canadian officials that Mexico was perceived as a strategic partner in the implementation of Canada's Americas Strategy. The recently signed joint plan of action states existing interest in the two countries to build on shared experiences to explore cooperation opportunities in Central America and the Caribbean, particularly in the areas of humanitarian assistance and disaster relief, maritime security, and peacekeeping (DFAIT 2010, Annex: 7).

What these examples show is how a trilateral shared perspective with regards to security in the region, particularly in the case of organized crime, has served as an incentive for bilateral rapprochement between Canada and Mexico. Although cooperation in this area is relatively new, and is probably best described as germinal, both countries have stated their interest in continuing to deepen ties

---

6   The other initiatives included a declaration on open skies that will give airlines greater passenger and cargo market access, and a Memorandum of Understanding on youth mobility (Office of the Prime Minister 2010).

7   Launched in July 2007 the objective of Canada's Americas Strategy is to re-position the role of the country in the Western Hemisphere under three main pillars: enhanced security, greater prosperity, and stronger democratic institutions. In a speech given in Chile Stephen Harper laid out the main pillars of the strategy, and framed Canada as an alternative model to the increasing polarization that was taking center stage in the region. Harper also spoke about Canada's interest in working with like-minded countries in the region, such as Chile, to achieve the goals established in the Strategy (Office of the Prime Minister 2007). On other occasions Canadian officials have also included the United States, Mexico, and Brazil as strategic partners in this endeavour.

among ministries and departments. This work also constitutes an important basis to reinforce North American efforts, as it complements other regional and bilateral initiatives (FOCAL 2010b: pp. 5-6). Moreover, positive exchanges and similar points of view–bilateral and trilateral–with regards to security outside of North America also facilitate cooperation in other settings, including the Americas and international fora.

Seen in this light, security, as an engine for integration in North America, has facilitated cooperation in an area where, until recently, Canada and Mexico had little in common. Security, however, is also creating tensions in the bilateral relationship, which are largely explained by the inexistence of strong North American governance mechanisms that establish trilateral guidelines defining how security should be enhanced. Instead the bilateral relationship that each has with the United States has become entrenched–even in mechanisms that were supposedly trilateral like the SPP–and national policies developed to deal with an increasingly inward-looking United States have the potential to pit Canada and Mexico against each other, weakening trilateral efforts to build a North American security perimeter.

North American Security, National Responses, and Sub-optimal Results

Let us go back to the aftermath of 9/11 and the US security paradigm shift, particularly in the area of immigration, to explain the argument. With over 80 percent of their trade going to the United States, the economic security of Canada and Mexico relied on having secure access to this country. Both nations understood that security cooperation was an essential precondition to dealing with the United States, but, in exchange, they needed to come to an agreement with the United States to ensure seamless flows of legitimate goods and people across the border.

This was the logic behind the eventual negotiation of the smart border declarations between Canada and the United States and between Mexico and the United States and the basis for any trade-off they would do with this country. Despite these shared concerns, Canada and Mexico did not act jointly to negotiate with the United States a trilateral North American border management arrangement as was proposed by Mexico (Pastor 2010: 11). Instead, Canada negotiated the Canada-US Smart Border Declaration in 2001, and a few months later, in 2002, Mexico and the United States signed a very similar document: the US-Mexico Border Partnership.

For a while it was believed that the two bilateral smart border declarations would eventually give shape to a trilateral initiative. The creation of the SPP in 2005 spurred anew some energy regarding trilateral cooperation–although not without a certain amount of skepticism and disappointment for those who expected a longer-term and bolder vision of North America (Rozental 2005). The SPP took the shape that the United States wanted it to have. Its ad hoc nature and the fact that its work was concentrated on building on existing bilateral and trilateral initiatives have become important weaknesses.

The SPP has been unable to achieve important trilateral developments (with few exceptions like the North American Plan for Avian and Pandemic Influenza), yet it became the target of civil society organizations, the anti-globalization movement, and media outlets that wanted to play out national fears on integration. As the public image of the SPP became increasingly compromised the three countries decided to separate it from the North American Leaders Summit (NALS). Currently, the SPP seems to have been shelved and it is unclear what the future of this mechanism will be.

Even though many of the initiatives comprised under the umbrella of the SPP remained at the bi rather than trilateral level, it was the sole mechanism that provided a degree of guidance in this matter at the regional level. Without it, US policies become the parameter of action, and Canada and Mexico are trying to respond to them, but unfortunately in an uncoordinated fashion. Canada's decision to impose visa requirements on Mexicans, and the impact of this action exemplify the potential negative implications of this lack of coordination.

On July 14, 2009, the Canadian government announced that Mexican citizens would no longer be exempted from a visa requirement to enter Canada. The argument to proceed in this way was the almost three-fold increase of refugee claims from Mexicans between 2005 and 2008–going from 3,400 to over 9,400. Mexican refugee claimants represented 25 percent of the total amount of requests received by Canada in 2008; of these, only 11 percent were accepted. According to a backgrounder produced by Citizenship and Immigration Canada (CIC), both these trends continued in the first half of 2009 (CIC 2009).

To defend his decision, Immigration Minister Jason Kenney argued that Mexican refugee claimants, which he constantly labeled as "fraudulent", were not only an onerous burden to Canadian taxpayers, but were also hindering the overall capacity of the Immigration and Refugee Board (IRB) and putting it almost at the brink of collapse.

The imposition of the visa requirement, and the way in which the decision was executed, no doubt strained the Canada-Mexico relationship, and continues to be an irritant.[8] Mexicans felt that the decision was made unilaterally without allowing for alternatives and bypassing the mechanisms of dialogue that were put in place to deal with consular issues. To mitigate tension Canada has repeated a number of times that the visa will be reassessed once the reform of the refugee system is

---

8   It is said that when Felipe Calderón called Stephen Harper to thank him for Canada's support with the handling of the Influenza A (H1N1) pandemic he personally informed him about the decision to impose a visa. Mexico later proposed a number of measures to better control unfunded claims, including screenings before departure and a crackdown on irregular "immigration consultants", but they were told that the decision already had been taken in the Cabinet (Ivison 2009).

passed by Parliament. However, even in the event of a reform, it is very possible that the visa requirement will remain in place.

It is important to understand how this decision in particular, and immigration reform in general, is also framed within the new North American security agenda. In many ways Canada's decision to impose a visa on Mexicans seems part of a continuum of national policies aimed at ensuring border security that goes from the US Western Hemisphere Travel Initiative (WHTI) to Mexico's decision to require of Canadian and US citizens a valid passport to enter Mexico (*El Universal* 2010).

Let us explore the other reasons behind Canada's change of visa policy towards Mexico in 2009. In addition to the staggering growth of refugee claims, CIC also underscored Canada's policy alignment with the United States:

> "Mexico was the last Latin American country for which Canada did not require a Temporary Resident Visa. The requirement is in line with the US, which has had a long-standing visa policy on Mexico (CIC 2009: 1)."

Moreover, in the *Canada Gazette*, the government's official publication for regulatory changes, the decision to impose a visa requirement on Mexico was explained on the grounds of the refugee claims, as well as identified risks related to travel documents (including passport fraud), organized crime, and corruption (*Canada Gazette* 2009: 2 and 6).

The imposition of the visa was seen both as a necessity to protect the refugee system from abuse and as a means to ensure public safety in Canada. This latter concern is the reason why the process to obtain a visa for Mexicans now includes security screening of people by Canadian authorities prior entering Canada–something that is not mandatory for all countries. The intention is to mitigate risks by removing the decision to allow people into the country away from the port of entry. This would reduce the risk of people's overstaying their permit or making an unfounded refugee claim and try to minimize potential security threats both to Canada and to the dynamics of the Canada-US border.

Some have stressed that prevailing problems at the Mexico-US border, including drug trafficking and human smuggling, could spill over toward the Canada-US border in light of differences in the level of securitization of the two crossings. In the past the visa exemption for Mexicans was framed as a potential risk to efforts made to control irregular migration at the Canada-US border, suggesting that traveling to Canada could be the least dangerous and cheapest way for undocumented Mexicans to enter the United States (Sands 2009: 56).

The allusion to having a visa policy aligned with that of the United States should not be taken lightly. Moreover, although Canada's immigration debate began prior to the terrorist attacks on the United States, the post-9/11 context has influenced it in important ways, namely Canada has tried to enhance policy harmonization with its southern neighbor to respond to the generalized US perception that it has a lax immigration system. While we do not want to argue that there are no domestic drivers for these changes, commitments to work on visa coordination policies with the United States made under the Canada-US Smart Border Declaration of 2001[9] and later under the SPP[10]–to jointly review visa waiver lists and share look-out lists of people (DFAIT 2001)–have certainly impacted immigration debates and reform in Canada.

Take for instance the progressive immigration changes undertaken in Canada. In 2002 the Canadian parliament passed a reform of immigration legislation, requiring immigrants to apply from their country of origin or a safe third country before traveling to Canada, and enhancing security screening and intelligence procedures for potential immigrants. That same year Canada and the United States signed a Safe Third Country Agreement to better manage the flows of refugee claimants at the shared land border; the agreement came into effect on December 29, 2004. Since then Canada has begun to have stricter measures regarding the evaluation of refugee claimants and their treatment during their *séjour* in Canada.

Additional proposed reforms to the refugee system, currently being studied in parliament, include an expedite evaluation process by public servants for a number of countries considered safe, without a hearing at the IRB. In these cases, decisions made would not be contestable in court and individuals deemed to be fraudulent claimants would be quickly removed from the country (Simpson 2010).

In the aftermath of 9/11 concern about the validity of travel documents has become a cornerstone of anti-terrorism measures to screen people and mitigate potential security threats. In addition to measures related to the development of compatible biometric standards and databases, information sharing of air passengers, search for harmonized visa criteria for third countries, and better management of refugee claimants established in the Canada-US Border Declaration and the SPP, the government of the United States went further.

The WHTI, which is part of the US Intelligence Reform and Terrorism Prevention Act enacted in December 2004, requires all travelers from the Americas and the Caribbean (including US, Canadian and Mexican citizens) to carry a valid passport to enter the United States as of 2008.[11] The initiative seeks both to strengthen US

---

9   Under the Canada-US Smart Border Declaration the two governments agreed to work to ensure secure flows of people. This included among others things: the development of biometric information for identity documents, pre-cleared traveler programs, better screening mechanisms for refugees to avoid potential abuse of loopholes by terrorist organizations, an agreement to deport rejected asylum applicants to a safe third country, sharing information on air passengers between the two countries, and the development of jointly-developed compatible immigration databases (Sands 2009: 11).

10   Under the SPP, the three countries committed to ensuring secure traveling in North America, and to that purpose they created a number of bilateral and trilateral initiatives, including the development of compatible immigration security measures (requirements for admission, visa decision-making standards, etc.) and enhancing the use of biometrics to screen travelers and develop secure proofs of nationality.

11   At land crossings, an enhanced driver's licence will also be accepted. For other crossings pre-screened traveler cards, including NEXUS and Free and Secure Trade

border security and to facilitate legitimate flows of people through the expedition of standardized citizenship documents. According to US authorities this would also help reduce the use of fraudulent identification documents, particularly by organized crime and terrorists.

In response Canada and Mexico are working to enhance security measures in the passports, including requiring biometric information in order to provide sufficient guarantees that they are reliable documents.[12] In Mexico a passport is considered the most generalized and reliable piece of identification given that it can be issued to all Mexican citizens regardless of their age (as opposed to other identifications, such as voter cards). According to Mexican authorities a passport contains 42 security features and as such cannot be "falsified" (Otero 2009).

Canada, in dealing with Mexico, preferred to undertake its own security procedures. The risk of fraudulent travel and identity documents was one of the reasons given by CIC to remove the exemption of visa requirements for Mexico in 2009. The language used regarding these risks is similar to the language that the United States uses:

> "In general, a [Temporary Resident Visa] TRV requirement reduces the risk that inadmissible persons could enter Canada by screening TVR applicants for safety and security risks before they travel to and enter Canada. The principal screening of travelers for inadmissibility will therefore be performed at a visa office abroad (not a Canadian port of entry) by CIC visa officers. [...] The removal of the visa exemption [...] will result in a shift of resources currently used for the removal of failed Mexican refugee claimants to high-risk individuals involved in serious criminality, organized crime and national security concerns (*Canada Gazette* 2009: 4)

With this decision Canada acted coherently to its interests. First, it sent a signal that Canada's immigration laws are not lax and, to the contrary, are increasingly becoming harmonized with those of the United States–with respect to both refugee and visa policies. Second, it stressed that Canada is doing its share when it comes to removing potential security threats away from the Canada-US border and safeguarding the North American perimeter, as agreed under the Canada-US Smart Border Declaration and under the SPP. However, the overarching emphasis on the bilateral relationship with the United States has led Canada to underestimate the importance of the bilateral relationship with Mexico to strengthen regional security.

Mexico also has made policy changes to align itself with the United States. Mirroring the requirements of the WHTI, starting March 1, 2010, Canadian and US travelers must present a valid passport or travel card (if they are US citizens)

(FAST), will be accepted.

12   However, both Canada and Mexico still face the challenge of ensuring that supporting documentation to the applications is not apocryphal.

when entering Mexico. This, Mexican authorities argued, would reduce security risks associated with the use of false identity by individuals related to organized crime. In the past Mexico had accepted the presentation of proof of citizenship and an official identification card with a picture as sufficient documentation for these travelers (*El Universal* 2010). The impact of this policy change is expected to be small, partly because having a valid passport to travel has already become a national requirement in these countries.

As was agreed in the US-Mexico Border Partnership, Mexico has also moved toward harmonization with the United States in visa policies for third countries. For instance, since 2005 Mexico has imposed visa requirements on a number of Latin American countries, including Brazil and Ecuador.[13] These measures intended to curb down undocumented migration to the United States from citizens of these countries crossing through Mexico. A rising number of Brazilian citizens–who entered Mexico as tourists–were using Mexico as a bridge to enter the United States.[14] The most interesting policy change, however, is Mexico's decision to waive its visa requirement to enter Mexico for those who can present a valid US visa and passport, regardless of their citizenship; insofar as the purpose of their visit to Mexico is for tourism, business, or transit to another destination (SRE 2010).

As in the case of Canada, these measures are coherent policy choices in the context of the relationship with a United States that is increasingly concerned with security. Greater convergence on visa policies with its northern neighbor allows Mexico to show its commitment to keeping security threats away from the US border and to ensure a secure North American perimeter.[15] Waiving Mexico's visa requirements if the person can present a valid US visa also denotes a high degree of pragmatism: If compatibility is the parameter, accepting the US visa allows Mexico to lower costs related to screening processes.

The problem is that these measures are conceived in relation only to the United States and not in relation to the needs of the entire region. They seem functional to deal with the United States and to show commitment toward a larger regional space–if by that we mean that each country does its homework as gatekeeper of the outer borders and that this function will be an extension of the bilateral dynamics that each has with the United States.

The biggest distortion of these uncoordinated national policies is the fact that dynamics at the two borders are not the same, and this creates incentives for people to look for loopholes on either side. In the absence of a an institution, or stronger

---

13   Mexico's unilateral decision to impose a visa requirement on Brazil came a year after the exemption of that requirement had entered into force in 2004.

14   In 2004 it was estimated that the US Bureau of Customs and Border Protection arrested 8,629 Brazilians trying to cross to the United States from Mexico (Friedrich Amaral 2005).

15   Mexico has assumed an active role in trying to seal its southern border to stop irregular flows of people coming from Latin America.

governance mechanisms, there is a need to ensure that securing the actual borders with the United States does not contrast with the shaping of a North American security perimeter.

The United States has reiterated the need for harmonized border management–even if this nation always opts for unilateral measures. In 2009, during a visit to Canada, Homeland Security Secretary Janet Napolitano stated that regardless of the differences between its two borders, the borders with Canada and Mexico would not be treated differently (CBC 2009). Although in Canada the notion of harmonized border management in North America is not well received (Peschard-Sverdrup 2010:6), it should be the standard from an efficiency point of view, especially if the goal is to build a North American security perimeter. This also means that Canada and Mexico should each strive to have bilateral initiatives and policies in the areas of immigration that converge with the management of the other, given that they do not share a physical border. The dynamics of the internal borders should reinforce the construction of the security perimeter and not the other way around.

The predominant view in Canada about favoring the bilateral relationship in the construction of North America creates a barrier to the development of the Canada-Mexico relationship. Under this lens the decision to impose a visa requirement on Mexicans was a price worthy to be paid if it served the purpose of strengthening the bilateral relationship with the United States. The full impact of the imposition of visa requirements is yet to be assessed both in economic and political terms.

What is clear now is that the decision has undermined to a certain degree bilateral efforts made to build trust and the mechanism of dialogue established to discuss consular issues; and by virtue of that the perception of Canada as a partner. Should this prevail, the foundations for security cooperation that were discussed in the first section may be weakened, jeopardizing the construction of trilateral cooperation.

Conclusions

The emergence of security within North America's agenda creates simultaneously incentives for more cooperation and coordinated action to ensure a larger North American security perimeter. It also requires other incentives that discourage trilateral cooperation, and therefore become dysfunctional. The Canada-Mexico relationship is determined and affected by the dynamics of the trilateral relationship as well as by the relationship that each has with the United States.

Since 9/11 security–and not economic relations–has become the driver of North American integration: the three countries are trying to undertake a number of measures to protect both internal and external borders of the region from potential security risks, including terrorism, organized crime, and irregular migration. This overall shared vision, in combination with domestic policy preferences, creates incentives to enhance cooperation among the three countries, be it through the set of three bilateral relationships or the trilateral one. This is illustrated in the emergence of security within the Canada-Mexico bilateral agenda and the relatively new mechanisms for dialogue. Although this cooperation is still at an early stage– it is an area that is growing, while other areas seem to have reached a plateau–it is likely to continue to grow as the two nations have pledged to work on it.

In this sense the determination of clear areas of cooperation is essential to maintain momentum, but more important to ensure continued interest and political commitment. The two countries express their interest in working in tandem not only to strengthen bilateral cooperation, but also to build on these experiences to complement other efforts in North America and the hemisphere. The inclusion of this security in the Canada-Mexico Joint Plan of Action 2010-12–providing the roadmap agreed by the two countries–is crucial, given that the Canada-Mexico relationship does not have many institutions to define its strategic vision. To support this vision, the Canadian government committed close to C$4 million to undertake different initiatives, including strengthening Mexico's judiciary system, that are compatible with the areas where the United States and Mexico will be working.

Despite the centrality of security in North America, there is still reluctance to create regional institutions to deal with it. Instead, a number of mechanisms of dialogue on security have been created at the bi and trilateral levels (e.g. the security consultations between Canada and the United States as well as with Mexico, and the SPP). Furthermore, Canada and Mexico have signed border declarations with the United States, pledging cooperation on a number of policy areas to ensure secure flows of people and goods. This patchwork of initiatives and declarations, and also US unilateralism, rather than helping build a coherent vision with regards to what needs to be done, have served to entrench the Canada-US and the Mexico-US relationships–even within trilateral mechanisms like the SPP.

Because it is clear to Canada and Mexico that the United States will usually act unilaterally, the two countries have made attempts to reassure the United States about their commitment to ensure US security. In practice this has meant greater immigration policy convergence between these countries and the United States, be it the management of refugee claims, criteria for visas for third countries, or ensuring the authenticity of identity and travel documents.While these actions may seem coherent in the context of the relationship each has with the United States, a lack of coordination has the potential to seriously damage the bilateral relationship between Canada and Mexico, especially if in the former there is a renewed interest in protecting the Canada-US relationship. The example is the visa decision.

References

Abizaid, O. 2004. *The Canada-Mexico Relationship: The Unfinished Highway.* FOCAL Policy Paper 04-8, Ottawa, Canada.

Canada Gazette. 2009, August 5. Immigration and Refugee Protection Act. Regulations amending the Immigration and Refugee regulations (Mexico). 146 (16). Ottawa, Canada. [Online: August 5, 2009]. Available at: http://www.gazette.gc.ca/rp-pr/p2/2009/2009-08-05/html/sor-dors207-eng.html [Accessed: September 16, 2009].

CBC. 2009, April 20. Interview with US Homeland Security Secretary Janet Napolitano. [Online: April 20, 2009]. Available at: http://www.cbc.ca/canada/story/2009/04/20/f-transcript-napolitano-macdonald-interview.html#ixzz0qKi6QSHT [Accessed: December 12, 2009].

Citizenship and Immigration Canada. 2009a, July 13. *Backgrounder. The visa requirement for Mexico.* Ottawa, Canada. [Online July 14, 2009]. Available at: file:///C:/Users/Owner/Desktop/bacgrounder%20from%20CIC%20on%20the%20visa.htm [Accessed: July 14, 2009].

___. 2009b, July 13. *Canada imposes a visa on Mexico.* News Release. Ottawa, Canada. [Online July 14, 2009]. Available at: file:///C:/Users/Owner/Desktop/press%20release%20kenney.htm [Accessed: July 14, 2009].

Dade, C. and O. Abizaid. 2010, June 22. Canada-Mexico: off to a new start. *Embassy Magazine.* Ottawa, Canada. [Online June 22, 2010]. Available at: http://www.focal.ca/pdf/Embassy%20Mexico%20June%202%202010.pdf [Accessed: June 6, 2010].

DFAIT. 2001, December 13. The Canada-US Smart Border Declaration. Ottawa, Canada. [Online; December 12, 2001]. Available at: http://www.international.gc.ca/anti-terrorism/declaration-en.asp [Accessed: June 6, 2010].

___. 2007, August 20. *Canada and Mexico: A Joint Action Plan for 2007-2008.* [Online August 20 2007]. Available at: www.canadainternational.gc.ca/mexico.../BilateralActionPlanfinal20aug-en.pdf [Accessed: June 2, 2010].

___. 2010, May 27. *Canada-Mexico Joint Action Plan 2010-2012.* Ottawa, Canada. Unpublished.

El Universal. 2010, February 16. México pide pasaporte a turistas de Estados Unidos y Canadá. *El Universal.* [Online February 16, 2010]. Available at: http://www.eluniversal.com.mx/notas/659128.html [Accessed February 20, 2010].

Embassy of Mexico in Canada. 2009, November 26. *Canada supports Mexico in strategy to fight organized crime.* Press release. Ottawa, Canada. [Online November 26, 2009]. Available at: http://portal.sre.gob.mx/canadaingles/index.php?option=news&task=viewarticle&sid=68 [Accessed: February 20, 2010].

___. 2010, January 22. *Mexican judges conduct working visit to Canada.* Press release. Ottawa, Canada. [Online January 22 2010]. Available at: http://portal.

sre.gob.mx/canadaingles/index.php?option=news&task=viewarticle&sid=75 [Accessed: February 20, 2010].

FOCAL. 2010a. *The Canada-Mexico Relationship: A Backgrounder.* A Working Paper of the Canada-Mexico Initiative. Ottawa, Canada. March.

___. 2010b. *The Canada-Mexico Relationship: A Canadian Perspective.* A Working Paper of the Canada-Mexico Initiative. Ottawa, Canada. March.

Friedrich Amaral, E.. 2005. *Country Profiles. Shaping Brazil: The Role of International Migration.* Migration Policy Institute. June. [Online: June 2005]. Available at: http://www.migrationinformation.org/Profiles/display. cfm?ID=311 [Accessed: June 7, 2010].

Governor General of Canada. 2009, December 7. Speech before the Senate of her Excellency the Right Honourable Michaëlle Jean. Mexico City. [Online December 8 2009]. Available at: http://www.gg.ca/document. aspx?id=13423&lan=eng [Accessed: December 8, 2009].

Ivison, J. 2009, August 6. Visa bungle tests Canada, Mexico friendship. *The National Post.* [Online: August 6, 2009]. Available at: http://network. nationalpost.com/np/blogs/fullcomment/archive/2009/08/06/john-ivison-visa-bungle-tests-canada-mexico-friendship.aspx [Accessed: August 7, 2009].

Joint Statement by North American Leaders. 2009, August 10. Guadalajara, Mexico. [Online: August 10, 2009]. Available at: http://www.whitehouse. gov/the_press_office/Joint-statement-by-North-American-leaders/ [Accessed: May 29, 2010].

Mayeda, A. 2009, August 9. Harper blames Canada's refugee system for Mexican visa uproar. *Canwest.* [Online August 9, 2009]. Available at: http://news. globaltv.com/money/Harper+blames+Canada+refugee+system+Mexican+vis a+uproar/1875552/story.html [Accessed: May 10, 2010].

Office of the Prime Minister. 2007, July 17. *Prime Minister Harper signals Canada's renewed engagement in the Americas.* Santiago, Chile. [Online July 17, 2007]. Available at: http://pm.gc.ca/eng/media.asp?id=1760 [Accessed: February 10, 2010].

___. 2010, May 27. *Backgrounder: Bilateral Initiatives Announced by Canada and Mexico during President Calderón's visit (May 27-28).* Ottawa, Canada. [Online May 27, 2010]. Available at: http://pm.gc.ca/eng/media.asp?id=3392 [Accessed: May 27, 2010].

Otero, S. 2009, December 27. El pasaporte mexicano "es infalsificable": SRE. *El Universal.* [Online: December 27, 2009]. Available at: http://www.eluniversal. com.mx/nacion/174200.html [Accessed: May 15, 2010].

Pastor, R. 2010. Should Canada, Mexico, and the United States replace two dysfunctional bilateral relationships with a North American Community? Paper presented at the Conference *North American Futures: Canadian and US Perspectives.* University of California, Berkeley Institute of Governmental Studies, March 12-13. [Online: March 4, 2010]. Available at: igs.berkeley.edu/ events/canada2010/pastor_berkeley_on_trilat.pdf [Accessed: May 28, 2010].

Peschard-Sverdrup, A. 2010. The Canada-Mexico relationship: A view from inside the Beltway. *FOCALPoint: Canada's Spotlight on the Americas.* 9 (4). May. pp. 5-7.

Rozental, A. 2005. The meeting in Waco. *FOCALPoint: Canada's Spotlight on the Americas.* 4 (3) March.

Sands, C. 2009. Toward a new frontier: Improving the US-Canadian Border. Metropolitan Policy Program at Brooking. March. [Online: July 13, 2009]. Available at: http://www.brookings.edu/reports/2009/0713_canada_sands. aspx [Accessed: June 2, 2010].

SRE. 2010, May 1. Supresión de visa mexicana a extranjeros portadores de visa expedida por EE.UU. [Online May 1, 2010]. Available at: http://embamex.sre. gob.mx/canada/index.php?option=com_content&view=article&id=164&Item id=2 [Accessed May 22, 2010].

Security and Prosperity Partnership. 2007. *North American Plan for Avian and Pandemic Influenza.* [Online: August 2007]. Available at: http://www.spp.gov/ pdf/nap_flu07.pdf [Accessed: June 2, 2010].

Simpson, J. 2010, March 20. Order out of chaos – why refugee reform makes sense. *The Globe and Mail.* [Online: March 30, 2010]. Available at: http:// www.theglobeandmail.com/news/opinions/order-out-of-chaos-why-refugee-reform-makes-sense/article1517695/ [Accessed: June 2, 2010].

Studer, I. 2009, July 4. Canadá-México: Adiós a la relación estratégica I. *Excélsior* [Online July 4, 2009]. Available at: http://cedan.ccm.itesm.mx/724-canada-mexico-adios-a-la-%E2%80%9Crelacion-estrategica%E2%80%9D-i-2 [Accessed: May 22, 2010].

Woods, D. and G. MacLean. 2000. A new partnership for the Millennium. The evolution of the Canadian-Mexican relations. *Canadian Foreign Policy.* 7. Winter.

Chapter 13

The North American Space Reviewed Under Bilateral Canadian-Mexican Relation[1]

Susana Chacón

Introduction

Canada is basic to Mexico, and it is a key player for Mexican foreign policy. Currently, the relationship with Canada must be distinguished from the one established trilaterally or bilaterally with the United States. Since 1994 the North American Free Trade Agreement (NAFTA) has established trilateral issues. Unfortunately, with the events of September 11th 2001, the United States preferred to strengthen two bilateral relations further rather than promote trilateral partnership. Mexico and Canada have not been able to stress the importance of our bilateral relationship, as both governments have chosen to refer to the other depending on what each has first agreed with the United States. Until today, the North American region has been built with the US perspective. It is essential to build Mexican-Canadian proposals to promote a joint future.

Since 1994 relationships between Mexico and Canada have been intensified under the NAFTA frame, and bilateral activity has improved on many issues: Trade, investment, tourism, labor mobility, and educational and research exchanges became more dynamic (Lawson 2005). Today it is necessary to find a different pragmatism that favors a strategic relationship. Academics, private sector, social networks, and governmental representatives from the two countries face a challenge to boost bilateral relations (Starr 2009). We must ask ourselves why this relationship is constrained, particularly because we are partners in NAFTA and this partnership has produced positive results from its launch. What has happened to our societies? Trade and investment have grown since then by at least 9%. It is necessary to reflect on the reasons why Canadians prefer to be closer to other actors rather than to Mexico. Additionally, the future of the relationship cannot be reduced to market dynamics or to the unilateral imposition of visas. We must build an integral vision, one that will improve with current and permanent care and with constant dialogue between the two countries.

---

1   A first version of this paper was published as The future of Canadian–Mexican relations: agenda for the 21st century, En *Latin American Policy–Volume 1, Number 1–Pages 151-160, Ed.* Blackwell, June 2010

Mexicans should consider the following questions: What do we know about Canada? Are Canadians familiar with Mexico? What are the limits and the obstacles of the relationship? Do we have common interests? What will our future path be? Do we know what alliances exist between the Mexican states and the Canadian provinces? How do these provinces relate to the Ottawa Government? How can we leverage what they have? What can we offer them?

Knowledge about the other country is required to draw a successful strategy. In this area we have a long way to go. Few members of each society have been given the task of working and meeting the other. Although there are still very few technological development, academic, or business agreements, there are some and they are gradually growing. The building of a New American Space invites us to consider six major issues that require a more pragmatic governance attitude for the 21st century: 1) Competitiveness, trade, investment, and new technologies; 2) Energy security and climate change; 3) Security; 4) The change in the demographic composition and in the labor markets; 5) Culture and education; and 6) Public policy, human rights, and multilateral diplomacy. The Canadian-Mexican relationship could be the breaking point of the new stage.

This chapter presents a proposal for recovering relations. Both countries, as part of North America, must decide on many issues together to offer a better perspective for the future of the region. We believe that now is the time for Mexico to design a strategic relationship with Canada. The two nations need to coordinate all the different actors who have interests in this bilateral relationship. The relationship cannot wait for the two Foreign Affairs Ministries, the Mexican and the Canadian, to make decisions. If we accept that the two countries share common interests in an increasing number of areas, it is necessary to include other actors in the bilateral decision-making process (Keohane 1988). The private sector, academics, and parliamentarians have a strategic role. Public and private actors, as well as civil society and the media, have to use another strategy to create a better and growing relationship.

The ideas introduced in this chapter will invite us to consider Canadian-Mexican relations in a different way. It is not our goal to offer just one path for building the relationship, but to offer some brainstorming to creating a better bilateral link. We offer a diagnosis of the current situation and introduce the necessary elements to build a strategic future and common relationship.

Current Situation

With the launching of NAFTA the Canadian-Mexican relationship improved, but after 9/11 this improvement disappeared (Lawson 2005). Revitalizing the Canada-Mexico relationship would strength cooperation in North America and other settings. The distancing over the last fifteen years has produced a negative reaction in both countries. They are facing an unexpected situation: On the one hand there is an incorrect perception in part of Canadian society, in particular in Ottawa, where a certain group accepts being tired of the relationship. This group argues that if the United States does not consider Mexico a priority, Canadians do not have to direct resources to a relationship that is unimportant for the United States. Canada's priority is to have a good relationship with the United States and not with Mexico (Government of Canada 2003). For this group, NAFTA is a mistake because it does not offer real and positive results. On the other hand, part of Mexican society is also upset with the Canadians. After the unilateral instauration of the Canadian visa last June 23, Mexicans do not consider these neighbors as they used to. After the visa requirement for Mexicans visiting Canada was instated, Mexican sensibility was affected, even though Mexico used to have a good relationship with Canadians. While there is agreement on the impact that negative perceptions in each country have on the relationship, there are differences with regard to how each country sees the state of the relationship. It is necessary to redefine these two negative perceptions by underlining common interests, so as to have a better perception.

To do this, the positive and realistic results of NAFTA must be recovered. This means considering what has been achieved until now. If changes in trade and investment are analyzed, the Canadian-Mexican relationship is much better now than it was in 1994. The focus and emphasis on these two issues are the more visible elements of the relationship. From there it is possible to understand other topics that allow the societies to get closer to improving common benefits. There is a positive increase in trade and investment, as table 1 shows in the data of change from 1998 to the 2008:

Although we can mention that the trilateral results are excellent, there are different perceptions. Those who are familiar with the relationship in Canada stress that Mexico is an important partner with whom there is cooperation at all levels of government in the economic, political, security, and social spheres. At a bilateral level, Canadian-Mexican trade has grown nine percent in recent years (Safarian 2001). Growth in investment has increased even more, as can be seen in the figure 13.1:

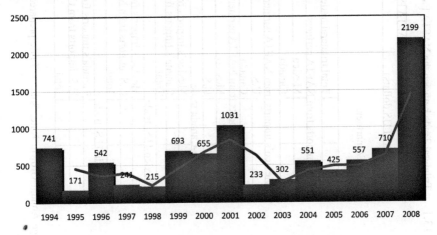

Figure 13.1   FDI from Canada to Mexico (Millions of US Dollars)

Table 13.1   Trilateral Trade between the NAFTA Partners

NAFTA partners		Year			Growth rate		AAGR*
		1993	2007	2008	08/93 %	08/07 %	08/93 %
	Total trilateral trade	288,812	894,413	944,891	227.2	5.6	8.2
U.S. imports from NAFTA partners							
	Mexico	39,917	210,799	215,915	440.9	2.4	11.9
	Canada	111,216	313,111	335,555	201.7	7.2	7.6
Mexico's imports from NAFTA partners							
	U.S.	45,295	140,570	152,615	236.9	8.6	8.4
	Canada	1,175	7,975	9,450	704.1	18.5	14.9
Canada's imports from NAFTA partners							
	Mexico	2,880	16,081	16,773	482.3	4.3	12.5
	U.S.	88,329	205,877	214,583	142.9	4.2	6.1
Mexico-Canada trade							
	Mexico's Imports from Canada	1,175	7,975	9,450	704.1	18.5	14.9
	Canada's Imports from Mexico	2,880	16,081	16,773	482.3	4.3	12.5
	Total	4,056	24,056	26,223	546.6	9.0	13.3
Mexico-U.S. trade							
	Mexico's imports from U.S.	45,295	140,570	152,615	236.9	8.6	8.4
	U.S. imports from Mexico	39,917	210,799	215,915	440.9	2.4	11.9
	Total	85,212	351,369	368,530	332.5	4.9	10.3
Canada-U.S. trade							
	Canada's imports from U.S.	88,329	205,877	214,583	142.9	4.2	6.1
	U.S. imports from Canada	111,216	313,111	335,555	201.7	7.2	7.6
	Total	199,545	518,988	550,138	175.7	6.0	7.0

Trilateral Trade between the NAFTA Partners (millions of US dollars)

*Average Annual Growth Rate. Source: Table prepared by the author and Itzel Barrera with information from BANXICO, USDOC, Statistics Canada

Since trade and investment have increased since 1994, it is worth analyzing in what other areas it would be possible to intensify the relationship. We will study the common interest issues in which legitimacy would be of help in carrying out decisions once we define the actors needed to participate.

Strategic Relationship

In order to have a better bilateral relationship, it is necessary to develop studies to present concrete advice that is easy to implement (Chacón 2008). There are some areas in which Mexico has a particular interest with Canada. If we compare the data of the last ten years, we can say that the Canadian-Mexican relationship is a good one but also that it can be improved.

Even though the existence of NAFTA has allowed both countries to have a closer trade relationship as well as new investment, an analysis is needed as to why Canada and Mexico have not been able to maximize bilateral results. There is still a long way to go so that the two societies understand each other. On the other hand, it is also necessary to understand why Mexico is not important to Canadians. It may be difficult to believe, but if we consider the exports and imports that Canada has with other countries, Mexico cannot do much unless it changes the strategy it has employed with this country until now (Hinojosa 2007).

It is necessary to understand why the bilateral relationship has been so limited. Why, if NAFTA is in place and Canada and Mexico are partners, can the two nations not improve the relationship by reducing the weight of other countries that are not part of North America, such as Japan, China, and Great Britain?

There is a low profile in the relationship that can be explained by the given decentralization among the actors involved. While it is useful in order to manage priority areas such as aeronautics successfully, decentralization also has limited the understanding of the whole picture of the relationship. We should learn how to link the different channels that already allow for daily communication between Mexicans and Canadians. We must see the whole strategy integrally, or there always will be actors missing the opportunities given by the bilateral relationship.

Another point is that traditions and history may have played an important role in impeding a closer relationship between the Mexican and Canadian societies. Do the British, even though they are far from North America, offer Canadians better prospects for the future? In the past the British Empire would not allow Canadian society to relate to groups other than those that always had been in place (Rugman 2001). If this is important, we must face the reality that migration has always been important in the country. As part of the Commonwealth, Canadians were used to migration, but from countries that were also part of it. Later, Canadians kept the tradition but entered into a stronger relationship with the United States because of the latter's power. This may be why Canadians prefer to relate to Mexico as part of their link with the United States. If this is so, the Mexican government and society

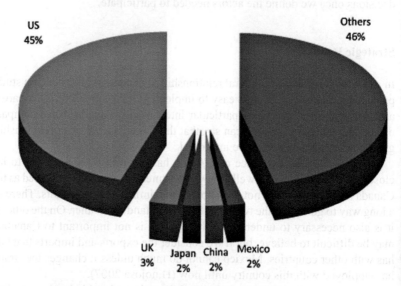

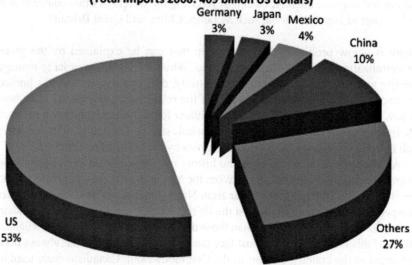

Figure 13.2   Canada's exports and imports markets

will have to work hard to change the situation. It is not just a matter of formal agreements; it will be necessary to build trust to design a different perception. The relationship cannot be limited to one of trade only. For this reason, it is necessary to define common interests aside from trade and investment. The future relationship should be integral and complex, with channels of communication at various levels. A constant and daily dialogue between the two countries should be included as part of the bilateral dynamic. Consider building from trade and investment:

Table 13.2   Mexico-Canada trade and investment relationship

From Canada to Mexico	From Mexico to Canada
Mexico is the 5th export market to Canada (US$9.4 billion in 2008. An increase of 19% over the year before 2007)	Canada: Second export market for Mexico (US$16.7 billion in 2008. An increase of 4% over the year before, 2007)
Products: Manufactured (cars and auto parts and machinery), mining, steel products, oilseeds, cereals, and meat.	Products: Cars, auto parts, electric machinery, furniture, textiles, mining, and fuels
Services: Banking, transport, tourism	Since the launch of NAFTA, bilateral trade has increased more than 500%
FDI: Canada is the 5th largest investor in Mexico: US$7 billion in 2008: More than 2,200 enterprises with Canadian capital	

Source: Table prepared by the author and Itzel Barrera with information from the Canadian Embassy in Mexico.

On the trade front, both countries aim to keep the North American competitiveness agenda from falling prey to Washington's overwhelming security concerns, which have taken center stage since September 11, 2001. More recently, both countries have voiced shared concerns over US economic policies that are viewed as protectionist and that add to existing barriers and border delays. These discussions, however, have not translated into coordinated action.

There is a high degree of convergence between the two countries with regard to the actions that could be taken to revitalize the relationship at the bilateral and North American levels and to take it to the next level, especially with regard to investment flows. However, the results are far from what could be expected. Regardless of government-to-government exchanges and the initiatives undertaken under the Canada-Mexico Partnership (CMP), there is a sense among stakeholders, including the private sector, that more could be done to enhance the relationship.

In terms of bilateral labor mobility, there are also good results. The same happens with education and culture, although despite these good results, it would be an excellent idea to motivate another dynamic to reinforce these three areas. Until now, the results are the following.

Demography and Labor Mobility

Immigration has a substantial influence on the size and growth of the population and the labor force. It also has an influence on the aging population (Beaujot 2003). For planning the population growth of North America it would be useful to consider the number of immigrants necessary to avoid population and labor force decline. What are the current migration flows between the two countries? There are 250,000 tourists and businessmen traveling from Mexico to Canada per year (2008); 1.5 million Canadian tourists visit Mexico per year; there are 16,000 temporary migrants under the Temporary Labor Program, and the total is almost 22,000 workers; there are 1,500 permanent migrants from Mexico to Canada per year (Rishchynski 2009).

On the other hand, over the last twenty years, there also has been a huge switch in the level of population growth (Fehr 2004). Since 1990 the Canadian population has increased nineteen percent, from 27.7 million people to 33 million in 2007. The Mexican population increased thirty percent in the same years, from 81.3 million people to 105.7 million. Here again, we should be interested in watching how this population will be of benefit to the Canadian-Mexican relationship (Grant 2004). There has been a significant Mexican migration to the United States, 450,000 people per year for the last ten years, and there will be a time when Canada will have to increase its active economic population and Mexico could be of help. On the other hand, if we relate the elements of education and population, it would be necessary to start planning a policy of return of migrants, but educated migrants, in order to have not just two but three strong populations in North America (Canada, Mexico, and the United States) and thus build the strongest region of the future world.

For instance, internally Canada is undergoing important changes. National economic power balances are shifting from the manufacturing heartland of the central provinces of Ontario and Quebec to the resource-based economies of the western provinces. Although economic growth has resumed, Canadian authorities identify an aging population and declining productivity as structural obstacles to achieve more robust economic growth in the longer term. At the political level, the sequence of minority governments since 2004 has added difficulties to the process of policy making and limited the possibilities of undertaking longer-term actions. These issues could help the Mexican government to have a better level of negotiation in the design of a different migration agreement.

Culture and Education

For the last ten years cultural links have also increased in a very important way. More than 10,000 Mexicans are studying in Canada per year. There are almost 250 academic agreements between universities in both countries. There are also a large number of cultural exchanges (Cirque du Soleil, Susan Hoeppner, Jeff Wall, Parfaits Inconnus participated in the Mexico City Historic Festival and in the Cervantino Festival).

In terms of education and technology, it is interesting to consider the data regarding Internet users in North America. In Canada and Mexico alone the increase has been enormous from 2000 to 2009 (Hinojosa 2007). Canada increased 97%, from 12,700,000 million people to 25,086,000, whereas Mexico increased 917%, from 2,712,400 users to 27,600,000. The use of new technologies changes the dynamics of societies. With such an increase in the number of Internet users, there is no doubt that Mexico and Canada could get together even if there were no national bilateral interest. Here we find a perfect tool for improving the bilateral strategic relationship, the use of technologies.

Energy security and climate change

Securing access to reliable energy sources is a priority if North America is to enhance the region's competitiveness. Since 2001, with the creation of the North American Energy Working Group, Canada and Mexico have explored a number of initiatives to foster science and technology transfers, joint research, energy efficiency, and development of clean technologies. They have also discussed the protection of critical infrastructure, including oil and gas pipelines as well as electricity grids. There is more that could be done to support those activities and also to resume existing discussions on facilitating movement of people to work in this sector.

A more recent discussion has also brought to the fore the link between energy and climate change, putting emphasis on the reduction of gas emissions, development of alternative sources of energy, and sustainable resources. There is an interest in identifying areas of cooperation to reach a joint decision on what kind of gasoline and fuel should be used. We have an opportunity because strategic joint energy public policy is not yet defined.

The Feasible Bilateral Future

Currently Canada and Mexico face a number of challenges. The most urgent one is the world economic recession that started in August 2008. It has led to a contraction of the market, lower consumption levels, and higher unemployment rates in North America and the world, creating pressures for a change of policy direction and a domestic push for protectionist measures. This is particularly evident in the United States but also has negative consequences for Canada and Mexico. Therefore, it is necessary to balance these measures by trying to build bilaterally adequate policies to counterbalance the US position (Lawson 2005). Given the levels of trade interaction that Mexico and Canada have with the United States, the recession could mean huge economic damage for both. This situation offers the possibility to build a new bilateral scenario impossible to imagine before the beginning of the crisis.

Considering this diagnosis, the proposal for the future agenda between Mexico and Canada would be to focus our attention not only on trade and economic relations, but also on the following issues: Trade flows, NAFTA, and services; natural resources, mining, and energy; borders and organized crime; migration policies and human rights; academic, cultural, and education exchanges; and diplomatic relations and the role of the media.

The real challenge is to not repeat the traditional way of formulating policy and decisions. It is necessary to define new tools for each of the six issues considered. It is time for a policy change. Although the United States is worried about the economic crisis and security matters, the nations need to think differently about the subjects they can use to build a new relationship together. All six offer channels for communication at different levels, from the governmental to the private sector and society itself. All of the actors should be thinking about how to relate together. Mexicans and Canadians face the possibility of losing momentum. As part of the international community and partners in North America, the two countries need to enhance cooperation, negotiation, and daily dialogue that will improve the bilateral relationship and the position of North America.

Coordination between actors is needed. Given the nature of the concerns and the common interests in all three countries, the relationship must be pushed at all levels. Doing so is the only way to define a new relationship. A new debate regarding foreign policy and the best ideas to cope with the recession are fundamental in the construction of a strategic agenda. For instance, Mexican states and Canadian provinces are engaged in a growing number of diverse state/province agreements that expand, amplify and, in some ways, shape the overall bilateral relationship. Sub-national linkages are also a source of dynamic examples of cooperation.

A mature relationship, one that was formally created sixty-five years ago, exists between the two nations. At thirty-five years since the launch of a labor agreement, fifteen years since the launching of NAFTA, and five years since the beginning of the Canadian-Mexican Alliance, the two countries now can deepen their bilateral agenda and improve bilateral benefits for the future and for strategic communication. What is currently being done is not enough. Definition and pragmatism in the design of policies is required for both countries. Neither Mexico nor Canada can continue without the other. The United States has its separate interests with both countries. There are also Mexican and Canadian interests aside from the bilateral interests with the United States. It is time not just to define them but, even more important, to defend them.

Mexico and Canada are located in a strategic region (Rugman 2001). It is time to think as partners and allies. It is essential that both societies become closer and that current and constant approaches build confidence between the two countries. The two nations can strengthen the field not only bilaterally, but also through NAFTA with a trilateral mutual perspective (Peschard 2008). This way, each can leave misguided perceptions about the other country aside and avoid unilateral measures affecting both.

Both Mexico and Canada have a close relationship with the United States. Currently this is not enough for the future of North America. Quite the contrary, sometimes it becomes a limit. It would be necessary to establish three bilateral relationships in the same region. The Mexican government can fully leverage its relationship with Canada to reduce the impact of US unilateral decisions. To do this, first we must learn how to build consensus and how to draw new dialogue spaces. As Michaëlle Jean, Canadian General Governor, said on her visit to Mexico in December 2009, "Only dialogue will remove all shadow in this luminous relationship which unites Canadians and Mexicans," (*Reforma*, 2009).

References

Beaujot, R. 2003. *Effect of Immigration on the Canadian Population: Replacement Migration?* Discussion Paper No. 03–03. Population Studies Centre, University of Western Ontario. London, Canada. http//www.ssc.uwo.ca/sociology/popstudies/dp/dp03–03. Accessed on September 9th, 2009 pdf.

Canada, Government of. 2003. *Opening Doors to the World: Canada's International Market Access Priorities-2003*. Department of Foreign Affairs and International Trade. Ottawa: Government of Canada.

Chacón, S. 2008. *La relación entre México y los Estados Unidos. Entre el Conflicto y la Cooperación (1940–1955)*. México: Fondo de Cultura Económica, (FCE).

Fehr, H.; Jokisch, S.; Kotlikoff, L. 2004. *The Role of Immigration in Dealing with the Developed World's Demographic Transition*. Working Paper 10512, Cambridge, Mass.: National Bureau of Economic Research.

Grant, J., Grant, Jonathan, Stijn Hoorens, Suja Sivadasan, Mirjam van het Loo, Julie DaVanzo, Lauren Hale, et. al. 2004. *Low Fertility and Population Aging: Causes, Consequences and Policy Options*. Santa Monica, California: Rand Corporation.

Hinojosa Ojeda, R.; McCleery, R.; Walmsley, T. 2007. *North American Competitiveness and Labor Market Interdependence*. Roundtable Presentation. North American Future 2025, Project. Washington, D.C.: Center for Strategic and International Studies.

Keohane, R.; Nye, J. 1988. *Poder e Interdependencia: La política mundial en transición*. Buenos Aires: GEL.

Lawson, C.H. 2005. *Building a North American Community*. Independent Task Force Report No. 53. Council on Foreign Relations, USA.

Peschard, A.B. 2008. *The Future of North America 2025*. Washington, D.C.:
    Center for Strategic and International Studies.
Reforma, December 18th, 2009
Rishchynski, G., Keynote Speech, December 10, 2009. CEDAN, Tecnológico de
    Monterrey, Mexico City.
Rugman, A.M. 2001. *The End of Globalization*. New York: AMACOM/McGraw
    Hill.
Safarian, A.E.; W. Hejazi. 2001. *Canada and Foreign Direct Investment: A Study
    of Determinants*. Unpublished manuscript, University of Toronto, Toronto.
Starr, P.K. 2009. Mexico and the United States: A Window of Opportunity? Los
    Angeles, California: Pacific Council on International Policy Special Report.

Index

THE INTERNATIONAL POLITICAL ECONOMY OF NEW REGIONALISMS SERIES

Other titles in the series

Robert G. Finbow

Latin America's Quest for Globalization
The Role of Spanish Firms
*Edited by Félix E. Martín
and Pablo Toral*

Exchange Rate Crises in
Developing Countries
The Political Role of the Banking Sector
Michael G. Hall

Globalization and Antiglobalization
Dynamics of Change in the New
World Order
Edited by Henry Veltmeyer

Twisting Arms and Flexing Muscles
Humanitarian Intervention and
Peacebuilding in Perspective
*Edited by Natalie Mychajlyszyn and
Timothy M. Shaw*

Asia Pacific and Human Rights
A Global Political Economy Perspective
Paul Close and David Askew

Demilitarisation and Peace-Building
in Southern Africa
Volume III – The Role of the Military
in State Formation and Nation-Building
*Edited by Peter Batchelor, Kees Kingma
and Guy Lamb*

Demilitarisation and Peace-Building
in Southern Africa
Volume II – National and
Regional Experiences
*Edited by Peter Batchelor
and Kees Kingma*

Demilitarisation and Peace-Building
in Southern Africa
Volume I – Concepts and Processes
*Edited by Peter Batchelor and Kees
Kingma*

Reforging the Weakest Link
Global Political Economy and Post-Soviet
Change in Russia, Ukraine and Belarus
Edited by Neil Robinson

Persistent Permeability?
Regionalism, Localism, and Globalization
in the Middle East
*Edited by Bassel F. Salloukh
and Rex Brynen*

The New Political Economy of United
States-Caribbean Relations
The Apparel Industry and the Politics
of NAFTA Parity
Tony Heron

The Nordic Regions
and the European Union
*Edited by Søren Dosenrode
and Henrik Halkier*

The New Regionalism in Africa
*Edited by J. Andrew Grant
and Fredrik Söderbaum*

Comparative Regional Integration
Theoretical Perspectives
Edited by Finn Laursen

Japan and South Africa
in a Globalising World
A Distant Mirror
*Edited by Chris Alden and
Katsumi Hirano*

Development and Security
in Southeast Asia
Volume III: Globalization
*Edited by David B. Dewitt
and Carolina G. Hernandez*

Development and Security
in Southeast Asia
Volume II: The People
*Edited by David B. Dewitt
and Carolina G. Hernandez*

Development and Security
in Southeast Asia
Volume I: The Environment
*Edited by David B. Dewitt
and Carolina G. Hernandez*

Thailand, Indonesia and Burma in
Comparative Perspective
Priyambudi Sulistiyanto

For Product Safety Concerns and Information please contact our
EU representative GPSR@taylorandfrancis.com Taylor & Francis
Verlag GmbH, Kaufingerstraße 24, 80331 München, Germany